POINT ZERO BLISS

POINT ZERO BLISS

A PRISONER'S QUEST FOR FREEDOM

SEAN LEGACY

GREATHOUSE

ISBN 0-9645561-1-1

Published by
The GreatHouse Company
167 Oak Drive
West Liberty, Ohio 43357
937-465-5400
937-465-5401 (fax)

The GreatHouse Company publishes books which explore unique and
provocative aspects of contemporary culture and thought. To be put on the
GreatHouse mailing list, or for information on future GreatHouse books
contact the publisher at the above address.

Cover and interior design by inari
Editing by Custom Editorial Productions

ATTENTION COLLEGES AND UNIVERSITIES, CORPORATIONS,
ORGANIZATIONS AND ASSOCIATIONS: Quantity discounts are available
on bulk purchases of this book. For information contact the publisher.

*This book is dedicated to
my father, who gave me strength,
my mother, who taught me compassion,
my daughter, who gave me purpose, and
to Marie, who brought me light
when there was only darkness.*

Contents

Publisher's Note

Because of the nature of the materials in this journal, the publisher and author felt that names of persons and places should be changed to protect the innocent . . . and the guilty. All of this is true, though, and comes directly from the personal journal kept faithfully by the author during his incarceration.

POINT ZERO BLISS

1993

kinds of physical and mental damage. Doing time is something each individual learns unto himself.

I met a lot of decent people during this time. And I met a few not so decent people also. I tried to learn as much as I could and I think I learned a lot between March of 1993 and December of 1995. In that 34 months I heard hundreds of tales, I listened and learned about people. I spent a lot of time learning about myself. I cannot say that prison life had much to do with bettering myself. I am not the same person I was when I "fell" in March of 1993. Yet the changes that have occurred were the result of my choice to face myself, accept my faults and to search for and find my strengths. And accept them as well.

I believe in myself today and I have confidence in my future.

Author Introduction

I was twenty five years and six days old when the police threw me into a jail cell. Shortly after that I was transferred to a county jail. I was sentenced by the State of Massachusetts to a year and 90 days. Four weeks later, I was sentenced by a federal judge to 46 months in federal prison.

I began keeping a journal in the county jail. Somehow, I found peace through writing and there were a lot of things on my mind that I felt I needed to address. The pages stacked up.

One of the things that really bothered me about prison was that there was no constructive rehabilitation. Incentives were cut and from what I've seen, prisons are now strictly places for punishment. Programs are offered, but there are no more good time awards for completing them in the federal system. I sensed that without a reward/incentive that hardly anyone was interested in rehabilitation. A few, but not many.

I had never been to prison in my life. I had let myself get out of control and made a very foolish mistake. I broke the law by robbing a bank with a note and it cost me nearly four years of my life. It gave me ample time to ponder my fate, to ask the questions that I did not have time to ask previously. Prison changed me, some for the worse, some for the better. It made me bitter, it made me look at my life a little closer. Most importantly, it made me face myself.

This book encompasses about three years of my journal: a year in the Hampton County House of Corrections, followed by several prisons in the federal system. By the time you read these words, I will have served my sentence and, hopefully, will be home with a girlfriend, a tan and a job.

Prison is not the end of the world. Although the environment is abrasive to one's psyche, it is possible to do time and survive without all

May 1, 1993

The motel was somewhere in the suburbs of Boston. Individual little cabins of various colors lay half-buried in snow.

There was a sudden heavy pounding on the door.

"Open up! Police!"

I lifted a blade on the venetian blind and saw three police cruisers and cops with their guns drawn. I could only speculate on how they had found me. But there was no time for speculation. They were outside ready to knock the cabin door down.

The dark-haired girl in the bed began to freak out.

"Get dressed," I told her.

I opened the door and two cops immediately came in.

"Sean Legacy, you are under arrest for bank robbery."

When they saw the girl they put the guns away after asking me if I had any weapons or drugs in the room. I had neither as I had just been released from a residential drug treatment program only sixteen hours earlier.

I took the few steps into the bathroom and began to brush my teeth. I was still in my underwear. The cops looked incredulous.

"What are you doing?" one of them asked.

"I'm brushing my teeth," I replied.

I knew what time it was. I was read my rights and handcuffed. I would become very used to handcuffs over the next four years.

No floor fell out from under me. Not yet. I was led to the police cruiser in just jeans and sneakers. It was 7:30 in the morning on March 9, 1993.

I ended up at the courthouse in Northampton, Massachusetts. But not on bank robbery charges. Rather on violation of probation. They used this charge to hold me until the Feds placed a hold on me.

I was convicted and sentenced to a year at the Hampton County House of Correction. On April 26th, I was convicted and sentenced to 46 months in federal prison according to federal guidelines.

For a reason not known to me, I've decided to start a journal to record these days. It will probably last about a week.

May 17, 1993

Another day locked away in the Hampton County House of Corrections. My first jail sentence. Forty-six months. I guess you can only play for so long before paying. There is no line you cross before they grab you.

"No, no, no, please, please," you plead with them, "I'll stop dancing. I promise."

But it's too late, kid. Away we go. No stops on this train. Say "hello" to the justice system.

And the band plays on.

You can't play anymore cause you'll be too busy trying to figure it out in that 8 x 12 foot cell. Sucker. Join the ranks of the downtrodden, the bitter, the worn, torn, hustlers, boozers, all around losers. Slashers, skinners, crackhead, better-off-dead, seventeen, fifty-five, black, white, red, pink. Come one, come all. Right this way. Step right up. Line up for the Mystery Tour. Its going to blow you away.

This jail I'm in right now is a damned camp. Inmates, P.C.'d from upstate. Concord. Shirley medium. Walpole. Other places like Ludlow. Cops hide here. I can't stand them. Especially the skinner cops who are in here for rape. But who am I to judge? I can't be much better. I'm right in here with them. But I've got to be better than that.

I get these feelings that clarify, intensify, perpetuate every day. It is part rage, part disgust. Anger they said comes from fear. Or hurt. In jail there cannot be any fear. Cannot be any hurt. There is only you and all the things that you carry in your mind. Your memories. You quickly learn your strengths, your weaknesses. You discover your friends. You find you really have no friends on the inside. No, unless you've got a buddy from the outside that comes in. And, from what I've seen, most of the time those guys weren't too close on the street anyway. But they're best buddies in here because two is a hell-of-a-lot better than one.

Anger. Disgust. Disgust because I'm watching the prime years of my life tick by. I always knew I'd stop at twenty-five. But I never thought it would be like this. Don't get me wrong. I'm not crying, though it may sound like it. Jail has a way of making you very cynical.

Lack of women. That's gotta be the worst. To go from getting laid all the time to not at all. There's no waking up to that smell of a woman's warm body next to yours. Nothing to reach out to in the middle of the night when you wake from a bad dream with bullets flying, people screaming, blood flowing and everything on fire. Yeah, feels like that big black cloud's coming down. Here, you wake up and what do you get? A smoke if you're lucky. Or a flashlight in your eyes. Better yet, maybe its light outside and they've unlocked your cell door, letting you know its after 9:00 AM.

No ladies in here. On the other hand you don't have to wake up, roll over and leap out of bed and beat the proverbial hasty retreat. And hope you didn't tell her your name or where you lived, if you were living anywhere at that particular time. How many names have I forgotten? How many more have forgotten mine? It's like playing Russian Roulette out there now. This is the 90s man. I've got my HIV negative results. I beat the odds. Ultimately I'm lucky in love.

In jail, they call AIDS the Ninja. Invisible, quiet, deadly. There was a kid in here that gave tattoos. Gave them to a bunch of guys. Gave them to himself. A few of the guys left before they knew. Maybe before he even knew. Now the Ninja got him. Probably a few others too. That's a subject wide open to discussion, theory and speculation. I'll pass by and pick it up at a later date. Not the disease, though, just the subject.

I think about my daughter a lot. Her mother hasn't let me talk to her since Christmas. I write to her a lot but recently found out that her mother is not giving her the letters. Not even reading them to her. I mean my little girl is only six and she doesn't know. But give me a break. More grief added to the files. Stuff that I don't need.

Mostly I think about Diane. Ours was quite a relationship to say the least. I've got a feeling it's fading fast but its probably for the best. I could spend the rest of my life with that girl. No problem. Yet I don't think she'll spend the rest of her life with me. She's the kind of girl that's not happy with one man and I'm the kind of guy that's not happy with one girl. Only the difference between us is that I could be happy with one girl. She's ten years older and I don't think she's going to change too soon.

So, by bowing out gracefully, maybe I'm giving her a chance. Maybe I love her so much I'm going to let her go. On the other hand, who knows. Being alone in jail is a drag. She knows I can't stand to do anything behind anyone's back. He was in jail when I had her. Now I'm in jail and he's got her back. I told her it's OK with me. I can't expect the girl to not get laid for four years. That's insane. I even told her to move in with him to cut back on her bills. She didn't do it. So now she's living with her sister and comes to see me once a week. Rips me up inside to see her though. Don't know what she's going to do with her life.

Me, I've got a million plans. All different facets on the big diamond. Now that I've got my head on straight I don't think there's much that can stop me. But that Diane, she's going to be on my mind for a long time. I'm still standing. For the longest time I searched myself and it was someone else I saw, someone else I wanted to see.

But I'm going to make it.

I'll be all right.

May 20, 1993

Sometimes you eat the bear. Sometimes the bear eats you. I've heard that saying a few times before and I'm sure I'll hear it again. You come in alone, you'll leave alone. You won't take anybody with you. Don't trust anybody. Mind your own business. Stay out of people's conversations. That's a big one. If it doesn't concern you then step off. If it does, take care of it quickly. Me, I try to be civil. That's my problem. I'm a sucker with no common sense.

I saw a guy come in here, he had nothing. He's Puerto Rican but he's Italian also. Came down from Shirley Medium where guys get stabbed as often as they pass out traffic tickets in New York City. He's here for a couple of days and they tried to ship him to the Mods but he didn't play that way. So they put him in the hole for refusal of a direct order. I got a D-report for that myself. I sent him smokes in the hole and when he got out, I helped him a little. I gave him a few t-shirts, some socks. He said he wanted to be my buddy. The next thing I know he wanted me to get him a pair of Reeboks. Goddamned fifty dollar sneakers.

"Yeah, OK," I told him, "I'll see what I can do."

On laundry day he's got nothing to wear to chow, so I gave him a pair of jeans to wear. He's still got them, although tonight is laundry night again and I expect them back clean tomorrow. Then, when I get jammed up in a poker game and owed about sixty bucks, he asked if he could help. I said sure. I'm short three Cokes. Three dollars and fifteen cents. Actually, I wasn't but I just wanted a pack of smokes and a bar of Irish Spring soap for myself.

What a mistake. You would have thought that three dollars and fifteen cents was a hundred and fifty. It turned out that the Puerto Rican guy tried to play me like a sucker, like I'm a friggin' squeeze. I told myself that I was too damn civil, that's your problem. A sucker with no common sense.

Usually I've got good insight. I can spot when there's some good in people and when there's not. But in here, no way man. Every guy is for himself. I thought that I met a few guys that were semi-moralistic. I was totally wrong. The bottom line is me, me, me. Just me. Only me. Me first. Me. Maybe I'll be like that soon. I've only been down five months. When a half year rolls around I will have served a sixth of my time. A half year may not seem like long but in this place its an eternity.

As the saying goes, curiosity kills the cat. In here its especially true. I heard of this kid who had just arrived at Walpole. He wanted to know something. He was probably scared and didn't know anyone and what to do or whom to talk to. He walked up to this guy and introduced himself. He didn't know the guy was a homicidal maniac and was tripping on acid. The guy opened the kid up like a Ziploc sandwich bag and spilled his guts all over the floor. The kid was eighteen and the guy was never caught although there were more than twenty witnesses. The bottom line is that the kid was only curious and it killed him.

Your instincts alone are not worth a dime in jail. Out there, you can trust your instincts because most of the time white is white and black is black. But in here, trust is part of a different world, a different culture. In here curiosity kills. Instinct doesn't cut it and there is no one to lean on or go to for advice. There is just you and the hundred other guys and the guards. The guards might as well not be here. They might as well be invisible.

In here, when you get in trouble you don't run to the guards and cry. You fight. There is literally no place to run. No place to hide. If you get screwed up by somebody and tell the guards you might as well plan on doing the remainder of your time in an 8 x 12 foot cell because once you're labeled a snitch, you're history. You will be beaten until you P.C. yourself for the rest of your bid.

Like H.G.Wells said, "The past is but the beginning of a beginning and all that is and has been is but the twilight of the dawn." Guess you can take that a few ways but what it means to me is every day is just a beginning of the rest of your life. I think every day can be like your whole life too. You start out doing one thing and end up doing something else. You go to run an errand, but never quite get there, and the next thing you know your whole life is like that. In short, a day is the sum of your life's existence. Give it half an effort and you sow half the results. Give it one hundred percent and, with a little luck, your life will fall in order and your wishes might begin to be fulfilled. And you can live in harmony and peace as opposed to disarray and self-torment.

May 26, 1993

I was in a substance abuse class today and the teacher explained the eternal circle to us. It usually begins when you feel bad. When you feel bad you drink booze. When you drink booze you create problems. When you create problems you feel bad. Simplified as it is, it made sense to me at the time.

My father, who has twenty-three years of sobriety, came to visit me in jail and, among other things, he dropped this bomb of wisdom on me.

"Son, I didn't get into trouble every time I was drinking," he told me, "but every time I did get in trouble, I'd been drinking."

Ain't it the truth.

It killed me when my father came to see me in here. I have the deepest respect for my dad and to know I let him down like this was really a drag. I know he's always expected a lot from me and I certainly expected a lot more from myself.

How could I let this happen? I look around and see all these guys and they are asking the same questions. I can't judge on such a broad scale, but I can speculate and say that at least eighty percent of the inmates are in here because of women.

There are several scenarios. A guy hooks up with a girl and they get strung out on drugs. The guy commits robberies to support his habit. A majority of guys I see are doing time for 209As, or some type of domestic violence. Now I know from experience how a girl can play with a guy's head until he doesn't know which end is up. And when both the guy and the woman drink, it is inevitable they will fight. There is absolutely no way that two alcoholic individuals can live together and not drink to-gether and not fight. And now, because of the increase in domestic violence, they are locking the guys up. Even if the girl doesn't press charges, the state or county will. The cops, always the cops.

Take the case of one of my buddies. I'll call him Joey. He's married and seeing this girl on the side. She and Joey are both lushes. They got in a fight and he threw something at her, a pair of vice-grips, an ashtray or whatever. She got a restraining order and the county pressed charges. Now to be fair, I will say that Joey has told me that they both used to knock each other around, that she was particularly violent when she was drunk. He also told me she would do things like kiss other guys on the lips and flirt with them heavily right in front of him when they went out drinking. Any guy who's had a drinker for a girlfriend knows the deal. Needless to say, this does not condone his slapping her around although when he told me she initiated it by becoming violent with him, I believe it one hundred percent.

They made up and broke the restraining order. They were back together and as a matter of fact, the morning he had court he was in her apartment, engaged in what he described as heavy sex. She drove him to court, also violating the restraining order. However, when she got on the witness stand she suddenly started crying and blabbering.

"I was afraid for my life, I thought he was gonna kill me," she said.

Joey can't believe it and leans over and says to his attorney, "Hey, I was making it with her an hour ago."

"Well, since there's a restraining order," Joey's attorney said, "I guess we can't use that."

Due to Joey's criminal record and her testimony, they gave him two years. When he was brought out of the courtroom in chains she was in the hallway.

"I'm sorry, I'm sorry, I didn't want to change my statement," she said to him.

"You bitch," he said. "Is this what you wanted to see?"

He held up his manacled wrists.

Joey spit in her face.

June 2, 1993

I was in substance abuse class again today and there was a kid in there who was busted with drugs and a gun. They gave him a six to ten, with a three to five on an after. Now I'm thinking that this kid's gonna do ten years no matter how you slice it, but a guy I play cards with said he'll do 50% of his time.

So I've got heaps of time. I've got nothing but time. I've got time to read. I've got time to write. Suddenly, I can watch entire car races, whole baseball games. I can play cards for eight hours. I've got time for three showers a day. Coffee at my leisure. Working out, playing Boccie Ball, basketball, softball, football, with my balls. I can lay in my cell and stare at the ceiling and no one will bother me.

I go to music class. I love music class and playing guitar. I'm not the best but I can hold my own. My buddy Randy plays the drums and he's OK but he's got to play a little softer. He's too loud. A guy named Tony just came in. He says he's been playing bass for quite a few years. Randy and I are gonna zoom his name to the top of the list and we'll have a regular three piece band.

Music is my escape. When I'm writing or playing something on guitar there are no walls. There is no razor wire, no cells, no fences. Whether I am plunking away on one of the beat up acoustics or screaming a lead with the amp jacked up high, I'm not here. I might not even be out there. I don't know where it is I go, but I dig it. I can't let them know that, though, because I'll probably get it taken away for one reason or another.

The last time I came back from California I formed a band called Breakaway. It took second place to other ideals I had at the time and fell because of that. But I realized how close I had come to love my music.

As a full blown alcoholic, I could put an open beer on my amp and it would just sit there and get warm, whether I was practicing or playing. In California I'd been listening to Pearl Jam, Temple of the Dog, Mother Love Bone, Jane's Addiction, Guns & Roses and thrash metal. Pearl Jam, TOTD and Mother Love Bone are kind of integral and interlocking but different, part of the whole Seattle movement of the early nineties and late eighties. My buddies turned me on to them a year or so before they were popular.

I believe the crowd I hung with in California were real trend setters. We certainly did not follow. We partied, we conquered, we loved, we fought. We hid from ourselves through drug and alcohol use. But we were very real people. Very there. On top of things, though only a few of us drove, we always had money, always had drugs and always had liquor. It was a paradise realized.

It was my third trip to California. I was running again. This time I was running from a relationship that fell apart from alcohol abuse. I watched everything my life stood for fall apart. I lost a good job. I lost a girl I really loved. I lost my daughter.

It was time to start over.

I arrived on a bus late in the summer of 1989. I was broke, hung over and needed a shower. My mother was there to pick me up. She had an apartment in Pacific Beach and had just separated from her last husband who later died of an alcohol related affliction.

She had a woman friend next door who was the apartment manager. The lady had a son about my age and he had a car and listened to Metallica and liked to do crystal meth. We hit it right off. We'd cruise over to Ocean Beach and hang out, smoke pot, do crystal and listen to thrash music. I picked up a full time job through a temporary agency and was making money working for a company called Conroy Composite. They made aircraft panels and things like that. The money was all right. My main concern was maintaining a buzz after work.

One time I disappeared for three days of parties. I was doing crystal which gives you the ability to stay up for a few days. When I came home, I raided the refrigerator, turned on the TV and fell asleep. My mom contends she came home and found me passed out on the floor.

The next day she told me to either go to a detox place or get out. I packed my stuff to go to Mexico. I was going to work on a boat for a few months. I found some weed while packing and stepped outside to smoke a joint. When I went back inside my mom was there with her new boyfriend. He is now her husband. I was getting teamed and after smoking the joint, Mexico seemed like a hassle so I said screw it, I'll go to the damned detox center and get it over with.

It was in downtown San Diego. I hated it. I cursed my mother and threatened her boyfriend. I told her to get me out of there. I stayed for three or four days. I saw guys pissing themselves, police in and out, fights and more hopeless cases in those few days. I couldn't wait to get out. They wanted me to go to a seven day program after that, but I refused. I swore I would go to a thousand AA meetings and would not drink.

The first thing I did when I got home was roll a joint. What a relief. I kept my promise and went to a few AA meetings a week and hung around with a few of the sobriety type people. I was hanging around a sober meeting house and was actually running a few meetings a week.

It was while I was hanging out there after a meeting that I found out about a plumbing job. I called the guy, went in and he hired me. His name was Bill and he was one of the greatest guys I've ever met. He still is. Leaving a $5 an hour job in Massachusetts at a hardware store I was hired on the spot at an $8 an hour job. I told him I'd give him a day's work for a day's pay and I set my mind on earning it. I ended up holding the job for two years.

June 17, 1993

So tired. I get tired a lot now. Tired of this place. Tired of these people. Tired of sleeping alone. Tired of cards. Tired of classes in substance abuse. Tired of running out of cigarettes. Tired of nothing to look forward to.

Maybe I'll lose my mind in here. I don't have long to go but this jail stuff just is not me. The joke's over. You can let me out now. OK? I've learned my lesson. Let me go. No? What's that? Three and a half years you say? My legal options are all gone. My attorney says the new Attorney General may do away with all of these federal guidelines. Give us first offenders a chance. My very first jail sentence. Four years. Bogus.

Got a letter from Suzy, one of my girls out there. She's really in love and she's going through some tough times. She misses me being there for her to talk to. And damn, I miss being there for her too. She was a player like me and when we ran together we ran hard. Now she's all cleaned up and I'm in jail and we're still buddies.

Yesterday, in substance abuse class, we were watching a film on recovering addicts called Circle of Recovery. It was about a men's group who met so they could talk about whatever and it pointed out the important fact that you can't do it alone. You have to have help, because if you could quit by yourself, you would.

This film goes on for an hour or so and the whole time the men in it are in this room talking and singing in a group. Then all of a sudden, there is this guy in a truck driving down the street. Busses, people, traffic.

And then it hit me. Not hard, but more like a whisper in my head, the slight breeze of some distant memory. I was missing something that was taken from me, something that I wouldn't see for a long time. I suddenly thought about all of the things I will miss, all of the things I won't see. People I won't meet. Opportunities I won't have. Women. Watching my daughter grow up. Fishing. Freedom.

My freedom is gone and everyday the sky is gray. Every night is a lonely one and every memory of a loved one painful. There is nothing like jail. They say it does many things to men. I can only wait to see what it does to me. Because now, I am left alone with myself. Now I face myself with a clear mind, with no place to hide, with no image to project that would fool myself.

I am here. I am OK.

I will make it through this nightmare and when I finally wake up, it will be August 25, 1996.

July 7, 1993

I didn't know what day it was. I didn't care. I had not been home in a couple of days and had not called and I was having a marvelous time. I was sitting on the wall by the parking lot, under the pier in Ocean Beach. I had been doing crystal meth continuously (a little bit goes a long way) but at the moment I was busy rolling a joint. I was with two psycho girls. I can't remember their names. Heather was one maybe. Fifteen or sixteen years old. I wasn't much older. Nineteen? I forget. Maybe twenty-one.

"Sean, are you going to jump the pier tonight?" asked Psycho girl number one.

Sucking on the joint I turned my head to look out at the crashing waves.

"How far?" I demanded.

Both girls immediately got excited.

"The end, the end!" they both screamed.

"You're crazy," I said.

"Freddy Kruger was my father," one of them replied solemnly. It was her favorite saying.

"Fifteen," I muttered peeling off my shirt.

"Fifteen!" the girls screamed.

This meant the fifteenth light on the pier. So far, I had only gone to the twelfth.

The parking lot was a great place. Sometimes it was crowded. Sometimes there was nobody around. But the police always came.

"Johnny comin'," someone would yell. "Ditch the joint in the sand!"

Once when I was playing hacky sack at two thirty in the morning the police questioned me. They waved a finger in my face and told me to follow it with my eyes. I did and they let me go. They suspected I was under the influence of methamphetamine (which I was) but they didn't bust me.

I left psycho girl number two with my shirt and drugs and climbed the stairs to the pier. A crowd had gathered now. Tweakers (people who use meth), trippers (people who use LSD) and wanna bes (clingers on to the drug culture thing). There were probably also a few straights in the crowd.

At the top of the stairs I paused. I remember wondering why I always do crazy stuff when I'm gone like this. It's pitch dark. I don't know if it was low tide or high tide. The last time the water wasn't very deep. Chest deep maybe. Would I be out in rip-tideville? I didn't know and didn't care. Carry on. Now this wasn't just a walk out to the fifteenth light and a vault over the side. It was more than that. At the first light I climbed onto the railing and began walking. Forty feet? Thirty? Over the sand would have been a broken leg anyway.

Halfway out I slipped. I almost fell but after waving my arms a couple of times I continued. I passed the twelfth light and moved to the fifteenth. It was a lot farther than the twelfth. I stopped. What lay below? Sharks? Jellyfish? Riptide? How deep?

And then I realized that I did what I did because I had to know. I had to find the answers for myself, not hear them from somebody else. I had to search, to do drugs, to take risks, to be different not just to be different, but to be better. To conquer fear. And the biggest fear I had was fear of myself. I was afraid of being afraid, of being weak. I was determined not to be weak.

I was not afraid. I jumped. The water was well over my head. I touched bottom and felt seaweed. I bent my knees as soon as my feet hit the bottom and launched myself forward towards the beach. I stayed under the water. I came up on the underside of a barnacle encrusted pylon under the fourteenth light. There was no rip-tide. No sharks. Just me.

I swam to shore where someone gave me a towel. Someone else handed me a bottle of tequila. For now I was a hero. The girls looked up to me because I was not afraid. The tweakers and trippers respected me because I was high and was not afraid. Not afraid of the unknown.

I did not go home for a week. I made friends. Some I will remember. Some I have already forgotten. Most have probably forgotten me. But somewhere, somebody remembers. We would take the girls in whoever's car we could get, me and the King Tweaker. He would drive and we'd go to the Mission Beach. We had a chair in the trunk and he would carry it all the way from the parking lot to the boardwalk. He would sit on the boardwalk and hawk meth to passersby. The girls would squeeze their breasts at strangers.

The night of my pier jump I don't remember where I slept. The next day I was selling meth for a girl. She gave me enough to last through the day. I never slammed meth or shot it up. But I met a few who did.

Anyway, some asshole guy was hanging out around the beach all day. He had a heavy-set girlfriend with him. I didn't say two words to either of them. The guy was big, vicious and I believed he had just been released from jail. I was talking to the girl who gave me the meth. The heavy-set girlfriend was on my right. She mumbled something but I didn't hear her.

"You're so rude," she said as she hauled her fat butt off the wall and began to waddle away.

I turned back to the girl I was talking to when the heavy-set girl's boyfriend sucker-punched me.

"Disrespected my woman," he shouted.

"I'm outta here," I said to the girl.

She gave me more drugs.

I ended up at a party. I got really drunk. When I woke up I was at some guy's house in Ocean Beach. It was a hell of a party. The first thing I saw was a bottle of VO whiskey. I immediately began to drink and wonder how to get back to the beach. I guess the guy who lived there woke up and got in a fight with some chick. His old lady? Who knows. He started drinking with me. Pictures started coming back to me from the previous night. Bare glimpses. I remember a lot of cocaine but whether I bought it, sold it or used it wouldn't come to me. I reached in my pocket. There was $400 in it and not a small amount of cocaine.

"Yeah," the guy said, "Cindy liked you. Everybody came here to buy coke from her. You screwed her in the spare room, then her pager went off. She left you a bunch of coke."

Must of been one hell of a binge when I can't remember getting drunk, getting laid and getting there in the first place.

I did some coke and packaged some.

A new day.

I got a ride from the guy to Newport Avenue which is the the big street in Ocean Beach. It runs from the hill to the beach and the pier. Once on Newport Avenue, I went to a hardware store. I bought about 10 inches of thick steel chain. It cost three dollars.

Then I went down to the pier and found the guy who hit me. He didn't remember me from the day before because he was so messed up. I took him under the pier to do a line, but rocked his world instead. He didn't come around anymore.

I snorted the rest of the coke with the psycho girls and spent all the money in the next two days. I got a ride home and once I got there I immediately feel asleep in front of the TV.

That's when my mom claims she found me passed out and unconscious.

July 22, 1993

Into the darkness. Nighttime is the only time I can find to write. It's not that I'm so busy rehabilitating myself during the day. I'm too busy gambling, playing cards and maybe shooting some pool or just screwing around. I read books so fast you wouldn't believe it. Three hundred pages a night is about average. I read the new Dean Koontz book in one night.

More and more, as each day goes by, I'm starting to notice it. Each day I see myself slipping a little more, a little more. I'm sick of the same old bullshit. It's only been six months and there's so much more time to finish. When I think of my family, my daughter, my girlfriends, my mom, I just get sick. Certain songs I hear, phrases I recall, dreams I have. It's all wear and tear.

Toughen up man, you're in jail. Yeah, well jail sucks and you're only here for a couple more months man so buzz off. It's like my mind is a big boulder and every day someone takes a pick to it and knocks out a little piece. I wonder if there is enough rock or will it run out before my time is up? Will my brain be so much dust leaving me a blabbering idiot?

Questions and more questions. They are like drops of water dripping on the same boulder. How long will I be in this particular place? What will the federal prison be like? How many times will they move me? What will I be like when I get out? How will people treat me? What if I get in a fight and mess someone up and have to do more time? What if I get greased? Am I gonna make it? What's today?

Over and over I curse every day that I'm in here. I do not get on my knees and pray for freedom because I know damn well that no amount of anything is going to get me out any sooner. Once in a while I kick a kite up to the Old Man in the sky. Tell him to watch out over my family, Diane, her sisters and a few others. This is my totally unbiased theory of God and jail. It's not his fault I'm here and he's not coming to let me out.

I see guys that come in here and all the sudden they've found God. Or they had this big religion before they came in here. Everybody creates God in their own image. Therefore, He is to them what they want him to be. Nothing more. Nothing less. But I can see that a few guys use religion to hide behind. I think more people turn to God when there is nowhere else to turn. Others use God as a kind of crutch. And some only turn to Him when they need or want. There are many different religions and I believe, though it will always remain a mystery, it is good to look forward to a Heaven.

August 15, 1993

This place is a zoo.

Another random urine tonight. The results of a snitch at work. A bunch of us got tested. This is the second time in a month that I've been tested. Always the same people. I am clean though.

Its been a fairly good day at the gaming tables where I seem to find myself day in and day out. I'm down four but up six so that leaves me about two until tomorrow which is the last day to break even, lose, or come out ahead. Sunday night is the night the canteen orders go in.

As deranged as it may seem, I find myself actually getting used to this place. I can only imagine what the federal penitentiary is like and it remains an ominous, unknown reality. A cell is a cell is a cell I guess.

My buddy Randy who plays drums in our little jail house band is quite the personality. Always full of piss and vinegar, ready for anything at the drop of a hat. It seems he's always got a comeback for everything. Tony, who plays bass in the band, lost all of his hair due to radiation treatments because he has leukemia. A couple days ago I heard Randy commenting at the dinner table about Tony and his baldness. We've all been getting tattoos done. I had my daughter's name and birthday done on my chest.

"Hey, lets tattoo some eyebrows on Tony," Randy says.

It was quiet for a second and then I couldn't help it and cracked up. I did stick up for him, though, and privately told Randy to lay off. He has.

I haven't been able to see my girlfriend, friend, or whatever she is, these days. One weekend she couldn't make it. The last two weekends I've told her not to come because of the tattoo work I'm having done. I had to shave my leg to get her name on it and now I have to wait for the hair to at least grow halfway back. Yesterday I had my daughter's name and birthday done on my left chest, over my heart where she belongs. I'm thinking of having another dragon done either on my leg or on my back or shoulder. Yeah, it's nuts to get a tattoo done in here, but as I am the one who gets the guitar strings, I know I'm getting a new one every time.

Things I miss the most. Sex, steak, the woods, my daughter, Diane, Suzy M., Tina, Susan, Samantha, Dori, Lisa, etc. All my friends, my family. Especially the ones that don't write me. I miss fishing, California, the beach, surfing, going to work every day, cranking tunes whenever I want. I miss going to the movies, going shooting, hunting, looking at the stars at night, playing the guitar by myself when there's no one else around. I miss waking up with somebody and the smell of good food. Apple pie. I miss being free.

Things I don't miss. Waking up and not knowing where I am. Waking up forgetting the girl's name I'm with, wondering where I'm going to sleep that night. Hustling money, taking advantage of people. Worrying if I'm ever going to get caught for anything. Wondering how long I've gotta run. Feeling empty inside, like I'm missing something and I'll be searching for it for ever, but won't find it because its me.

August 28, 1993

Music playing on the radio. Another Friday night. More of the writing that will probably never be read. More shitty pens. One of them has gotta write.

I'm beginning to see a lack of control in my life again. Gambling, gambling, gambling. It's not that I lose all the time. I don't. Actually I do fairly well. Yet it seems that gambling is all that I do. Up in the morning, gamble all day, go to bed. Cards, cards, cards. Spades, pitch, poker, seven stud, low in the hole, forty-four, fifty three, No Peek, the "L" game, the "X" game, criss-cross, In Between, football games, baseball games. It's tough just keeping track of it all. But then comes the commissary day. You pay your debts, you get paid. And when you come out ahead, there's nothing better than getting ahead.

But I see myself falling into the proverbial pit. I'm losing weight, not going to my classes, screwing off and shirking responsibilities. I never call Diane when I'm supposed to. She's getting fed up I'm sure. Damn, though, that's tough. My life doesn't revolve around her and her life sure the hell doesn't revolve around mine. I think about her a lot though. The inner sense of loss is still there. Yet I'm happy because I know she's doing OK and can take care of herself. And, she's got Mike looking after her.

I saw her last week. She looked good. Damn good. It made me

realize how long it's been, maybe a month, since I've seen her. There were those two weekends I told her not to come because of my tattoos. When they strip search you they look for stuff like that. I got two new tattoos and I didn't want to do hole time, so I told her to lay back a couple weeks. It is funny that I saw her more when she was in New York and she would drive down every week to see me. Now she's practically next door and I never see her. Dames are too much. If you put an infinite number of guys in a room with an infinite number of women, you'd still never figure them out. They're put here to torment us, I believe.

Anyway, the Giants, the Saints and the Raiders look pretty tough this year. Cleveland looks good too and this weekend I think the Eagles will beat the Redskins. But the spread is seven points. It's a tough call. Tony, the bass player, is a football fanatic. He's a statistic nut. He knows what he's talking about though. He hit the ticket we have in jail for a carton last week.

The band's doing good. A concert is coming up in a couple of weeks. I can only imagine how that's going to go. It's either going to hit big or crap out. I'm hoping we can pull it off. The songs we are going to do are "Layla," "Wild Horses," "Wonderful Tonight," "Johnny B. Good," "Little Wing," "Crossroads," "Pretty Woman," and a blues song I wrote on the beach in San Diego.

Tomorrow is Saturday and its always a busy day. Tom is coming to see me. I haven't seen him in a while either. Tom is my guardian. In all aspects of the word. The one guy in the world that I will always trust. But Tom and me, that's another night, another page, more ink to be used. And right now I'm just too damn tired.

September 30, 1993

Tomorrow is October first. Fall is here. This morning they opened the door to the little yard and I could see my own breath. Mornings are chilly.

Band practice is tomorrow morning. We're supposed to have a show on the first Tuesday of the month. I hope I'm still around.

Sad and lonely, sad and lonely. These words echo in my ears. Like a bottomless pit I've fallen into watching a circus world go by while I slowly die. I am only beginning to "climb the hill" and I hate this place so much. If I didn't get into so much trouble I'd probably feel better about it. But right now it sucks. Sad and lonely, sad and lonely.

I remember the woods and the scent of pine. The leaves in the breeze and my twelve gauge loaded as I slipped through the thickest of the scrub oaks trying to flush a pheasant out, usually with some success. Knowing I could go and get into my truck and go home to my old lady and my daughter, knock back a few and play a little guitar. Crawl into my waterbed and go to work on Monday morning and dream about a house.

I remember my dog Angus who would almost knock me out with his leaps at me because he was so happy to see me at the end of every day. He would jump on me and bite me a little and jump more as if he was saying, "I thought you'd never come home." I'd race him to the house and wrestle around with him for a while. He was a magnificent animal who lost his marbles somehow. He was so gentle with kids and he loved me more than anything in the world. He bit a couple of people and got out of control though. He was wild like me.

There came a day that I had to put Angus down. I couldn't let them kill him. Not their way. No. I took responsibility and did the right thing. It was one of the hardest things I ever did. I took him out in the woods and let him run. He loved to run and chase tennis balls. He loved tennis balls. I led him to a spot on the edge of a field and fed him and then talked to him. Then I pumped a few hollow points into his head and dug a grave through the frozen ground with a pick and shovel. It took a while. She never forgave me.

October 2, 1993

Diane is going to kill me when she finds out the fifty dollars I borrowed from her isn't going to be paid back. The money I owe her was used to pay other gambling debts. She will probably tell me to get lost. I suspect she is seeing somebody else besides her Mike. I know the girl like a book and something is definitely wrong.

As long as I live I will never be able to figure out women. There was a time when she would have told me what's up, but now she leaves me guessing. Sometimes I feel so close to her, sometimes I am discouraged by the direction the relationship is leading. When we were together before I came to jail, everything was right. Sure we had arguments, and I maybe misled her a little, and she maybe misled me a little. But we had this thing.

I believe that some people go their whole lives looking for what I have (had?) with Diane. To see it slipping away is just a total drag. Like in the Road Runner cartoon where Wile E. Coyote looks down and suddenly realizes that he's standing on nothing but air. He overshot the cliff and its a long way down. Beep, beep. I love that girl much too much I think. Maybe I'm driving her away. Maybe its for the best.

I told her when I came to jail four years was too long to wait for me. It'd be ridiculous to expect her to wait for me. Do what you gotta do, I told her. I knew she'd be back with Mike and when she moved back from New York, she told me she was going to move in with him. I encouraged her. I wanted her to save money on the bills. In the end, she moved back in with her sister. But that's another chapter.

I told myself I must face the fact that I would lose her, lose the girl I spent my life looking for. I told myself not to get too involved, to hold on loosely. Girls like her, though, have a way of turning iron will to mush. I don't care if you're the strongest guy in the world, if you pull freight trains with your nose hairs, some way, somehow, some girl is going to work her way into your life and, before you know it, bang. You're just cruising along in life, a girl here, a girl there. Party, party, party. Maybe you're working. You got a car. Some extra cash put away. (This was not the case with Diane and me.) Everything in life is going pretty smoothly. Then love comes to town. Common sense? Out the window. Friends? See ya. There is only one thing in life to exist for and that is her. And then comes the worst part. She finds out about it. Then you're all done.

So my strategy for this woman trap was simple. Don't get too close. Touch and play, but don't let them in or else. I had learned my lesson. You could not tell me because I knew. And for three years or more, it worked perfectly. And there I was, cruising along, playing in a band. Sure I had trouble. I had the cops and the FBI on my ass and I knew I was going to get busted soon. But right then, everything in my life was cool. Then, here she came along. My knees got weak, my mouth got parched and I knew it was all over for me. I think I actually said to myself after I kissed her the first time, "Oh shit."

Of course I wouldn't change a thing that ever happened, except I wish that I never got into so much trouble. I wish I never came to jail and that I could be with her right now. But you know what? That's what every guy in this place wishes for. Nobody in here wants to get out so they can go rob people, or steal things. No one wants to get out so they can drink and drive or kill people. No, I think that for the most part that they're a lot like me. They just want to be with their woman, go back to work again and see their kids. That's all I want. To see my little girl, go to work and settle down. My days of rage are over.

I think there's too many guys in here that made five minute mistakes and are paying for it in years. Short of murder, that makes no sense to me. I was talking to a guy that runs the football tickets the other day at chow. He just got paroled.

"How long you been down?" I asked him.

"Thirteen," he said.

"Months?" I asked.

He just looked at me with a strange look on his face. Then he laughed.

"Years man, years," he said.

"What the hell did you do, Johnny?" I asked him.

"A breaking and entering," he said.

I shook my head.

"You must have done a lot of B & Es," I said. "A whole string of them or something."

He held up one finger.

"One?" I asked.

"Mayor's place," he mumbled and then walked away.

Thirteen years. One breaking and entering.

My bass player Tony who just left here has done some time but not much. I think he was here sixty or ninety days. He showed me his record. It was four pages long. Tony was forty three and had charges going back to 1973. Small stuff at first. Possession of marijuana. Stuff like that. But as the list went on I saw larceny, DUIs, breaking and entering, kidnapping, assaults, more kidnappings, more assaults, more breaking and enterings, driving with no license, and on and on and on.

One of the kidnapping charges was his kids, which I can see. The other one was a drug deal gone bad. This is how he explained it to me. A friend of his had ten pounds of pot. I remember him telling me it was worth about five grand. This guy came over to his friend's house with a bunch of pills. He got his friend all whacked out and when he woke up all his pot was gone. This guy called him up and got him to admit it. He went over to his house and he was gone. Tony and a bunch of guys cleaned the guy's house out and took everything.

The guy called Tony's friend and asked where his stuff was. He agreed to come over and bring the pot. The guy showed up. It was a brownstone type of building. Tony's friend meets him at the door but the guy wouldn't come in. Meanwhile, his friend's brother is on the second floor looking across the street at the car the guy came in. He had brought two friends.

"They've got guns! Get him in the house!" the brother starts yelling.

They drag the guy in the house and he starts to fight. Tony said he was pretty big and put up a hell of a fight. Tony had this jack handle and kept whacking the guy in the head but the guy wouldn't go down. Finally, he gave him a good one and he went down for the count. The brother then pulls out a pair of handcuffs and cuffs the guy. The guys outside with the guns must have split.

They put the guy in a car and they all piled in and drove off. They guy is on the floor and really freaking out. He is bleeding badly and tells them that he will take them to get the dope. They pull up to a stop light and a state cruiser pulls up next to them.

"What should I do, what should I do?" says the driver.

They are in a Volkswagen so they obviously can't outrun the cops. All he could do was just to drive real cool. There was blood on the car's windows and probably blood outside too. The guy was bleeding from a pretty bad wound in his head. They pulled away from the light and the cruiser, sure enough, pulls in behind them and hits his lights. They pull over. For a few minutes they thought the cops wouldn't see the guy but, of course, they did. They drew their guns and did the old hands in the air bit and in a matter of minutes there were cops everywhere.

They were charged with kidnapping but the guy was so scared he never showed up in court to press charges.

October 17, 1993

Today was a good day. I woke up in time for lunch which is about usual.

I should say I arose for lunch because I am always awake by then. Around 7:00 AM I am awakened by the guys getting up for breakfast. I hardly ever go to breakfast. They buzz the door to your cell at 7:00 AM.

They come into the block and open your door. They make sure you didn't enter the slip-knot zone since their last check. It always wakes me up. Then, just as I am going back to sleep, after the guys come from breakfast, they lock all the doors again.

Lunch was chicken, peas and ice cream. I watched a little college ball on TV and then I went to the gym at around one. I had a relaxed work-out alone and at my own pace. I was satisfied.

Diane of course didn't come to see me. But that's OK. She's pissed because I spent the hundred bucks I was supposed to give her. She didn't show. I didn't call. Obviously, she was busy.

When I came back from the gym there was a letter from mom on my bed. Complete with pictures of my brother Tony and my cousin Peter. She also sent me a picture of Suzy Q, a friend of hers with whom I became sort of friendly. The letter was good. At the end of the letter, she says that when I come home she'll have a limo pick me up at the airport.

After I read the letter I studied my music theory book for a couple of hours. I found an excellent book called *Programmed Rudiments of Music*. It had superb information on the technical aspects of music presented in an ideal manner so that you could learn quickly and easily. It was just the book I've been looking for. Next to it in the library was another little gem called *The People's Songbook* with a Forward by Alan Lomax. He is known to me by another book called *The Delta Blues* in which he travels to the deep south in search of Robert Johnson to record his works for the Library of Archives or something like that. Anyway, while he's looking for him he stumbles on Muddy Waters.

When I read *Delta Blues* I remembered reading one of the songs that Muddy Waters wrote. It had a common chord progression that everybody shared. This was the way the blues were played back then. Only Muddy could have written the lyrics, though. The song was called "Worried Man's Blues" and the music to it was in *The People's Songbook*. It says folk song choral arrangement by Waldemar Hille. Another song I took the book out for was "Midnight Special." Credence does that song. A lot of people don't know it but that's a prison song you know "with swing and strong accent" or, in the case of "Midnight Special," with "sentiment, in a steady beat." For "Worried Man's Blues" there is one word above the first staff and it says "Worriedly."

I studied music for a couple of hours in composition format. My mind was boggling over octave registers, so I quit for a while and played a couple games of cards until supper. It is the same every Saturday night. Hot dogs and beans. Every Sunday night it's cheeseburgers. After chow I played a couple of hands of cards but I didn't gamble.

Then I went to the gym. Terry worked me hard tonight like he always does, and I felt good after the gym. I owe Terry two cartons and Dave two cartons. They both told me that they wanted a store order this week. Well, that's fine but I didn't have any money in my account because I had just paid $150 in canteen. So I didn't know what to tell them, although I'm sure it will be all right.

After gym I took a shower and flipped the house movie on. There is a movie every Wednesday, Friday and Saturday. They rent a movie and you just flip the TV to channel three and its on between 8 to 8:30. It was a Van Dam flick. A good one. I didn't catch the name though. In the beginning, he escapes from a prison bus and goes on to be a good guy until the end when they catch him and send him back to jail. After the movie, I played a couple of hands of rummy until lockdown at 10:30 PM.

This day may sound boring to you and it kind of was. But it was a good day. It was a good day because nothing bad happened.

Now we'll see what tomorrow will bring.

November 2, 1993

Another day locked away.

I'm in a block with six other guys. One of the six is a former NBA basketball player. He's a nice guy who ran into a streak of bad luck. Got hit by a car. A hit and run. He went into a coma and came out of it with his equilibrium all messed up. He then caught a couple of assault charges. He came to jail and found out he has cancer of the mouth.

There is Tommy Giani, an Italian dope addict. They feed him tranquilizers like candy and he seems dazed most of the time. He sleeps a lot. Old man Stan never comes out of his room except to go to chow, the shop, and occasionally watch TV.

"Everything I need is in my cell," he tells me.

There is a new guy by the name of Al. He's got those heroin eyes. I think he's a junkie but until he admits it, I wouldn't swear by it.

By far the most interesting character in here is Charlie. Most of the time you try and figure out if a guy is full of shit or not. Jail is not exactly the kind of place where you take somebody's word for anything. Charlie, however, I'm still trying to figure out. He is an ex-CIA zombie spy, who has had countless experiments done on him starting at a very young age. He is also haunted by demons and visited by angels. He claims to have relations with saints and extraordinary paranormal experiences. Spying on cops was where he ended up, he says. This put him on the police shitlist and they pursued him relentlessly. They arrested him on no charges, locked him up and basically messed with him.

One time in his apartment, he heard a crashing at the door and went to the corner of the bedroom and sat there with a high-powered rifle. He said he didn't know it was the police. When they finally broke the door down (without a warrant) and saw him with the rifle, they left rather quickly.

Charlie wondered what was going on and went outside where he found mass confusion. His house was being surrounded and there were police everywhere. No one noticed him come out of the house. There was a cop crouched down loading shells into a shotgun next to a cruiser. He walked over and crouched down next to the cop.

"So what's going on?" he asks the cop.

"Keep you head down buddy," the cop says. "There's a gunman up there."

"Up where?" Charlie asks.

"Right there," the cop says, pointing to the window of Charlie's apartment.

"No, there's not," Charlie says.

"Yeah?" says the cop. "How do you know?"

"Because that's my apartment and there's no one in there," Charlie says.

At this point he was arrested.

This is a light story from Charlie, yet I found myself drifting into his cell more and more. Charlie has a genius IQ of 160 or thereabouts and conversations were occasionally boring. I would tell him a few of my own and it was not long before he compared me to the likes of "The Fabulous Furry Freak Brothers." We have discussed the Don Juan books, Nietzsche, *The Book of Five Rings*, pondered politics, renounced religion, put down philosophy and both shared the dislike of any law enforcement official. Inevitably, the conversation seems to drift back to his CIA zombie days.

"I was tied to a chair," he tells me, "and made to drink a glass of orange juice with huge amounts of LSD, after which an electrode was placed over my heart, with another inserted into my penis. The electrodes were connected to a variable controlled current with a range of 0 to 18 volts and unlimited amperage."

The details of an experiment begin to unfold.

And today there is another story.

"I was told I was to meet an Indian shaman," Charlie begins. "I was given a large amount of LSD and all my clothes were taken away. I was put into a room that was pitch black, though after a time, I could make out a silhouette of the left side of a man. He was utterly terrifying. His left eye was giving off a light and then he did something that was totally beyond comprehension."

"What did he do?" I excitedly asked.

"I don't know," Charlie said. "It was beyond comprehension."

Charlie's "control" told him that he had been given a demon and an angel.

"But I already have an angel," Charlie said.

What a lucky guy, I thought. He's got two angels when I've never even seen one. I can only take so much before I steer the conversation towards a more rational line of thought. Charlie has a particular way of droning on using four, five and six syllable words that can, in effect, be kind of hypnotizing.

At some point, before my brain overloads and my ears start spewing sparks, I deftly slink from the room, remembering a phone call I'd forgotten to make. Yet, again and again, I find myself compelled to go talk to the man with the gold rimmed glasses, the self-proclaimed Ghandi philosopher.

To continue what I have dubbed "The Cell Eleven Chronicles" I see that all of the sudden it is 1:43 AM. I am not tired, or if I am, it will be an hour yet before I turn over for the twentieth time to go to sleep. Music class in seven hours. I imagine I'll be dragging ass.

My time here is ticking away. With good time, my last day will be December 23rd, two days before Christmas. So the feds come to get me on the 23rd. Christmas will be bleak. They don't tell you where they are moving you. By the time I get there it will be the 24th and I won't even receive a letter Christmas day. No cards, nothing. Merry Christmas.

One of my favorite Christmas songs I sang as a kid in front of a lot of people. I was attending a Christian Academy and it was the Christmas Pageant. I had a solo and the song was "Noel." It still sticks in my mind.

"The first Noel, the angels did say, was to certain poor shepherds in fields as they lay. In fields as they lay, keeping their sheep, on a cold winter's night that was so deep."

And then thirty kids began the chorus behind me. Then the first verse began again. Only this time it was staggered with one group singing the first line while the second group sang six or eight beats behind them. Then the third group began singing behind them. It sounded beautiful and I will never forget it.

November 10, 1993

"I believe this house is haunted," she said.
"Are you the ghost?"
"What I am is a mystery," he replied. "Even to myself."
Clive Barker.

More reading.

At night I used to long for my dreams. They were the only things that would take me away from this place, from behind these walls. Dreams of escape came often. They were so realistic yet teasingly bizarre. I would be free, see the wind blowing through the trees, taste the air. And through my dreams, I found freedom.

Now it is not so. More and more I find myself waking in the early hours of morning trying to shut out the images and pictures that are still fresh in my now tortured mind. Change the channel. Click. I stay awake until at least two in the morning. Sometimes much later. At first I wanted sleep but could not sleep. I would stay up until I was so exhausted I couldn't keep my eyes open. Then toss and turn for another hour or two with them closed. Finally, sleep.

But now my dreams haunt me. Is it all my past sins which have laid down in my conscious now leaping to life, to pluck at my sanity? To rob me of the one escape I had? Or am I the ghost? Do I only torment myself? Could it be somebody is out there right now suffering because of me? It is, as the quote suggests, a mystery.

Jail is historically a place of suffering. People attack you when you go to jail. They will tell your secrets, abandon you, even make up stories to make you look bad. Maybe because you are not there to stand up for yourself. Maybe there is a gap in the circle you once belonged to and people need to make excuses for the hole by citing incompetence. If somebody got hit by a car and went to the hospital for six months, people would say "Poor so and so, he'll be healed soon." But go to jail and its "That no good scum bag went to jail." They talk of you like you're never coming back. Ever. I am using examples of other inmates although it has happened to me to a certain extent. You find out who your true friends are.

Jail is a place where many men find the true meaning of loneliness. Even if you come to jail to straighten your life out, once you're in it seems that everything you've had deteriorates. Guys in here talk to me, they reach out, they want to know what to do. Because even though we don't know one another, we're all going through the same shit.

There is a sense of camaraderie. We all help out each other but there is a limit. And its not even a gray area limit. It's a thick black line you do not cross. Got a cup of coffee? Sure. Smoke? Maybe. Can I trust you? Absolutely not. If you find yourself in trouble, you got yourself there, you get yourself out. There are cases where guys spend a lot of time together, I imagine they get tight. There are exceptions to every case. The jail I am in is a medium security facility but inmates are doing longer terms. Maybe it's just me but I doubt it.

Seven more weeks to go before my time here is up. Then I'm off to who knows where for another three years.

Time ticks by. I sit and wait for the end of the nightmare. In between the beginning and end is, for now, only time served.

And, a mystery.

November 13, 1993

Gotta ramble on. Find the queen of my dreams. Ramble on.

"Hey Paul, whatcha doing?"

"Nothing Sean. What about you?"

Me? Well I'm gonna ramble on over to the library. Today I rambled on out the door to the yard. That's the extent of my rambling. Tomorrow I will ramble on down to music class and maybe tomorrow night I will ramble on down to the gym. And besides the chow hall, I have no other place to ramble. Oh, once in a while, when I get my dander up, I ramble on down to pod five to listen to Paul pour his heart out about how his woman screwed him over or maybe scare up a game of spades for fun. No more gambling. It's been almost two months since I gambled.

It really sucks because B.T.C. (Before The Clink) I used to cruise everywhere. When I was growing up, I knew people who had spent their whole lives in their hometown. I just couldn't fathom it. I might stay in one place for maybe a few years, but eventually I gotta ramble. Even if it's just a road trip, skiing or going to Mexico from San Diego to surf. Usually, though, it was a three thousand plus mile jaunt. Massachusetts to San Diego or San Diego to Massachusetts. Every time I came back to Massachusetts I seemed to get into trouble, though. The last time, I was way out of control. Probably because I knew I was coming to jail and didn't want to deal with it in any way, shape or form.

I feel pretty miserable most of the time. Now I'm realizing my bid is just beginning. Ten months into it and it just makes me sick. The same food over and over. The food is good but there comes a point when you eat it only from necessity. I've begun to forget what day it is sometimes, which is OK. And I forget what month it is, which is not OK.

I believe I am on the verge of an emotional collapse. Every step I take I expect to go crashing through the floor and find myself in the dirt with a mock-up prison of cardboard above me and the director yelling "Cut!" while the actors break for lunch. Days and nights become equals. Neither is better nor worse than the other, though I prefer the night because it is predictable in that I'm locked in my cell. Days are all right, but they take too long. What they have most in common with night is that they pass.

Time.

My nemesis. My whore. My lover. Sweet, deceitful time.

I found out today that a friend of mine caught a real smoker. His name is Martin Thompson, a really cool kid. Mellow, laid back with long, hippy-type hair. Armed robbery with a mask, otherwise known as Masked Armed Robbery. Here's a little lesson kiddies. If you're going to stick up a place don't use a mask because you get ten to fifteen years in Walpole (rhymes with hellhole). For the uneducated, my friend Martin will do nine to ten years. He's just a kid. Another one of my friends, Tommy, got nailed for trafficking. Bing. Seventy-six months federal time. That's six years anyway.

And here's the kicker of the month. Little Sal wanted to be in a gang. Little Sal joined the Latin Kings. Little Sal took part in a murder. Little Sal got busted. Little Sal believed the cops when they told him he would get hardly any time if he cooperated. Little Sal went to court and testified against all his buddies. Guess what? They gave Little Sal a life sentence along with the rest of them. Little Sal is in big trouble. He caught a natural at the ripe age of eighteen.

They are placing odds on the length of his life.

In days.

November 21, 1993

Out of my head. That's where I'm going.

I have this urge to write somebody but I can't figure out who. I had some envelopes done up by one of the talented local artists on the tier above me. Now I can't think of who to write to. So I'm writing to myself. I wrote a poem, a song, something called "Hours." Depressing as hell.

I actually had two visits yesterday. Diane came to see me today for the first time in two weeks. I'm still crazy about that girl.

Bob Seeger's on the radio yelling about that "Fire Down Below."

I had music class today. We picked up the song "Needle and the Spoon" by Lynard Skynard. It sounds excellent. The teacher is bringing me in a fuzz-wah hopefully for the next practice. I'm trying to get enough songs together for a concert before Christmas but I'm running out of time. We are moving right along though.

No new tragedies in the block lately. Trey is locked up. He's a Jamaican kid who outwardly appears rational and educated but he has a history of just freaking out. Blitz is the word. He stabbed a guy eight times in here. That is not why he is locked down now though.

Three weeks ago they brought in a twenty-two year old kid. He pulled out these pictures of a girl in a skirt and pumps and somebody asked him if it was his girlfriend.

"Oh no," he said, "that's me."

He was wearing a wig in the picture and is a flaming cross-dressing queen. I always refer to him as "her" or "she." She likes it. She has the cell next to mine and after lockdown I heard her talking to me through the vent.

"What?" I demanded.

She tittered. She actually tittered.

"This is 555-OPIG" she said. She said it just like that, not five-five-five-oh-pee-eye-gee. She said "pig."

I have dubbed her Piggy and I think she just adores the name. She's all right although I had to backhand her once. She touched me on the shoulder in a casual way but it was obviously a feminine gesture. It wasn't just that, though. I don't like anybody to touch me for any reason at all. So I backhanded her and knocked her on her ass. She looked at me in surprise and put her hand to her cheek.

"You terrible man," she squeaked as she ran to her cell.

Sunday came and football was on. Now this is jail and we are all in a six man unit. Trey, Gary, Kevin, Al, Piggy and me. Sunday is football day. Period. Well Piggy threw a tizzy because she wanted to watch something, I don't know what, I wasn't here. I had rambled on down to pod five.

When I came back the cable box was in pieces, Trey was locked down and Piggy was pouting. Trey blitzed. He didn't smack Piggy but ripped the cable box out and threw it down to my tier. I tried to fix it and thought I actually might have succeeded. But that sucker was toast. No more MTV. Bogus. Hopefully, I will be moving to pod five soon. I've only got about five weeks left here anyway. As I close this, Lynard Skynard is on the radio singing about a free bird. Lord help me, I can't change.

November 26, 1993

Today I finally got out of the six man pod. They moved the six of us into a much larger pod, a twelve man unit. The last pod was six cells. Three upper, three lower with enough room in the so-called day room for a TV, a table with four chairs and a trash can. No shit. Now there is much more room to pace if need be. The six of us, Al, Piggy, Kevin, Trey, Gary and me, all took upper tier rooms. Six cells upper, six lower.

They moved in a regular plethora of inmates. Jose, who escaped from a van with mere weeks to go, will be receiving a new sentence I'm sure. Then there's Earl, a regular powerhouse of wit and wisdom with sayings such as "Licker in the front, poker in the rear." There are two other men who are older. One is a skinner who I have not had the pleasure of meeting yet. His name is Peter and his tastes run pathetically towards kids.

The other guy they moved in to the tier below is my old friend Charlie, the ex-CIA zombie of the famed "Chronicles of Cell Eleven," my intellectual stimulator, the spark of intelligence in a void of fried minds. Already we have begun the "Chronicles" again. He is extremely intelligent and most of the time his statements are beyond my ignorant comprehension, yet I cling to the discussions of society and its subjects: art, politics, religion and literature, with all the fervor of a man at sea clinging to a life preserver after the ship has sunk.

An incident today centered around Pat. I couldn't believe it was Pat. They came in the middle of our AA meeting and did a head count. Pat had tried to escape and got caught real bad in the razor wire. I heard he was pretty torn up. They shipped him upstate today I believe. Pat was the last guy that I thought would try to escape. He was a nice guy who got along with everybody. When we had an inmate meeting once about Randy and me howling like dogs after lockdown, Pat led it. I've heard he claimed that it was a spur of the moment thing. The guards left the north door open and he saw his chance and went for it.

I have to wonder if I would do the same thing. I don't think so. Pat and my circumstances are different. I know he just got done doing a long bid. I believe I heard it was five years. I can't say I blame him and actually several people thought it was me. I think if I was doing a lot of time that after a while escape would be on my mind.

Tonight at AA I ritualistically flicked little balls of torn up napkin with my spoon at people. I sat in the back row, denial isle, and talked quietly, but still talked, with my friends. On the way back from the meeting I was walking behind Tim, a guy from Boston who clapped whenever someone at the meeting mentioned how long they've been sober. This led the sheep into a round of applause. My friends and I looked at each other and laughed and rolled our eyes because before Tim came, this never happened.

"Don't you know how to act at those meetings?" Tim asked me in the hall.

"Sure," I said and shrugged my shoulders.

"Then, why don't you?" he asked.

I didn't answer him because I couldn't.

When I got back to the block the house movie was on and the block was full with twelve inmates. Something was eating at me. Something still is. I have the feeling that something is very wrong. I need to focus more. I need to think positively and lay low. I can't do it. What will this mean when I get to the federal pen? I feel like my mind is really screwed up. I'll be reading a book and thinking of something and will be so engrossed in my thoughts that I will have to go back four paragraphs or a page. This has happened before but not with such intensity.

I feel like I am becoming unstable, that the foundations of my mind are beginning to weaken, perhaps crack. I am beginning to wonder if I will just snap. Visions of me fighting and beating the shit out of a bunch of guards trying to subdue me dance in my head. I can feel it and I am afraid. I cannot say that it is fear that is eating me up. Maybe it is. But I believe that it is the isolation, the lack of freedom, the loss of loved ones, the endless soul searching and "what ifs" that are doing it.

And this feeling of uselessness.

That's it, that's exactly how I feel.

Useless.

Louis L'Amour wrote from the lips of Bendigo Shafter in his book *Bendigo Shafter,* "It is easier to destroy than to build. It is also easier to scoff and turn away than to continue and do what a man knows is right." Or something to that effect. I tried to look it up but couldn't find the passage.

I am even contemplating throwing myself at the mercy of God and asking Him to straighten me out. But, as with most things in life, I know I must make the choices that correct myself, that the answer lies within. Maybe it is because I look at myself and do not like what I see. I cannot drink away my self-proclaimed inadequacy. I cannot drug it away either. It is not because I can't get drugs but because I have sworn off both while incarcerated and hopefully thereafter.

So maybe all the reasons I began to drink and run and hide from myself are now surfacing again. But if they are they are, not exposing themselves. Maybe they are just obvious problems that have always been there but one's I've deemed "conquered" long ago. Maybe they have been solved and now I have no problems so I need to create some? That's stupid though. I have witnessed people who thrive on turmoil and cannot function without creating some kind of trouble or hassle for themselves. I know people who set themselves up to take a full fall and I am sure that I am not in this category.

No, I believe that there is something deep within me that is crying for recognition. Maybe something in my childhood. I can't put my finger on it but I sense it is there. It is the answer to the question that I do not know that haunts me so. It dances beyond my grasp and I believe it comes to me in my dreams every so often just to taunt me.

However, I'm a determined man. Hearsay and menial obstacles won't subdue me from my true course. I know what I want and will pursue it. I think I will just stay on track, try to stick to the positive aspects of everything and set my sights as high as they will go. But uppermost, I will start to try harder to give everything my best. No short-cuts. I will be a man people will remember and, most importantly, respect.

And I will pursue my dream of being a musician to the very end.

December 3, 1993

It has been a while since I've written. Exactly how long, I'm not sure. I am certain I wrote last month. Now it is December.

I asked for and received my projected release papers from this jail.

My time here ends on December 25th, Christmas Day. So Christmas morning I will pack up my belongings and move back to maximum security. Probably A or B block. It kind of sucks because it will be all unsentenced inmates. The feds came yesterday and removed another federal prisoner. I believe I am the only federal inmate left in the whole jail. I will be put into maximum only until the federal people show up to move me. I believe that will be around the first of January.

I'm a little apprehensive about the upcoming move. Apprehensive? Maybe a little. Since my gambling debts have been paid I've hung pretty comfortably. Plenty of cigarettes. I bought a killer tie-dyed Harley shirt for five packs. This is a county jail and so many people come and go. Most of the guys are short timers and I've been here now almost a year. All the screws know me. All the inmates know me or know about me.

Lately things have been very easy it seems. Music class is going good and we got the OK for our Christmas concert on the 21st. Three guys: Mark on drums, Paul on bass and me on guitar. We all sing different tunes. I am only singing one, "Born To Be Wild" by Steppenwolfe. My guitar playing is coming right along. I am studying music religiously. Composition and theory. I like it very much, although it is extremely hard at times. It is like trying to learn a foreign language. There is a tremendous sense of accomplishment to it after studying and then looking at actual sheet music and being able to know. Mom sent me a way cool 100% cotton Turkish towel bathrobe. Its white and comfortable.

It is good to see degrees of self-control coming back into my life. My self-esteem is returning without alcohol. This is amazing. Tuesday I had a visit and I went out looking for Diane. Lo and behold if it wasn't my father who had come to see me. He looks damned good for his age. He just had his fiftieth, or somewhere over fiftieth, birthday. Diane came while he was here and she looked devastating as always. I realized that she still comes to see me after all this time (how long has it been?) and that it's nothing to take for granted.

In actuality, I have a lot to be grateful for and there are so many others who have it so much worse. I know because I've got to look at them every day. Nobody really envies me going to federal prison to do four years, or three more anyway. I think I have begun to really accept this mess and realize the steps that I have to take to straighten myself. I think I am going to surprise everybody when I get out.

I hope the world will not slam the door in my face.

December 11, 1993

When was it actually? When was it exactly that I stood at the crossroads and looked around? What point in my life did I choose the wrong direction?

Many cultures expound on the four directions, or the four winds. Maybe I have only just arrived at the crossroads? Or do I stand here again? Maybe my destiny is already cut out and I am like a leaf, blowing in the wind, buffeted in one direction only to swirl in circles and race back to where I started. It could be that the leaf has come to rest somewhere and will lie upon the ground until it starts to die and decay. From earth into earth. All things return to Mother Earth.

I feel I am rotting already in this stinking jail. How clearly it becomes when one abstains from the use of alcohol and drugs, the things we turn to when we want to run and hide. All the ugly truths of humanity become so grossly apparent. The inadequacies of the people as a race. Selfishness eats away at the society. When every man lives for himself there can be no progress as a whole. Slowly the world is deteriorating. Things are not getting better. They are worse. Why? Because we are all dying. Every day brings us closer to death so we spend our lives trying to become wealthy or gratify the self.

Live a full life it is said. Men turn their backs on other men for their own personal gain. Some men have millions while others starve. To live a full life. What is the point? To die with the most toys? A good man should live to attain knowledge and to utilize that knowledge to benefit not only himself but his neighbors and his nation. I sit in jail and my life seems such a waste.

Never has my head been clear enough to possess such thoughts nor untangle the knots of confusion that bound me as surely as the chains which they will place me in for transportation to the federal prison on Christmas Day. I find myself so ignorant of the world around me. I lack an educated mind. Yet my fears and dreams are equal to those of any man. I see my limitations. I am aware of my faults. Though I am in denial about my stupidity.

There are instincts and urges deep inside us beyond our comprehension. There is a realm that all of us walk in, all of us know. Yet no one can quite put their finger on it. It may come to us in dreams, or in sudden visions or strange feelings. But it is there. You know it is. It is a peaceful place, although chaos sometimes dances through it. At times it may have guided you through times of difficulty.

Have you ever dreamed a dream that you can't quite remember, but was so outstandingly clear you know you must have gleaned knowledge from it, but don't know what? A dream in which something important happened but that you forgot? You felt you had to go back to discover that which is missing but you can't go back. And you find yourself looking forward to dreaming again that night. Maybe the next night. Then it is gone for a while only to reappear. A nudge at the back of your mind demanding attention.

Maybe that has not happened to you. But I think it has.

Maybe I'm just crazy.

December 24, 1993

Well here it is, my first Christmas Eve in jail. A lot has happened since I last wrote. I am now back in maximum security. They moved me over here this morning.

Tom and my brother came to see me in the early afternoon. Diane came later at about 2:30. She could only stay fifteen minutes before they called my time because Tom and Jimmy were here for forty-five minutes. I guess as an inmate on federal remand my visits are limited to one hour total. It kind of sucked.

Latest news. Piggy received a serious beating last week. Someone stole a carton of cigarettes from her and she ran right to the cops.

As I write they are strip searching an inmate next door to me. I think he cut himself or something. They are asking him where the razor blade he used is hidden. They leave at 11:00 in about fifteen minutes. I'm sure its just another hassle for them on Christmas Eve. I think they found it because I just heard a toilet flush. They leave.

"Screw you! Bunch of assholes!" the kid yells after they are gone.

Merry Christmas.

I turn my headphones back on. The action is over.

Back to Piggy's beating. It happened around noon. No one knows what was happening until she started screaming. We all ignored it and avoided looking up at her cell as called for in proper jail etiquette. It was a prolonged beating and went on for ten minutes. That is a long time to take a beating. After the first five minutes I thought it would end but it didn't. I know it was ten minutes because I was wearing my new watch I received from my mother. It's a cool watch and shows the circles of the moon.

I could do nothing for Piggy because it was none of my concern. I honestly had mixed feelings about the whole thing. First, you have to observe and ignore things like that and there is an odd sense of detachment that becomes inbred. On the other hand, to turn your back on another human being who is being traumatized like that is a tragedy. You have to realize that things have been this way for years and will remain this way. I have a feeling I will see worse at the federal places. However, the sound of Piggy's screams will remain with me for a long time.

Moving back to jail block is a trip itself. Just before I came in, Big Bob came back to jail. A guy that was released from jail back in March is back and he remembers me. I've seen them come and go and come again. There are more than a few men in jail block that were here when I came last March.

Today I began a rigorous workout schedule. I have let myself go soft and that's something I can't afford to do where I am going. I had a light workout today and realized how pathetic I have let myself get. Tomorrow morning I will be at full force. I also played squash today. I beat the guy I played 11 to 9 the first game. I was kind of feeling him out. The second game I shut him out 7 to 0. All day I wondered if the feds would come. But at about 4:00 I realized I would be spending Christmas here.

As far as my personal thoughts, I've got a lot on my mind. After being here ten months I've finally gotten to know all the guards on a first name basis. Anything that is available in the jail at all is available to me. Just when I got the system under control to the point which I could use it to my advantages, I am through. Now its like I'll have to start all over again.

It is now 11:25 PM, thirty-five minutes to Christmas.

Over and over in my mind, I turn over the set of events which led to my being in jail. Over and over I wish I could somehow make restitution or go back in time knowing what I know now. Guess I need a visit from the Ghost of Christmas Past. It is with a heavy heart that I sit and write these words. Cut off from family, my lover, my daughter, my friends. I know that I have committed a crime and must do my time just like the next guy, or the next, or the next.

An outrageous percentage of guys are in here because of women, which I wrote about earlier in this journal. I have met more than a few that are here for beating on their girlfriends or wives. That to me is screwed up. If the situation is that bad you have to remove yourself from it or you end up like Shawn, one of the guys that has been here in jail since February. He stabbed and killed both his woman and baby. Or Danny the singer in my first jail house band here who stabbed his wife thirty-six times.

Elvis is on the radio singing it'll be a blue Christmas without you. God, I think one Christmas in jail is enough to suffer for one lousy note-job bank robbery. I mean come on, I only got $1,300. That's like three and a half months for every hundred dollars I got away with. However, when you add up all the bad stuff I did and got away with I guess four years is about right. But I should get parole in two. No such luck though. Federal time has no parole.

Nine minutes until Christmas.

My watch calendar is between the 24th and 25th. I guess if I wonder how my next two Christmases will go I'll have to remember this. On the radio "The Little Drummer Boy" is playing. I'm wondering what Diane is doing. Wondering if anybody is thinking of me. I miss the fresh air. Its snowing out for the first time on Christmas Eve in a long, long time. The smell of a Christmas tree, the crinkle of Christmas wrapping being torn apart by kids.

One minute until Christmas.

Christmas all over the world. I remember . . . it's here. Christmas is here.

I guess I will escape to dreamland to seek my freedom. My eyes are too blurry to write.

1994

January 1, 1994

Last night was New Year's Eve. 1993 is behind me now. So is ten months of County Jail time. The feds still haven't come to get me and I am back in Cell 8, the six man pod that was once designated only for sentenced inmates. But they made it a jail block and I am back.

Cell 8 is on the lower tier which makes it extremely cold. As a result, I have a cold and stayed in bed and slept away the first day of the new year. I did get up for breakfast (French toast) and again for lunch (ham) and smuggled a ham sandwich back to my cell. It was a monstrous thing. Two giant slabs of ham and mayonnaise on two slices of bread. I ate it at about three o'clock and fell asleep. I slept through Saturday night dinner of hot dogs and beans which I have vowed never to eat again. I woke up at 9:00 PM and it is now past 11:00 PM.

Last night I stayed up and played cards with George who is in the cell next to mine. We talked through the night about crime, scores, drugs and how bad things are. George is a professional B & E man. His last score netted him about $14,000 in cash. We talked about alarms, about sensors, about cracking safes, robbing banks, big scores that were waiting to be done. Invariably, it all led back to cocaine.

When I robbed the bank back in '91 I hadn't even been on the stuff yet. That came later. But the more we talked the more I realized how powerful crack cocaine is. I have seen the horrible things it can do to people. I have lived through it. Just to mention it still makes my guts tighten and I feel that old urge. I have met quite a few junkies in here too and, though I have never touched heroin, know that once you become hooked nothing else matters. I have heard junkies tell me that crack is more addicting than heroin. Some may argue the point but for every one person I know addicted to heroin, I know twenty addicted to cocaine.

Crack is an evil drug because there is no escape. Crack is not prejudiced. It doesn't care how old you are or how wealthy you are or how intelligent. There is far too much crack and it has taken over my town with quiet but deadly efficiency. It is everywhere and it is breeding like a virus. No one is immune to its call after you've been hooked. The only way to avoid its power of total destruction is by abstinence. I have seen too may good people go down because of it.

My personal drug of choice was always alcohol. It was my first love and reigned over me even until the end. When I was young we were always moving and I never had friends for too long. But alcohol would always be there for me. At the age of twelve I ran away from home to Boston and never returned. Marijuana was still hard to come by at that age. Though I came across it every now and then I never had much for myself. But I found that alcohol solved all my problems. Intoxicated, I could choose to be whatever I wanted, go where I pleased and my thoughts were my own. No one could tame me.

After about six months in Boston I went before the courts where my mother gave custody of me to the state. At this point I felt I owed nobody in life anything. The state could not control me. I went from foster home to foster home before they placed me in an asylum in Greenfield, Massachusetts. I was thirteen years old. At fourteen I was appointed a legal guardian and at fifteen I hitchhiked across America to San Diego, California from Massachusetts. All this time I did pretty much as I pleased as long as I stayed on the right side of the law. There wasn't much anyone could do. Except for drinking and smoking pot, I pretty much walked a straight line.

Back in Massachusetts (my guardian kind of extradited me) I hung out with the "in" crowd. All of us drank heavily. I realize now (but didn't realize then) that I always ran, and was always running from was myself. I read somewhere that when we run away we are most likely to stumble. Alcohol had this hold over me and ultimately led me to jail.

There came a time when I stopped using alcohol and it started using me. Booze is very patient. It just sits there and waits. Its made me look foolish and incompetent more than once. But I know something that may save my life before it is ruined. I know alcohol can be beat.

The alcohol monster, like the cocaine monster, is a powerful and destructive enemy. Through disguise it pretends to be your friend. But once you become enslaved your number's up. You have no choices and you enter a downward spiral, sucked into a vortex with all the power of a black hole in space. And, you wind up dead or in jail.

I'm lucky. I'm in jail. Many times I should've been killed. Maybe this is what it took to open my eyes to see that through. I thought I was strong. I am weak. Awareness of my faults and adjusting to correct them will be the key to my success. Perseverance and dedication to honesty within myself will help me see this through. I will conquer my fears, and through my search for inner peace, I will come out on top.

January 2, 1994

The dream began like it always does.

I was eating something when I felt a filling in my tooth loosen. Another bite and the filling came completely out, a piece of metal in my mouth. I spit it into my hand. It was a small spider web-like chunk of silver. Then, my whole tooth crumbled and all of my fillings fell out. I couldn't get them out of my mouth fast enough. Big chunks of metal.

I reached in and pulled. The first large piece of silver looked like it had been cast from the lower jaw. My teeth were imbedded in the silver. The other piece was very large, too large to have come from my mouth. It was silver also, though this piece was cast in the top half of a skull and even my teeth were imbedded in its upper jaw. There was an ominous sense of foreboding.

January 4, 1994

It snowed last night and today. Not a really big storm but around a foot with up to twenty inches in the hill towns of the Berkshires.

I stayed awake until three in the morning and didn't get up until two this afternoon. Since I slept through breakfast and lunch I didn't get a look outside until dinner at 6:00 PM. By then it was dark. In my block you can't see the outside. But on the walk to the chow hall the courtyard and the yard are visible through glass. I saw the snow on the walk to dinner.

There was snow on the ground when I came here and now three seasons have come and gone and there is snow on the ground again. I guess it means more to me than most others, though it seems many inmates are more content with the coming of winter. Jail means a hot meal and a place to sleep out of the cold.

There is not much to do in the winters of Massachusetts but drink and work. I remember when I worked as a superintendent of maintenance for a college area apartment complex. Snow meant work, hooking the plow up to the truck and hiring a local kid from my town of Montague to shovel walks. John was his name. A good kid, although a little light in the head. He did like to drink though. I'd pick him up and we would head to work. He loved the snow blower like a little kid. After everyone was dug out and the complex was clear we had condominiums to do up towards Turners Falls.

Snow meant a full day's work. Samantha used to have coffee on for me in the morning. Usually she was up with the baby by the time I got up for work. And after the day was done, I'd reward old John and myself with a few beers and maybe some whiskey. More than once we made a few extra dollars plowing someone's driveway. Sometimes we'd stop at a bar to have a few though I was not yet of age. I was big for my age and had a man's job, a man's responsibility, and I drank like a man, too.

Looking back on those days I remember them clearly. Samantha and I lived way up in the hills of Ashfield when we first started out. We both worked. I worked for a department store and then a moving company. In those days I was always working. The winter in Ashfield wasn't easy for us but it wasn't really difficult either. I received my F.I.D. card from the chief of police there. He charged me two dollars and typed it up on an old manual typewriter.

"Never been in trouble with the law have you Sean?" he asked.

"No sir," I replied, not quite sure.

When it snowed in Ashfield, it really snowed. I loved to hunt and Ashfield's mountains were right behind my house on Main Street. Actually, Main Street was at the top of a big mountain. To go hunting I would simply grab my twelve gauge and walk down Main Street, take a left and hunt Ashfield Mountain.

My father taught me to hunt that mountain and I knew it like the back of my hand. I remember going out early one morning. By mid afternoon it was raining and the rain quickly froze. Trudging miles through hip-deep snow I headed home. The ice on my gun was half an inch thick.

It was in our apartment in Ashfield that Samantha became pregnant. I was eighteen years old when I found out I was to be a father. I accepted the responsibility. I did tell Samantha I thought I was too young, that it was maybe too soon. But she made the decision and I stood behind her one hundred percent once she made it. If it was a family she wanted then, by God, a family we would have. At this time I was very much in love with her. And she was very much in love with me.

Everyone knows that it is difficult for a young couple starting out with nothing. I didn't have much money but I was a determined man, determined to provide the best I could. Things were made a little easier when we moved to Montague Center. Her uncle had some money and owned an apartment house there. I helped him fix it up.

The apartment on the bottom floor came out very nice. Samantha set her mind to having that apartment. Her uncle wanted more money for it than I could afford and Samantha couldn't work being pregnant.

But Samantha could be a very persuasive and stubborn girl and when she made up her mind to get something, she got it. We got the apartment and had a shepherd dog named Angus.

Samantha had this way about her. I remember when I was in high school and dating a girl from Wendell that Samantha set her eyes on me. I was only a junior and she was already twenty-two. She worked at a pizza place and me and my friends would go there to check out her ass. I never dreamed she would take to me. We had a few encounters. She was the best friend of my best friend Doug's girlfriend, Debbie. Those two have since married. At first Samantha was just hanging out at Doug's. Then one night she asked me to go drink a couple of beers and smoke some grass. I said sure.

Everyone knew that my friend Chris and I grew the best grass around. Chris had a green thumb but I was into the marketing aspect. I'd borrow Samantha's car to bring the weed up to the University of Massachusetts to sell to the students. I would pick up Chris and we'd fill the trunk with pot and off we'd go. I was like sixteen and didn't even have a driver's license. The security guard would have us sign in to the dorms and we'd use funny fictitious names. The deal done, I'd fill her tank with gas and give her some weed.

After that first night when Samantha and I went out, we started going out some more. We'd park the car and drink a six pack and smoke up. She had a bunch of tapes and we'd listen to Motley Crue and hard rock. She had a Prince tape and after I got really buzzed, I'd find the Prince tape and play "Purple Rain" and make her swear not to tell any of my friends.

Then one night, drinking Bud bottles and parked up by the water tower in Sunderland, she asked me to kiss her. I couldn't believe it. Then she seduced me. I couldn't believe that either. I was young and un-schooled in the ways of women. But I was to learn quickly.

About this time I was living with my guardian, Tommy. Chris and I made a few bucks selling weed and Tom was upset because I was drinking and partying all the time. So, Chris and I split for California. Samantha wrote me every day. She sent me cards and told me she missed me. I called her and we talked on the phone for longer periods of time than her parents probably liked.

Chris came back first, and not too long after, I also came back. At the airport I couldn't believe it—all my friends were there: Tyronne and Kimberly, Chris and Chris, Big John, Troy and Debbie and Doug. And, of course, Samantha. She wanted to know where her hug was. Carrying my Vantage electric guitar and surrounded by friends, I came home.

Between then and the time Samantha and I got the apartment in Montague I remained somewhat a rebel. Samantha decided to tame me and that she did, for a while. With our apartment in Montague I was always working. When I wasn't working, I was either fishing or drinking or playing the guitar.

I used to drive Samantha crazy with the guitar. I guess that most women can't stand it when their man's attention is focused on something besides them. She never had much to say about it and only once did she say something good. I was playing something and she must have been in a good mood.

"Sounds good Sean," she said.

Little did she know how those words would continue to echo in my ears. I haven't laid down my guitar yet.

On August 11, 1987, my daughter Stephanie Diane Legacy was born. It is something I'll never forget. I believe that the birth of a child is a personal thing, but I was there in the room when it happened and nothing could stop the tears in my eyes. After the baby was checked, I was the first to hold her in my arms. I was a father now and I had a big responsibility, for with my daughter's first cries came not only the birth of a girl, but the birth of a family. I was never so proud and so scared at the same time. Allen's Ginger Flavored Brandy helped me through that one.

With a nice apartment, a new baby and a good job (I now had the superintendent job) it seemed like my life was off to a good start. In a matter of two years everything would deteriorate. All that I believed in and loved would vanish like an illusion. Slowly, things went bad one after the other. I can blame alcohol. I can blame myself. I could even blame Samantha. But the fact of the matter is, it just didn't work. Whether I tried too hard, or not hard enough, maybe I'll figure out some day. I do know this.

Those first few years with Samantha until Stephanie was two years old were probably the happiest of my life. I never wanted anything to work out so much as I wanted it to work out with her. They say a woman falls for a man then sets out to change him. Once she changes him she doesn't want him anymore. I've also heard that one person in a relationship always loves the other one more and that there is no such thing as equal love. I believe that Samantha started out loving me the most, but in the end I loved her the most and would do anything for her. I think once a woman knows she's got you to that point, you're beaten. She loses interest once she has you conquered.

On April 31, 1991 I robbed Pacific Mutual Bank in California. In June of 1992 I met a girl named Diane S. Beryl and we immediately fell in love. Madly, deeply, in love. My life was a hurricane of chaos and I was in for the run of my life, soon to be arrested by the F.B.I. I became an outlaw. Diane and I became caught up in the force of the wind and somehow, some way, we would find ourselves totally inseparable.

That ride lasted eight months and inevitably led me to New Hampshire, Vermont, New York, Massachusetts and all the way to Florida. I crash landed into a rehab from which I was directly ejected into jail.

The story of Diane and Sean is a good one. But I'll save that for another day.

January 10, 1994

There was a big snowstorm this past week and last night it snowed about sixteen inches. I lost six pounds while battling the flu and am down to 194. If I could only break 190 I would be really happy.

I had an argument today with Diane. She didn't come to see me again. This time she told me she had to go to dinner with her boyfriend, Mike. If they come to get me this week I won't see her for a while.

I am really beginning to despise being in jail and the pure helplessness that comes along with it. Anything or anybody on the outside is totally beyond control. A feeling of rage is building inside of me, a bitterness that evolves from being denied freedom.

The feeling comes slowly. First you go through the numbness of being in jail. It is a detached kind of feeling, a denial that you will be here so long. Then, there is an adjustment period where acceptance is the key to holding your sanity. Days tick by and then the remorse comes. Especially over the holidays. Man, you say, I wish I never did that. You find that truly in your heart you are sorry for what you've done. You make peace with yourself and face yourself. When I did this I realized that I was a screwed up kid turning into a screwed up man. But I also realized that it was not too late, that I was still young and there was so much I could do to make myself a better person. I began reading the Bible to myself late at night and struggled to regain a relationship I had with God and then lost many years ago.

And through all of this, I am still alone yet I am fighting to gain an edge, an edge that will keep me out of the prisons in the future. I'm searching for inner peace. I feel that I am doing well, that I am accomplishing something for myself.

Then comes the kicker. Struggling to find all the answers, and actually finding a few of them, I realized that no matter how much I accomplished, no matter what great heights of mental awareness or self-satisfaction I found, I still was in jail. It was extremely disheartening. So, while struggling for inner peace, I got really pissed. I didn't feel like being peaceful anymore.

No, that's not true. I just got knocked all the way back to the first step though. It's really aggravating to come to jail, go through the whole process, end up being aware of your mistakes, feeling remorseful for your crime, forging whole new planes of consciousness, stripped now of alcohol and drugs. Accepting the fact that you need to adjust certain ideas and control your urges to run and hide from everything. All this new knowledge overwhelms you and you can't even apply it.

Now I sit in jail and become bitter. Three more years to go and by then all these thoughts of inner peace will be gone. What's going to replace them? Rage, that's what. Pure rage at the system. Rage at being robbed of the prime years of my life. I'll be a friggin' hardened criminal. Won't I? Would you? Would you be pissed? Of course you would. And

I think that's the problem with these so-called "correctional facilities." There is no rehabilitation. You stick a criminal in with three hundred other criminals and expect him to rehabilitate? Yeah, right.

The group I'm with now is composed of Dennis (armed robbery), Walter (violation of a restraining order, repeat offender and general nuisance to society), Tony (accused child molester), John (being held as a fugitive from justice pending escape from New Hampshire), and George (professional B & E man). I can classify us like this: Dennis (alcohol and coke); Walter (alcohol, coke, heroin, whatever); Tony (soap operas); John (alcohol and coke); George (coke and probably alcohol) and me (alcohol, coke and pills).

The six of us are together all day, every day. We play a lot of cards, watch the house movie, go to the gym, and play a lot of cards. There is a sense of camaraderie which is greater than being in with forty other inmates. Or even a dozen for that matter. There is always that unbreakable code of every man for himself and not getting too close. But it is much easier to be socially accepted. Inmates are social critters. Each knows the other probably led a lifestyle that was somewhat similar to their own lifestyle. Being a drug addict, a thief, dealer, whatever—with the exception of Tony.

Every guy has a hundred stories. Every guy wants to hear a thousand more. Nothing in jail is better than a good story because a good story offers one of the two truly valuable things in jail.

The first thing a good story offers is knowledge. Jail is a virtual encyclopedia of criminal knowledge: how to hot wire a car, how to disconnect alarms, how not to get busted and how to clear yourself if you do. The latter two seem to be the most important things to know, yet are kept by some as secret knowledge.

The other valuable thing a good story offers is laughter and laughter is sometimes more important than knowledge. By laughter I don't mean just a chuckle or snicker, but rather all out uncontrollable laughter. A story told by an inmate will most likely bring a good laugh. Rarely will it bring the unstoppable hilarious laughter that carries a little bit of freedom to the heart. I've found that such moments are more likely to occur at the spur of the moment and are brought on by the quick wit of the con.

These moments are priceless. We had one of them today while sitting around playing five man cutthroat pitch and watching the Spanish channel. Even though none of us speaks a word of Spanish, we watch it because they show a lot of gorgeous women wearing next to nothing.

While we were playing cards, the Spanish equivalent of The Price Is Right television show was on. This blonde girl was on the show. She wasn't very attractive and someone commented on her voice. But in a few minutes our card game had come to a complete halt with all eyes glued to the TV. Realizing the foolishness of it all, we all had a good laugh. Like I said, times like that are hard to come by. Maybe being in a six-man pod makes it a little easier to laugh.

Daniel, the guy I sold my Saint Jude medallion to, tried to take me for what he owed me for it. I went down to see him and straightened him out. Well, I suspected, but had it confirmed later, that he's got the Ninja or Aids. And he's dying. The other day, on the way to chow, he stopped in front of my door and slid an envelope under it. The envelope had my name on it and I stuffed it quickly into my pocket, thinking it might be contraband. It is illegal for sentenced inmates to have any contact at all with the inmates of a jail block which is considered maximum security. I opened it in my cell and, to my surprise, I found my Saint Jude medallion and a note.

"Sean, this medallion belongs to you, not me," the note read. "Wear it in faith. Daniel."

This is another rarity in jail. I think that Daniel is doing a lot of soul searching right now, he is obviously dying. What was it that possessed him to give the Saint Jude medal back to me? It was compassion. If I was Daniel right now I would be doing everything I could to insure my soul from going to hell. As it is I am soul searching, but Daniel is obviously on a much higher plane than I am on right now.

What can I do?

I can do this. I will never lose this medallion. I will keep it forever and I will ask God to bless Daniel in my prayers. Maybe Daniel will go to Heaven, if there is one.

I am beginning to struggle with religion again. I read the Bible late at night and have even begun to pray. Many people tend to portray God as an all powerful being and believe all sinners are doomed to fire and brimstone. But I would like to paint God as peaceful, a God of compassion and forgiveness, one who loves us all, no matter what we may have done.

January 15, 1994

I never will be able to figure out why I keep writing like this. I never have any idea of what I'm going to write about. At least one thing is consistent—I always have to smoke while I'm writing. Right now its eleven thirty at night and I'm sure I will be writing for at least an hour which is why I dated this the 15th of January.

Maybe I'm writing this so someday I can look back on it and read it. Maybe some day my grandchildren will read it, or even their kids. I will type it someday and have it bound in leather and undoubtedly it will sit in a box in an attic, basement or closet for years. The chances of getting it published are about five zillion to one I figure. I think that by the time it is finished it will portray an accurate account of both prison and my life.

It is cold in my cell. Damned cold. In the morning there is ice in the toilet which I piss little "X"s into. Sometimes "O"s. I am still in Northampton and jammed into that little six-man pod. I'm sick of playing cards, although I do like playing George in cribbage for push-ups. I always skunk him for double so he has to do sixty instead of thirty. I've hit the floor once or twice myself in the past couple of weeks.

Today I saw a classic movie on TV. I had flipped to it during a commercial in the Kansas City-Houston football game. The movie was "Ragtime" and it was based on a case of extreme injustice dealt to a black man in the thirties or forties. I've seen the movie a few times and liked it. Near the end it finds the hero holed up in a fortress type of building that he and his cronies have taken by storm. Surrounded by police, ready to do him in, they send in a man to try to talk him out of it. Though I can't remember the whole conversation, it was very powerful and the moral of it was that vengeance can only perpetuate more vengeance. Somewhere the chain must be broken. Somewhere, someone must turn the other cheek and say, "No." The hero in the movie laughed at this and was killed in the end.

I hope I don't run out of stuff to write and just draw a blank one day. Maybe in four years I can say all that there is to be said in the life of Sean Legacy. Somehow I doubt it. I believe there is curiosity inbred in us all to question everything, to learn more, to advance forward, always forward, searching for our dreams. They say a man has ceased to live once he has lost his dreams. Me? I guess I've always been a dreamer. In these pages you will find all of my dreams, all of my fears, all of my personal victories. And, you'll share my losses, too. May they be few.

Speaking of victories, I received a gift the other day. The property guy came around and handed me a bag. When I opened it I saw it was from my daughter Stephanie. Talk about spirits being lifted making a heart soar! In the bag was a letter from Stephanie. Although she's only six and the letter only a few sentences, the words were the best of the thousands I've read since I got here. She also drew me a picture of her as a butterfly and sent me a book she made. One side of the book said, "The Book of Stephanie" and inside were pictures cut out from construction paper and taped together. A man, a woman, doggies and stuff. Little girl stuff. "To Dad, Love Stephanie" was written all over everything.

Let me tell you, it made my heart feel good. I also received six photographs of her with her bear that I sent her for Christmas. "One picture for each year old that I am," she wrote. Bless her grandmother, she is the one behind the scenes that made it happen. I guess now she likes to hear my letters and demands that every time I send one her grandmother must read them all. Well, she won't be able to do that after a little while I'm sure. As a matter of fact, I'll be writing her a letter tonight. She is a beautiful child in these pictures. I am sending one to my father on Tuesday if no mail goes out tomorrow.

Yes, that little package I got from my daughter was really a heart burster, bursting with happiness that is. I really do love that daughter of mine and someday I will be a father that she is proud of. I want to give her everything she wants, not just what she needs. Between Stephanie and Diane I've sure got my work cut out.

January 18, 1994

Night time. I am struggling through my music studies. Intervals above notes which can't be parts of major scales, enharmonic intervals and it was finally inversions of intervals that fried my brain. Music theory is hard. I tell Diane that it is like learning to read Chinese. I am almost done with my basic music theory book which is sixteen chapters and three hundred and fifty pages of torture. My next book is *Harmonic Materials in Tonal Music,* an advanced teaching of harmonic theory. I just look at it and get discouraged but I continue to plod ever onward. Music has always been a part of my life.

Ever since my grandfather showed me a basic country and western chord progression, I was hooked. I think I was around eleven when I received my first guitar. It was an acoustic guitar that my mother bought for me. I remember having it when I lived on the farm in Colrain, the house I ran away from, never to return. I was twelve when I left so I guess I was eleven when I tried to bang out "Iron Man" by Black Sabbath. My older brother Tony was a Kiss freak. Disco music had come and gone and was replaced by the likes of Gene Simmons, Ozzy Osborne and Randy Rhoades, my all-time favorite hero. My mother had remarried to a guy who had three kids of his own. I don't think they all lived with us. If they did, it was off and on.

My mother had fulfilled a promise that she made to us as kids. The promise was that we would live on a farm and have chickens and cows and, wonder of wonders, my very own horse. Sheeba was her name and she was a quarter horse. Our relationship was tenuous at best. She liked to jump the fence and go up the road to see our neighbors who owned a stable and boarded horses. At our neighbors she would hang out with the other horses. Once I got my boot caught in the stirrup while dismounting and she danced around and scared the shit out of me. Another time while I was saddling her she nonchalantly stepped on my foot and didn't seem to notice me howling for a few minutes.

I've always liked horses though. There is something very earthy about riding. It makes you feel like a man to have your own horse and ride her when it pleases you. I had to study a lot to learn about taking care of her and though I only had her for a few years, I'll never forget her.

The farm was way out in the sticks of Colrain which meant going to yet another school. I had attended a private school in South Deerfield but I was thrown out after a nasty little incident involving cold pills that somehow got reported to the authorities there as Blues. My new school was packed with hicks and all the hicky things that went along with it. I hated it and used to cut school a lot.

Sometimes I'd leave the school and walk across the mountains to get home. The first time I did that I thought I was lost for sure. But my sense of direction was good and I'd end up home before mid-day. Other times I'd get on the bus just to jump off a mile or two up the road, then hike back through the woods and watch the house until everyone was gone. Whoever had lived in the barn before had left tons of old stuff. This stuff was treasure in any kid's eyes and just poking around through all of it was a blast.

There were chickens to feed, cows to feed and Sheeba to hay and change the sawdust. A massive wood heater burned in the basement and heated the whole house in winter. I split many cords of wood in summer and winter. It was hard work but that makes a boy feel good.

I think it was there that I developed a sense of hard work and saw the benefits that came from it. I was the one who would shovel all the sawdust into the barn after they dropped it off. I was the one who cut the wood and would get up in the middle of the night to throw wood on the fire in the basement. It was a dangerous job. If you ever dropped a chunk of maple on a cold toe you'd curse for days. I fed the chickens, the cows, the horse and shouldered most of the responsibility of running that farm. My little brother Jimmy was just too young. And my older brother Tony would rather be blasting his stereo.

My mom's new husband was a hard worker too. I liked the guy. He liked to drink but I never saw him get out of hand. But somewhere, somehow, the relationship ended and he moved out.

A funny thing happened on the farm one summer night. Across the street from us lived a house full of Jehovah's Witnesses. When I lived in Oklahoma, I'd been raised a Christian and Mom saw to it that we went to church every Sunday and were baptized as good Christian kids should be. Religion was not forced upon me. To the contrary, church on Sunday was just part of a normal life.

The Jehovah people were nice enough. They had a little daughter about my age but her parents wouldn't let her associate with us very much. One night my brother and I made up some costumes. We were into the comic book scene. Batman was Tony's favorite comic character and Spiderman was mine. We had costumes of Batman and Spiderman with capes and masks with horns stuffed with newspaper.

With a couple of pitchforks from the barn we would get their attention by throwing light bulbs at their house. Then we'd dance around in the street that separated us and used an aerosol can to shoot some flames. When they came over after us we ran and screamed at them to get off our property. We laughed and laughed.

My twelfth birthday came and went. Bad things always happen within a week of my birthday. With Mom's husband gone, things were a little wild. One night I took a pretty good beating with a banister pole. "Screw it," I told myself. "Colrain's not for me."

I left school one morning and hitchhiked to Turner's Falls. I was a great hitchhiker. In Turner Falls I went into Cumberland Farms and asked to borrow a Magic Marker. I made a sign that said, "Boston or Bust." After I left Cumberland Falls, I walked over the bridge spanning the Connecticut River and onto Gill. The highway through Gill ran to Boston. A guy picked me up. It was the first car that pulled over and I'll be damned if I didn't get a ride all the way to Boston.

The guy asked me why I was going to Boston. I told him I was going to see my mother. Besides being a great hitchhiker, I was also a great liar. He had a few packs of Marlboro's in his car and I kept bumming cigarettes until he broke down and gave me a pack. We started talking and by the time we had reached the city I'd told him everything. He was pretty cool.

"Look kid," he said to me, "I'm either calling a priest or I'm calling the cops."

"Call a priest," I told him.

He called a priest from his mother's house. The priest directed us to a place in Boston called "Bridge Over Troubled Water." They would, with no questions asked, place you in a home for an indefinite amount of time. We first went to the an adoption clinic which was the wrong place. We finally found it and he said, "Good-bye" and I said, "Thanks." That was one righteous dude.

At the new place they asked me where I was from and I told them I was from Tulsa, Oklahoma. They raised their eyebrows. "Address?" they asked. I told them it was 11425 Newton Place. This was in fact the actual address of one of the houses I lived at in Oklahoma. They gave me the address to the house. They gave me subway money and I beat feet.

I was in Boston. I had made it and I was going to a temporary foster home, my first of many. It was a nice house, a nice Catholic family. We prayed before each meal. There were four or five other kids there. I stayed about a week.

Then I guess they gave me the boot and directed me to a another home called "Place Runaway House." I gave them the same story about leaving Oklahoma and they gave me a bed. There were girls there too. My stay at Place Runaway was extended. I don't know how long it actually was. A couple of months anyway. Kids came and went. Or they came, looked around, and split. Or they came and stayed. I met several characters.

This home was on Marlboro Street right next to the Combat Zone. During the days I would walk around and check it out. I began to jog in the mornings. A few times I wasn't allowed to go because someone had just gotten killed a block or two away. Finally, I stopped jogging entirely. A kid overdosed one day. He was about thirteen, maybe fourteen. He used to talk to me and tell me how cool Boston was and all the things that he had done growing up there.

Then he died.

One girl I remember was deaf. Her name was Wanda and she was black. She started to teach us sign language and we got along pretty good. One day I came back from walking around and she was gone.

Around then, the staff of the place approached me and said, "Look kid, we know you're not from Oklahoma, so come across." I did and soon was visited by Tom and my mom. They asked how I was and I said, "OK." Now that I think about it, nothing was mentioned about me coming home. Then again, that was fifteen years ago and while some things stand out crystal clear, others are kind of fuzzy. Soon I had to go to a court in Greenfield.

A few days before going to court, I was attacked by killer squirrels from hell in the Combat Zone at the Park. I had gone out looking for a girl to save. She had left the Runaway House after a few days and I had a crush on her, so I went to the heart of trouble looking for her. I remember someone telling me where she might be. At the park were lots of friendly squirrels. At least they looked friendly until you grabbed them by the tail. Two of them jumped on me and clawed the shit out of my hands.

I had to get a tetanus shot the day I went to court in Greenfield. When I got to court, I stood in front of the judge and he told me that my mother was giving me over to the custody of the state.

My ride had just begun. For two years I would be shipped from foster home to foster home, from shelter to shelter, until I ended up in an asylum. It was all high adventure to me. It was life in hell, belonging to no one, not staying long enough to establish any friends.

Through it all, though, I felt no sense of loss. There were no personal victories during that time. I was isolated and it was this period that I had to watch out for myself. And it was good that I learned so young how to take care of myself.

I've been doing it ever since.

January 20, 1994

Nighttime.

Reflections of the day.

At breakfast there were waffles. Because we are jail block, we eat last and therefore get any extra food. I had ten waffles with lots of syrup.

Cases and more cases. I'm in here with the inmates who are not yet sentenced and all I hear about is this one's case and that one's case. There is constant speculation about how much time they are going to get.

Being back here in jail block maximum security feels like I am going backwards. They still haven't moved me and the days are becoming monotonous. It's the waiting that's killing me. My sentence here was up a month ago and I still sit here. Time is passing so much slower. I wake up each day and wonder if today will be the day. And then, nothing happens.

I cut my hair short on the front but left it long in the back. I began to grow my beard again. I've taken to smoking cigars and speaking with the mouth of a gutter tramp. I can't help but feel that maybe, once again, I'm projecting a false image. Just blending in. At least I hope that's it. I hope I am not slowly being molded into the proverbial convict. I wear a bandanna. I have an attitude. I'm really freaking out is what I'm doing.

Being in this tiny cell block with six guys day in and day out I feel like smashing a couple of them in the face repeatedly to vent this feeling of frustration and rage. I feel disgusted. I feel tired. I want to go home. I want to be free. I spoke with my old boss at the plumbing company in California today. He told me that they would most likely hire me back when I got out. I constantly feel that a major part of my life is missing. It is that feeling of being my own man. Something deep inside is rebelling at the nature of incarceration.

I've always believed in hard work, in contributing somehow to leading a normal life. Go to work. Pay your bills. Go to work. After being self-supporting for so long having all your independence stripped away is extremely aggravating. I never dreamed that somebody would tell me, "Go live in this small box. You cannot leave the box except to eat and go to the gym for two hours a day. And at 10:30 every night you will go to this smaller box and remain until 9:00 AM." I remember a time when I swore I'd never go to jail. "It'll never come to that," I said. I was too smart to go to jail. I was too slick to go to jail. I would never put myself in a position where I would do anything that could ever result in me going to jail.

Well, here I am in jail. And it sucks.

My cellmates and I had a conversation about getting out.

"I can't stand being in jail," said Johnny. "There's just something in my blood that makes me want to get out." Johnny has twenty-four escapes, although twenty are from juvenile hall facilities.

"You've got a rabbit in your blood," says Dennis.

"No one wants to be in jail man," I say. "These places aren't right for anybody."

"You've got rabbit in your blood," Dennis says.

"Yeah, but no matter where I go, I'll always try to escape. If they ever give me a chance, if I see an opening, I'm gone."

"Escape just ain't worth it," says Andy. "Unless I had like twenty years or something. It messes up your whole life."

"Like when I escaped from New Hampshire," says Johnny. "You know the riot was going on and once we broke through the skylight I said, 'screw it man, I'm outta here.' What would you do Sean?"

"I don't know man," I said. "It's a tough call. I ain't really got that much time to do. But you know, you'd be looking over your shoulder your whole life and that's no way to live."

There are mumbles and grunts and solemn nods of approval.

"Yeah, yeah," they say.

A Rolling Stones song called "Angie" is playing on the radio.

"You know man," says Johnny, "I really like listening to music in jail. But sometimes it makes me sad because it reminds me of things I've done and times I'm missing right now."

"Yeah," agrees Denny, "and girlfriends and ex-girlfriends."

"And screwing," I add.

Music is a carrier in jail. Its like a briefcase, or a personal computer with files of your past. All songs have different memories to them: a different girl, a different age, a different stage in your life. I don't know what's harder, to listen to a song that reminds you of a woman and how good you had it made with her, or a song that reminds you of a loss. I can name a couple of albums that are directly tied in with the separation of the mother of my daughter. I can also name a few that bring back good memories. Then, there are party songs that just remind you of having a good time. These are probably subconsciously the worst. A song might remind you of a certain person, a particular event. Either way, its like Johnny says. In a way it's good. In a way it's bad. I guess the radio kind of takes the place of a woman in here. Only this one's got an "On" and "Off" switch. Every guy's dream.

I studied triads today. Major, minor, diminished and augmented. Got bored and played cards. Skipped lunch. No mail. Went to the library at 1:30 to be greeted by the grimacing librarian.

"What's the matter?" I asked her.

"Nothing," she said.

A few minutes later she broke down.

"Sean, come here," she said. "You'll appreciate this. I know you are a book fanatic and respect the library. You won't believe this."

I approached, perplexed.

She led me into the sacred Librarian's Office.

"Look at this," she said inside her office as she opened the Secret Librarian's Drawers. They were utterly empty.

"While I was on emergency medical, family emergency leave," she said, "they cleaned me out."

I tried to look sorrowful.

"A sad thing," I said. "You have been violated."

"Yes," she said, "I knew that you would understand."

I slowly walked out of the revered office of the Librarian.

"I think that this is like the 11th Commandment," I told her. "Thou shall not desecrate the hoarded books."

She sniffled, almost tearful.

"Thank you for understanding, Sean," she said as I departed.

I skipped lunch for two reasons. One was that I had too many waffles for breakfast. The other was that for lunch there was the dreaded macaroni and cheese. I did, however, go to the gym at 9:30 this morning, mostly to try and sneak into the music class which is down the hall from the gym door. In order to do so, though, I had to walk by the door of the Captain's office. He saw me, so I ducked in and pretended I had stopped to ask him permission.

"Can I please go to the music class for just two minutes?" I asked.

"No, beat it," he said. "How'd you get down here? Where are you supposed to be?"

"Aw, come on, Fred," I persisted. "Just two minutes."

"No, beat it," he said again. "How'd you get down here anyway? What are you doing wearing shorts in my office. And put that god-damned cigar out in the hall, Legacy. Jesus Christ."

"Yes, sir," I said. "Right away, sir. See ya."

I beat feet.

As with any situation, I seek the boundaries and limitations. I see exactly how far I can go, and then I go. But now, all my little pushes are on the humorous side. After all, this is a jail. There is a line that cannot be crossed regardless. They are "them" and we are "us."

And never the two shall meet.

January 25, 1994

Tempers are hot and patience is wearing thin between all of us. This block is too small for six inmates even though there are six cells in it. A small pod is OK if you are sentenced. You can come and go as you want. But you can't do this if you're not sentenced.

Tony never comes out of his room except for meals. But the other five of us, John, Dennis, Andy, George and me, are always playing cards or watching TV, for the simple reason that we have no choice. If we are not in our cells, which are freezing, we are forced to sit at the one table that barely fits.

Day in and day out we have tolerated each other but it is hard not find faults in the others. Dennis has a big, obnoxiously loud mouth that seems to flap a lot, especially early in the morning. George seems to take forever to shuffle the cards and he's so slow because he's either in the middle of a story or he's spacing out. Sometimes, I could choke him. Andy is a snitch, period. And John? John's all right.

Violence erupted today during a game of hearts when John called Dennis an idiot.

"What'd you say?" Dennis said.

"I said, 'you're a stupid idiot,'" John replied.

"Well, shut your mouth," Dennis said.

"Screw you. Shut you're damned mouth," John said.

Dennis began sputtering and I could see was starting to lose it.

"That's it," he shouted, as he slammed his cards down and stood up. "This ain't damned New Hampshire. That's it!"

John was still sitting down.

"What are you gonna do about it?" he said.

Dennis took a swipe at John who blocked it to the surprise of Dennis. Dennis is glaring now and John glares back.

"If you want to continue this we can go to my cell right now."

"Sit down, play cards and shut up," I said.

"This ain't damned New Hampshire," he said.

John has escaped from institutions in New Hampshire and this is why Dennis keeps bringing it up.

Later on, after me and John beat Dennis and Andy in spades, George had the winners. However, he didn't want Dennis for a partner because he sucks and Andy didn't want to play. George and Dennis started a serious shouting match and I was certain someone's head was going to roll, but they were shouting at each other so loud that his Royal Highness, Lt. Ortega, came in followed closely by the Testicle. He yelled at them and that was that.

The lesson I learned from this was, if there is to be a confrontation with either of these two, then it is necessary to strike swiftly. Strike hard and strike first. If I was to get into it with one of them, it would be Dennis. George and I get along fairly well. Dennis has a serious attitude. He doesn't really try any shit with me, though. I don't think he knows quite what to make of me. I'm sure he has heard rumors.

Last Thursday night I wrote my daughter's mother a letter. I wish she would stop being the way she is. I haven't even talked to her in over a year. In the letter, I told her that I felt we had to work things out. It's our responsibility as parents. I told her that I still cared about her and what happens to her and that I'd like to hear from her. She told her mother I threatened her life. That's a crock of shit. I would never harm a hair on that girl's head or threaten her in any way. She's really being off the wall but, then again, she's always been like that. I can't imagine why she's making up stories like that. When her mother, Inge, and I talked she said she didn't know either. I said she's mad at me because I screwed up enough to come to jail and now that I'm here she's upset that I screwed up my life. Maybe she wants to see me do better. Maybe she really hates me. Maybe I'll never really know. I sure wish I could talk to her.

God, I hate jail. I'm really starting to get tired of it. As I sit and wallow in self-pity and agonize over my wait to move, I must do two things. I must smoke and I must write. I don't really feel like writing to anybody in particular though I should. I started to, but just couldn't. I feel only I understand the true depth of my feelings. I have begun to shun the girl I love with all my heart. I feel like everybody is slowly turning their backs on me, rejecting me as a loss.

"Oh, Sean, yeah, he's in jail. Too bad. Tisk, tisk."

Nobody writes to me. I look back and see that I have burnt my bridges. Now I'm paying the full cost. The one thing I've feared the most in life has begun to take place. I am utterly alone. When I needed Diane the most, it seems she let me down. I have this bad habit of pushing people away and treating them badly when I don't get my way, or if I really need someone. The slightest rejection sends me into spasms of negativity.

Excuse me while I light another cigarette.

Puff, puff.

I believe my mind is deteriorating, falling apart. Every day now I wonder if I'll make it. Three years, three more damned years.

I go into these fugues when I lay in bed for hours. Today it was the whole day. From 10:00 AM until 5:30 PM. I don't really sleep. Rather, I doze on the edge of insanity. Visions play through my head at high speed, like a tape on fast forward. They mix and jell but never seem to match. They are not happy pictures and thoughts. They are not sad ones either. They are nothing thoughts. The worst kind of all. No direction. No purpose.

It reminds me of when I did drugs. No, this isn't really true. At least when I did drugs I had things to think about. The knowledge I have nothing to look forward to for the next three years is a real beast of a burden. The mother of my child refuses to let me even talk to her. She tells my daughter I am scum. The girl I would die for would rather go out drinking with another guy than come to see me once a week. Add to all this the fact that without her I have absolutely nobody in the whole world to talk to and this is what you get.

Me, sitting here, writing to myself and smoking.

Through it all, I try to convince myself I'll be OK. I try to convince myself that I believe in myself, that someday this whole nightmare will be over and I can go on living my life. That someday I'll be changed. I tell myself I won't be alone forever. There is a rainbow out there somewhere with my name on it.

Everybody seems to be waiting for success.

Maybe it is all an illusion?

I remember seeing some graffiti written on a wall which said, "I look around but see nothing." This is how I feel. Jail is like an empty canvass that cannot be painted. The yellow of sunshine, the green of grass and the blue of sky are just words in here, not actual colors. There are no Twinkies in here. No steak, no lobster, no link of any kind to the freedoms all of us are accustomed to.

Some claim jail is a place of rehabilitation. That's garbage. I've heard that putting a sane person into a lunatic asylum makes that person a lunatic. How can you expect jail to be any different?

Even if you're not a criminal when you get here, you're sure to be one when you leave. All you hear about all day, every day, is drugs, scores, scams, rip-offs, past cases, future cases, getting high, hiding out, escape, doing time and how to do it. You are surrounded by rapists, child molesters, murderers, armed robbers, burglars and people of a general unethical attitude. Most are drug addicts. Many are alcoholic. All are lost, yet find themselves sharing the same common thread with the man in the cell next to them. They are all in jail. Its the end of the world as we know it.

I think society has discarded me. It has decided I have the mind of a trash can and placed me in the giant dumpster with the rest of the trash heads. If you accidentally throw out something good and it is surrounded by garbage, it is too late. It is in a dumpster and, therefore, becomes trash. Even if it has some gold in it.

I am locked in a parody of time. It used to be that the future was like clay to be formed and molded while only the past was inscribed in bedrock. To live, breathe and be free. To travel, drink and cheat life of its pleasures. To follow the heart blindly and without question. Even if the heart lied. Inner demons were meant to be conquered by frantic boozing. Faster and faster you ran until after attaining top speed you slammed into that proverbial brick wall.

How many nights of altered states, of mindless drunks, did I cheat death while trying to find myself? Trying to find myself, but running away from myself at the same time? Will I ever attain the knowledge that I so truly desire? Why are there so many more questions than answers?

Everyone races to beat others towards an unknown future. But what is the prize? Don't they realize we're all dying? The "e" at the end of the word "life" is exactly that. The end. If I only had another chance.

Maybe it is not the future that scares me but the past that haunts me. We race in a world where the past can decide your future. I hate my watch. I hate the calendar. My future is now carved in stone. It is the very substance of the walls that now surround me.

My dreams haunt me. Shadows of the past. Evil creatures that lurk in the darkness and feed off the subconscious. My mind is like a dusty museum. I tread through the museum's halls lightly. This memory may be painted on canvas hanging on the wall but over there is one locked in a glass case. It is shielded even from myself. A childhood toy, a faded photograph, a lock of hair. One entire wall of my museum will be blank.

For out of nothing comes nothing. The thief has now become the victim, robbed himself of something far more precious than money. I wonder why they "give" you time when they sentence you, when what they really do is "take" time away?

What happened to Sean Legacy, climber of mountains, swimmer of oceans, wild and free mountain man, guitar player serenading women all across the continent? What happened to the pursuit that once seemed so important? Where are my family values? I had it all figured out. Once, I held it in my hands and overflowed with joy with what I possessed. A woman. A child. A job. That is what any man deserves and I was so happy to have gotten that far. I reveled in my success. I sensed flaws but was too foolish to act quickly to correct them. I celebrated and I took advantage. I also took it for granted.

Then one day it was just gone. Like the trick of the magician David Copperfield when he makes the Statue of Liberty disappear. It was agony and I'll never know how many pieces my heart was shattered into. Blindly, I stumbled forward. But the past is an unmovable rock.

Abandoning my sense of direction, I simply rambled aimlessly. Avoiding any kind of commitment, I set out to forget. All I really wanted to do was forget. I didn't want to start over. I didn't want to conquer the world. I didn't even want to play the guitar for a while. I just wanted to forget. But the more I tried to forget, the more I realized I couldn't. I was a fool in a fool's world, playing the inevitable fool's game. I was pissing away my life. Outside I was happy with too many friends and was never alone. Inside, though, I was suffering a thousand deaths.

Every day was a nightmare. Every night was pure torture. Women came and went, came and went, came and went. I stumbled on, searching for something. I had no idea what I was looking for, but I knew it was important I looked. Days turned into weeks, weeks turned into months and I became an expert alcoholic. I was not happy unless I was totally miserable. But when I was miserable, I was hysterically happy.

I became reckless in my search as I grew more frantic. Time was running out. I had to find it, that key that would solve everything and bring relief. I swam in an ocean struggling to keep afloat while dodging the anchor I kept throwing at myself. Mental anguish, self destruction, alcohol poisoning, suicidal tendencies, self torment and inner suffering.

These were my friends. Nothing could replace them because they were so goddamned dependable.

My head was spinning. I courted desperation. Death seemed imminent. Something saved me. Maybe it was God. Maybe it was Diane Beryl. Wonder of wonders, maybe it was me. Maybe it was because I ran out of money. Maybe I got tired of beating myself up. Maybe it was music that finally showed me the way. Maybe it was fear.

Something saved me, though.

The year I came to jail became a new era, the dawning of a new age in my life. The past and future of my life was suddenly etched in stone.

At least for a while.

January 29, 1994

I've been sent to a new place called Johnsville F.C.I.

Saturday 4:00 PM.

Head count.

Woo has left and moved to another block. I share my cell with a Dominican and he seems like an OK guy. They want to give him sixty-five years he says. A lot of guys here aren't even designated yet. I am in a holdover block. Inmates come and go by the busload everyday. I hear a lot about M.C.C. which is like another holdover place in Manhattan, New York. I've heard bad things about that place. They shuttle inmates between here and there for court. A lot of these guys aren't even sentenced yet.

There are people from all over the world in here. Chinese. Koreans. Japanese. Dominicans. Puerto Ricans. Blacks. Jews. Italians. Christ, half of the mob's in here! The Asians keep to themselves and take care of their problems as one. I am unsure about the rest as I have not been here long enough to really see anything firsthand.

In the chow line the other day, I heard a voice calling "Sean, Sean. Is that you?" It was my friend Tic-Tac Tommy. He's Italian and instantly I felt at ease because Tommy has one of those happy-go-lucky carefree attitudes that makes a lot of friends quickly.

He immediately introduced me to several people. One was from my unit and was named Peter. He was fat and Jewish and walked with a cane because of a bum leg. Through Peter I met several other inmates. One was a crazy Russian guy named Yok. Another was a Frenchman whose name I don't know yet.

Though I have met several people here, I trust no one and stick to myself. I have found the gym and been there twice. I went last night after dinner and today after lunch. There are no attitudes here as there were in the county jail I was in. Everybody respects everybody else because I think nobody really knows who the next guy is. Here, there is a much stronger sense of "us" and "them."

"He stick him in head. Try to kill."

"Who? The Puerto Rican guy?"

"No, the black Jewish man. He snitch."

"The black Jewish guy was a snitch?"

"No, no. He stick snitch. He stab in head you know. Try to kill but couldn't kill. Head too hard."

February 2, 1994

I just watched a late night movie called "Unlawful Entry." They let us out at 12:30 AM to watch it on HBO in the TV room.

Today (actually yesterday, Saturday) I swore I'd write a couple of pages and study the book I took out from the library, *The History of Western Music.* I did neither, so it is now I find myself jotting down a few lines in the wee hours of Sunday morning. Mostly I played cards today. I still have not seen a counselor since I arrived here. I put in a request form to attend AA meetings while I'm here. Monday I have an appointment for medical at 1:00. I dread the visit because I'm sure it means getting stuck with needles.

I made a mistake by turning in my laundry on Friday. They only gave me three pairs of uniforms to wear. From what I gathered of the laundry schedule, you hand your stuff in during the morning and get it back in the afternoon. So, I handed in two of the uniforms they gave me and both of my towels and was told I wouldn't see my stuff until Sunday or maybe Monday. This left me from Friday until whenever with the clothes on my back and no towel. I was pissed.

I've washed my socks in the sink with soap and dried them hanging from the bed. When I'm not wearing them I hang them out the window to air out a while. Tonight, while I was reading before the count, a big gust of wind came up and blew my sock right out the window. Now I have one sock to wear tomorrow to Sunday brunch. I saw Tic-Tac Tommy at chow and he gave me a towel. Before that I had taken a shower and dried off with about 80 paper towels. The second time I used my face cloth and just kept wringing it out. Then I used my t-shirt. I have since studied the laundry schedule.

I slept all day today. I got up for lunch and had a semi-big breakfast. The syrup was orange and tasted like cough syrup. I suspect it was doped because when I came back I tried to study but fell asleep and slept until chow time at 5:00. After chow I got my laundry. Hallelujah! Clean clothes at last. I was unable to retrieve my sock. When I went to get it, I found it was in a fenced in area. Oh well. I will bitch at the laundry that they lost it.

Already, I feel myself bored with the holdover. It's like being at the airport and having your plane delayed and delayed. I can't wait to get to my designation, Spartanville, Pennsylvania. However, I'm preparing my-self to stay here for months if need be. You never know with the Federal system.

I am picking up bits and pieces of Spanish and trying to learn it as a language. I have a few black neighbors and never get tired of hearing them talk to each other in their own language. Nothing is as funny as a black guy in a good mood.

"Yo, my little man Shorty. He's one crazy little mother. He be messing the house all up, man that Home Alone dude, he got nothing on Shorty."

Shorty is one of the inmate's four year old sons. From what I gathered, he was born three months premature at a pound and a half.

"Yo, Shorty at the doctor and doctor stab him with a needle. He calls the doctor a 'bad ass' and laughs."

"You know my little girl ask me, she says, 'Daddy, will you go to my kindergarten graduation?'"

He looks all remorseful.

"I said to her, 'But baby your school goes up to the eighth grade.'"

We all crack up.

"This other bitch, I knocked her up and she starts talking about having the kid and I said, 'No way.' This bitch knows my wife and daughter. I said, 'Here's five hundred dollars for an abortion.' She asked me why. I said, 'Baby, you know. I don't love you, we wuz just screwin', that's all. You wanted something and I gave it to you and that's that. Now get the damned abortion.' Bitch says, 'But the doctor says it won't be good for my health if I have an abortion' and I said, 'Bitch, get that damned abortion or its gonna be real unhealthy for you cuz I'll have the boys come over and slay yer ass.'"

"Shit, I'll have Shorty do it. Shorty go to his grandma's the other day and guess what he say. Called her an ol' bitch. Little Shorty messin' up the whole damned house."

It goes on and on.

February 7, 1994

Today I had my medical check up. They stabbed me with a needle for a T.B. test even though I just had one last year. It came up negative. Then they wanted to jab me for a tetanus and I drew the line. I had one not long ago so I signed a piece of paper saying stating this. Then my physical. I had a temperature of a hundred and something. It seems I caught the flu. I've got a sore throat too so the doc wrote me out a couple of prescriptions. I have to go back tomorrow for my blood work and then Wednesday so they can look at my arm and tell me I don't have T.B.

I went back to my unit for the 4:00 PM count and then skipped dinner to rush to the commissary. I bought cigarettes that I can't smoke because of my sickness and chicken soup and vitamin C tablets for my flu. Q-tips, razors and stuff like that. Tomorrow I'll have some more dough coming in so I can buy a pair of Reeboks. Money is something there is always just barely enough of it seems. It looks like I'll have to forego a radio until I get more cash.

I panic if I have less than fifty dollars in my account. I can't fall behind on my financial obligations. I've set a goal and I intend to keep it. I was told today that when you leave they give you a certain amount of money. Like $100 or $500. My source wasn't quite sure.

I met the source in the waiting room at the doctor's office and he proved to be a regular wealth of information about the federal system. He said Spartanville is an excellent place to be, one of the best. I am not sure if he is from India, or some Asian country, or what. He claims to have traveled a lot around the world. Although he seems educated, there is definitely the unmistakable air of a con-man about him. I think that comes from being in a system for a while. We talked about sentences. Mostly, I talked about mine.

Nobody here wants to tell anybody else about their crime. I think this is because most are not sentenced yet. I don't blame them. On the other hand, I have no problem telling people that I'm in for bank robbery. I believe this is an accepted crime. During our conversation the story of another monster sentence came up. This guy just finished doing fourteen years in a state jail and now he's got twelve to do federal. That's twenty-six years straight. Damn that's a lot. I don't know if I could hang on through that.

I was talking to a guy named Anthony who seemed confident we would be leaving Wednesday on the same bus. He said we might stop at Clayton for a day or two before we get to our destinations.

The name of Clayton rings an immediate bell in my mind. It is one of the most nastiest, cutthroat, killer, federal prisons in the nation. I can hardly wait to see the inside of those walls. Maybe I won't though. Anthony says if we go to Clayton they will keep us separated from all the real hard core guys.

It's now midnight and my roommate is sleeping. I'm going to turn out the light and try to get some sleep. I have a doctor's appointment tomorrow morning at 9:00. I hope I can get up that early. I think I'm getting the flu.

February 9, 1994

A new Chinese guy came in and moved into Dee's cell, the cell next to me. The Chinese guys are mostly here for doing big kilo quantities of dope and heroin. The new guy doesn't speak English. Most of them don't speak English.

Hassan, a black guy has the cell on the other side of Dee. He's a cool guy, always ready with something funny to say. Hassan and me went into Dee's cell to say hello.

"How you doin', m'man," Hassan says.

The Chinese guy says something in Chinese we can't understand.

"You speak any English?" asks Hassan.

The Chinese kid shakes his head.

"Well, screw you," says Hassan, smiling broadly.

Then, there's Comacho. I think they got him on a homicide beef. He's a small guy with a big chip on his shoulder. Hussan, Dee, Pooh and me are up on the third tier looking down at the floor while Comacho is yelling up to us and telling us what a bad ass he is.

"I mess up the biggest, baddest mothers anywhere bro."

"Yeah, in your neighborhood Comacho."

"Man, you don't even know my style. This is my style."

He pretends to pull out a gun and walks over to a black guy sitting on the table. He sticks his finger up to the guy's knee.

"Bang! Now I say this is a stick up," he says to the guy. He takes his imaginary gun and pretends to smash the guy in his face. Little Comacho looks like one rough little guy.

This brings up a very important point. Most guys in the street that play tough are tough. They hang with tough guys. Guns make them tough. Booze makes them tough. Women piss them off. Drugs make them tough. By selling drugs a man can achieve a level of respect he could not have attained otherwise.

But when you come to jail, all that shit is stripped away. There is no booze and no drug problem to capitalize on. There are no guns and there are no women. Under these circumstances, most men become docile and even scared. They are scared of all the things they've heard about prison, those preconceived notions I mentioned earlier.

I am speaking about the first time offender and not about the hardened con. The con that has done a lot of time doesn't want to mess with you. He just wants to do his time and get out.

The average guy who comes in off the street is no tough guy. He is just someone who got caught up in his own little world. Someone who thought he could pull something off and get away with it and he couldn't. He got caught and goes to prison. Like the kid who was twenty-two and got life plus forty. He was just a little fish, a small time guy. I was told that he didn't even own a car.

Comacho represents a minority, I think, because he's homicidal. He's young and doesn't give a damn. Maybe he's been in prison before. I don't know. I do know that when you come to prison you learn a new kind of tough. You learn that if someone screws with you, you bust their head. Right then. Right there on the spot. No gun, no courage from a booze bottle, no acting violent to support your habit. You fight for your respect because without all the other things, the booze, drugs, guns, cash, you are only a man. And you might go your whole sentence without fighting. I bet it happens a lot. You stick to yourself and mind your own business and you're not going to have problems.

I am polite to people and I'm getting along marvelously in here. I respect them and they respect me. I mind my own business and don't ask any questions. You never ask a convict about his case. I also have a desire to get along with everybody. We are all prisoners doing time for our crime.

I guess prison is only as tough as a person makes it.

That's it in a nutshell.

February 11, 1994

In the early hours of Friday morning, the C.O. came into my cell and woke me up.

"Legacy, pack it up," he said. "Go to R & D. You're outta here."

It was 4:30 AM.

I packed quickly but thoroughly. I didn't want to leave my few possessions behind and never see them again. Everything has its value in prison, no matter how small or trivial. Things that have absolutely no value behind the walls become connected to you. Property is an important commodity. It symbolizes everything you are, your entire existence. I made sure to pack everything.

At R&D they took all my property. I mean everything. Even my religious medallions were taken. I was put into a cell with about ten other guys. I thought we were all going on the bus to Spartanville, Pennsylvania. In actuality we ended up in Clayton, the original Big House.

From the first cell, we were taken to a second cell and placed with another seven or eight guys. Nobody had cigarettes. Everybody was trying to sleep because it was so early in the morning. Right about the time we became complacent, we were placed in yet a larger, third cell. There were now almost thirty of us in a room with only one urinal.

After a couple of hours, we were led from the room by fours. We were stripped of everything and put into khaki clothes that didn't fit. A

thick chain was placed around our waists. It had a special link for handcuffs. Dressed like this we are deemed ready for transport. We were led
back to one of the first cells. This time sixteen of us were jammed into
a small cell. We were all chained up.

They gave the Black Box and leg chains to a guy with a loud mouth.
The Black Box is a machined steel device that fits between your handcuffs,
entirely restricting your movement. I've heard they are painful and used
in security situations, as well as for troublemakers. This guy was a beauty.
A lot of stories go around when you've got sixteen guys jammed in a small
cell like that. Prison stories. This guy seemed to want everybody to think
that he was a real killer. But later I agreed with a couple of other guys that
he was scared shitless. He was, after all, designated to do time in Clayton.

Securely shackled, we were led through the door we all came
through upon entering Johnsville. It was cold and snowing really hard.
They gave us a jacket to walk from the holding cell to the entrance/exit.
Once in the Admissions Building, before boarding the Clayton bus, they
took the jackets. It was only a few feet to the bus. They gave us a bag
lunch for the trip.

The bus looked like an ordinary Greyhound on the outside. You
couldn't see in. All the seats were new and vinyl. The bus driver tuned
the radio to a rap station. There were eight speakers in the ceiling. It was
snowing like hell but the bus driver went about eighty miles an hour. All
over the highway tractor trailers were overturned and cars were flipped
upside down. Occasionally, the driver was forced to slow down because
traffic had come to a complete stop. But once past the accidents, he put
the pedal to the metal again. I was sure we would crash.

It was like being on a bus to hell. And, when we finally arrived at
Clayton Penitentiary, at around four-thirty that afternoon, I found that
Clayton was kind of like hell. It was 1:00 AM before we were once again
stripped, issued clothes, processed, fed another stale sandwich and assigned a bunk.

Clayton Penitentiary has a wall. Or "The Wall" if you prefer. It was
the original Big House and in many respects resembled a dungeon. It
was made entirely of stone and housed only the worst criminals. Most
guys were doing life. And the ones that weren't, might as well be. We
were placed in the hospital ward. I was in a common area with sixty-

eight other inmates. You were allowed ten minutes on the phone every other day. There were showers and two toilets with urinals.

I met a couple of good guys there and we stuck together through the nightmare that was the Clayton holdover. No property or any money followed us because we were there for an undetermined amount of time. We could not buy cigarettes or coffee. They gave out free tobacco. The "roll your own" kind. We were grateful for anything after not having smokes from 5:30 AM until midnight.

After a few days at Clayton, I took an orderly job because we got coffee and an extra phone slot. I stayed at Clayton for exactly one week. I met a couple of good guys and didn't have any problems.

I was awakened at 4:00 in the morning on the 18th of February and led to the chow hall for breakfast. Then I was taken downstairs with others and stripped again. They took my hair bandanna that I'd had since Northampton. They handed me the usual dull brown traveling clothes and secured a chain around my waist and again the handcuffs through the chain.

I left Clayton for Spartanville in the early morning hours of February 18th. I hope its the last time I ever see that place.

February 25, 1994

F.C.I. Spartanville.

I find myself writing late at night again. It's a little past midnight, but today is Saturday and I plan on sleeping late. I probably won't be able to because my bed is in the common area of 4B. I'm tired a lot, maybe because they turn the lights on at 6:00 AM and everybody is up making noise by 7:00 AM. I can't fall asleep until 12:00 for the same reason. I keep trying to catch up on my sleep because I feel tired all the time. Either I'll have to adjust or someday get caught up.

There's so much to do here. I have a job in the plumbing shop which is really cool. I also have a couple of bands that I'm in. One of them is working out really good. I've discovered that I can actually do back-up vocals and harmonize. I've never had the confidence, or the ability, to figure out when and how to harmonize, but my drummer's good at pushing me in the right direction. I was told that we will be allowed to make Mother's Day videos of the band playing to send home. I'm psyched.

My schedule has been unbelievable since I left Johnsville. Hell, since I left Northampton. I've only been able to write bits and pieces here and there. The pages I have written are unfocused. A little here and a little there. A lot of times I've said to myself I've got to remember this and write it down, but of course I forget.

Now I'm settled in and I've got a cell and a nice psychotic cellmate. A self-proclaimed homicidal cellmate. We get along great as long as I don't bring any roommates over. My cell is located next to the T.V. room which blares on late into the night. The movie on right now is called "Blood In, Blood Out." It's a prison movie and my cellmate and I were discussing what garbage most movies are that try to portray life in prison. Movies about prison are made in far-away sunny Hollywood, written by people who have absolutely no clue what prison life is really like.

I immediately got involved in several programs when I got here. The predominant program was music, of course. I joined a couple of bands and was appointed Secretary of the Music Appreciation Club. I have drawn up a proposal to teach a guitar workshop. There will be two of these—Workshops I and II. They will be 40 hour programs that offer certificates of accomplishment. I still have to get permission from the Recreation Specialist. Then it has to be blessed by the Education Department.

I got a job in the plumbing shop. I signed up to apply for my Pell Grant to go to school and get my Associates Degree. I'm also trying to take a course for my Physical Trainers Certificate. I haven't had time to find out about the A.A. meetings. I mentioned it today, though, when they called me out to see the psychologist. He told me it was "intake screening."

"Do you feel suicidal?" the psychologist asked.

"No," I replied.

"Do you feel homicidal?"

"No."

"You can go," said the shrink.

Back on the block things are active as ever. Surrounded by over a hundred inmates I realize I am not afraid of them as much as I am afraid of being like them. Bitter, angry scowls are etched on their faces. It seems like we all lose touch with the positive aspects of life. Day in and day out we live in a cold environment where emotions are things to be hidden.

Becoming institutionalized is a simply brutal and brutally simple process. All you gotta do is exist within the system. Just be.

Today is Thursday and I have the afternoon off. There's a few things I have to do. One thing is to go to see Tazz, my drummer, who messed up his back. I'm thinking of going to the music theory class at 1:00 but that will wreck my Thursday afternoon practice, which is canceled because of Tazz's back. I also have to talk to Bill next door about moving in with him.

My cellie is leaving tomorrow and going to Fairton, so I advance to bottom bunk, a much better deal. I'm thinking about moving out of my cell but I don't know yet. I've grown accustomed to it. My esteemed roommate corrected my spelling on his destination in his own unique way. Reading my stuff, my fault for leaving it out.

I went to music class today at 1:00. It was very interesting. Most of the stuff he taught, I already knew so I kind of kept one step ahead of him. My knowledge was recognized by the professor. Way cool.

March 11, 1994

They recalled us today from work around nine thirty. I've got the rest of the day left. I moved into my new room and hope I can get this guy Bill to move in with me. He's got a Gibson Les Paul and a set of really nice keyboards. I'm trying to learn piano. I really love the instrument. Its got such a pure sound. I'm starting by learning the beginning to "Free Bird" by Lynard Skynard.

The Rec Department is giving me a hard time about getting a guitar in here. I went down to I.B.F. to see what kind of guitars they sold there and found out it was a bunch of junk. A Mexican Stratocaster and a Gibson SG copy are the only decent things they have. They also have a cheap Les Paul copy. But it is so outrageously priced I could get a new Les Paul for the same price. It's almost twelve thirty and I'm going up to the music room to practice playing the piano. Maybe I'll just stick around until the roommate situation is resolved.

I think I'll write my daughter a letter. As far as I know, her mother still does not want me to write her. But I do any way and send the letters to my daughter's grandmother. She will hold on to them until Samantha comes around and then maybe she'll read them to her again.

March 15, 1994

Today is Wednesday and I'm at work.

It snowed again last night.

Snow, snow, snow.

That's all it ever seems to do here at Spartanville.

Last night I went up to the band room to work on some stuff but ended up hanging out with people I know up there. There is a horn section in this one band. They do some pretty cool things from the Blues Brothers, some Chicago and other saxophone-related music. There are two saxophone players besides the bass, drummer and guitar players. The guitar player is leaving next week and I have been nominated to fill his shoes. He is also in a blues project on Wednesday nights and I will also be playing in that band.

My personal band is working out very smoothly. It is always a pleasure to play with talented musicians. My bass player and drummer are both of high caliber. We are thinking about bringing in a keyboard player to round out the sound, but I don't want to lose the particular sound we have right now. There are drums, guitar, bass, a singer and then all of us singing harmony.

I am very pleased with my progression as a back-up vocalist. Although I need much work, I really like to sing, even though I'm scared shitless about what I sound like. I guess I sound OK. Otherwise, the guys wouldn't keep giving me a mic to practice.

Since I began playing piano I can't get enough of it. Although I'm only a beginner, I've developed a strong sense of attraction, a kind of magnetic pull, to the piano. I have only learned two songs, but I have learned them right and I learned them well. The first song was "Freebird" by Lynard Skynard. It is a flowing, pure sounding melody in the key of G with heavy overtones of D. The second song I am still learning. It is the classic "Mr. Bo Jangles." The original version actually surprised me. It is a prison song. "I met him in a cell in New Orleans" and also "He danced a lick across the cell" not the floor as sung in the popular version.

I stopped in the chapel yesterday. I've been dying to get in there to play the only piano in the compound. There was already a guy in there practicing. He was playing some awesome piano. I can only hope to be that good some day.

My new roommate is an excellent musician. He has the ability to play anything by ear, even if he doesn't know the chord progression. As long as he knows the vocal melody line he can figure out all the chords exactly, including all the 7ths, 9ths, suspended or augmented. I am extremely envious of his perfect pitch, although I am learning and bettering my musicianship every day.

I am still having problems sleeping and it is difficult to get up on some mornings. Sometimes I walk around in a daze. People notice this and tell me I should stop taking my medication. I am going to take their advice and stop taking it for a while and see what happens.

There are no problems getting along with the guys. I get along with mostly all of them, white and black. My unit is 4B and it is notorious for all its action. It has the most fights, the most drugs, the most wine, the most blatant homosexuals (two transvestites) and the biggest gambling ring. It goes on and on. A really happening place. Of course, things are exaggerated like everything is in prison. Anytime you are hungry, though, you can find food. Even at three in the morning.

The most common thing is called the "Hustle." Everybody has got a Hustle. No matter who you are or how much money you have, you've got to have a Hustle. If you don't, you are a Chump and Chumps are the guys who are the prime targets for the Hustle. The Hustle comes in varying degrees. Most Hustles are food related. Guys hustle sandwiches, pizza, milk, juice. Anything you want can be bought. Even steaks.

Outside of food Hustles, there are all kinds of ways to make money. The primary object of the prison businessman is to end up with actual cash. Preferably the cash is sent from someone on the outside into your account, or to a third party who will hang on to your hard earned dough. Gambling is big in prison and is done through cards, sports, numbers, pool games, dice. It all pays cash if you win, or you pay cash, if you lose.

Credit is not a good thing to receive. And credit is not a good thing to give to somebody. Suddenly you find yourself on D-Day when payments are collected or paid. You find yourself chasing one guy to collect to pay another guy you owe. When the first guy you're trying to collect from comes up with an excuse he can't pay, you have to cover yourself and prepare for that.

March 30, 1994

Spring is coming.

For a while the snow melted and grass and flowers started to come up. Then it snowed again and I woke up to a fresh few new inches.

Spring is temporarily on hold.

I got all screwed up playing cards this month and lost around six hundred dollars. I don't know how I am going to get out of this situation. I don't know how I keep getting in to it. I suppose its better than doing drugs or drinking. It costs too damned much though.

So, once again, I've sworn off gambling. It's going to take three months to pay off all the shit I owe. I am glad that I am not sitting at that damned card table every night any more.

Now I can get back to my music again. My roommate is shredding on his Les Paul right now. They had a big shakedown and took the speaker we played our electric guitars and radio through. The only radio you're allowed is the kind with headphones. My cellie is running his guitar through the speaker in our Yamaha PSR-27 keyboards.

The Warden was here today inspecting stuff and he poked his head in our cell.

"What's this?" he said. "The music room?"

He's right. It does look like the music room. It's absolutely packed with music materials: sheet music, Guitar magazines, the Les Paul and keyboards and an acoustic I took for practice from the Recreation Department. Add to all this the poster of the Doors and the cutouts of Robert Plant, Jimmy Page and John Paul Jones. There's music stuff everywhere.

I turned on the demonstration song on the keyboards just to have something to listen to. It's a drag without the radio speaker. Maybe we can rig the amp receiver up to the keyboards. I'll have to mention this to my cellie.

April 1, 1994

I had the day off from work and didn't wake up until around noon. I heard them announce last call for lunch, so I ran down and almost got beat out of chow. After lunch, I went up and worked out for a little while, then came back and took a shower.

It was a pretty nice day. All the snow melted again and I actually saw flowers in a flower bed.

I cruised up to the music room to jam and ran into Miles. He's fifty one years old and used to play with Roy Orbison, Johnny Cash and probably a few others. He showed me a couple Johnny Cash songs like "I Walk The Line," "A Boy Named Sue" and "Folsom Prison Blues." He's

a real good dude and he's from Massachusetts. He also knew where
Greenfield, Massachusetts was, which surprised me.

April 4, 1994

Thank God spring is actually here. I was beginning
to lose my mind with all the snow. It seems I almost forgot what the sun
and green grass were all about.

I was able to get out on the yard and play some hacky-sack the other
day. It's been over a year since I've had a full body work-out like that. It
was so warm I had my shirt off and actually got a mild sunburn. The
next day it rained and snowed all day, but the day after that all the snow
melted away. It was like waking up from a bad dream.

Speaking of waking up, I've been getting better about being at work
on time. I have a new method where I drink a glass of water before I go
to sleep. When I wake up in the morning I have to take a piss bad enough
to get out of bed right away. The method is working splendidly.

I was asked to join another band as a bass player. I accepted. My
friend Jimmy is also a guitarist in a band called Bad Attitude. I made a
commitment to join one band, which is currently my top project. That's
a rock band. At the same time I came in, another guitar player was
leaving. He played in two different bands. One band was a horn section
band and the other a so-called blues band. Songs that you love to hate.
The guy from both of those bands asked me to take the other guitarist's
place in both bands. Even though the music wasn't really my style, I
agreed. I made it up to a few of their practices. Man it was boring. So
then the dude leaves and I show up and find out what an egotistical dick
head this guy was. Enough said, so I quit.

While all this is going on, I was approached by Bad Attitude about
joining them as a guitarist. I accepted and the first night of practice my

friend Jimmy was playing the guitar. When I showed up they gave him the boot. I guess he had just showed up to jam a little. Still, he was pissed. I could tell this when he handed me the guitar. So I said "Look man, why don't you guys let ol' Jimmy play in your band?" At this point I was already committed to three other bands and this band would make four.

I ended up jamming that night and everything went pretty well. A few days later I found out that the drummer had quit, the singer was about to quit and old Jimmy had been hired to replace me. It was kind of bogus, but that is the politics of bands in prison. So, I was out of the band I figured and then quit Mr. Bass's bands. Now I have been hired to play bass in the band that hired and fired me just a week and a half ago.

I was happy to see my friend Jimmy get into a band situation. He's been tense lately and I knew he needed something to focus on or he was going to end up freaking out. Jimmy's an excellent musician. And, he's also a bank robber like me. He's also got a good voice and we're always talking about music and scales and the guitar.

It was pretty funny the way he asked me to play in their band.

"Man, I gotta a favor to ask you," he said, "and you're probably going to say 'no' but I want you to think about it." Then he added "I'd do it for you if you asked me."

I'm thinking to myself, "What the hell is he talking about?" He must have been thinking that I was still all pissed off about that other bullshit of the hiring and firing. The other guys must have decided to have Jimmy ask me because he's the closest to me. Actually, they already have a bass player, but he's a homo and they can't wait to get rid of him. At the least, I hope I get to be a shredding bass player. It will be another addition to my musical abilities with guitar, keyboards and bass.

Saturday night was a trip in my unit. I was playing Scrabble and the guy sitting next to me was getting shelled on home brew. The cop on duty was watching us play the game. He got a whiff of the stuff and took one of the glasses, but left one. It was enough to drive me to get a quart of the stuff for myself. I got shelled and called my brother on the West coast at around one in the morning my time. They sell grapefruit concentrate in the commissary and it isn't good for anything but making home brew. The stuff tastes like floor wax but it does the trick and gets you through a lonely night.

Easter came and went. We got olives with our Easter turkey dinner. The music room is closed today, but I think its open tonight. I have been working on a classical piece by Randy Rhoads called "Dee." It's a great piece but difficult and has to be played in an exact manner. The classical style of fingering is an art in itself.

I wrote a letter to my brother and included the music to "November Rain" and a couple of other songs. I also sent a letter to my mother and mailed her some newspaper clippings that I cut out of *The Bradford Era,* the local rag. The articles were on violence here at Spartanville. They discussed some stabbings and other stuff. I wanted her to realize that, although this is a soft joint, it isn't that soft. It's still prison.

The cops here are real assholes. For doing the stupidest thing they throw you in the hole. For example, my singer got a scratch on his neck at work and they threw him in the hole over Easter weekend on suspicion of fighting. That's ridiculous, especially since he went to the doctor after it happened. I guess they have the right to lock you up with just a suspicion of doing something rather than any proof.

Some guys get outright nailed. One guy in my unit got hit for having a still in his room. He wasn't making just home brew, but liquor. He did 75 days in the hole. That's not too long. Another guy I know did 140 days. He said there was snow on the ground when he went in and there was snow on the ground when he came out. He'd missed the whole summer.

April 6, 1994

I'm waiting to go to dinner and then to the commissary and get a few things. I have $13 in my account but owe $10. It's enough to get a pack of cigarettes. I'm struggling to get my debts paid and at a precarious point with everything two thirds paid. Right now

$550 is paid and $325 owed. I can't wait to get out of this financial hole. I'll be smart enough to stay out of this situation. By June I should be all right.

The rain has arrived but it might get cold again and snow. A guy told me all it ever does is rain and snow here.

Riot season is coming and certain procedures are being taken. Work was canceled today and they made us go to our cells for count and then came around and took all the metal trash cans, metal chairs and wooden furniture. Everybody has these in their cells. To replace the trash cans they gave us a heavy duty plastic trash can. It would probably hurt just as much as the metal trash can if someone got hit with it.

I guess that things pick up around here during the spring and summer. I hope something exciting happens so I can write about it.

April 26, 1994

Sometimes things can change without you ever noticing. It might be a good thing slowly turning bad. The best thing is when something bad slowly gets better. Doing time is rough on anybody. It doesn't matter how tough you are. If you are doing any serious amount of time, I could see how it would be hard to adapt.

I remember rock climbing with my friend Doug. There always comes a time when you get stuck. You're in the middle of a cliff and it seems you can't go up and can't go down. You see lots of rock above and lots of rock below. Things look bleak. But you tell yourself that the cliff has been climbed before. Someone has gone before you. If you concentrate and look hard enough you find the move to reach the next position.

There is that one moment of terror when you are sure that you are all done. Courage prevails. I think there is a chemical reaction that induces courage once your fear level has peaked. On the cliff, you delve into the consciousness which has a difficult terrain to map. Somehow I've gotten myself out of these positions.

Whatever possessed us to climb rocks? I saw my friend Doug fall over a hundred feet. Maybe we were possessed by that demon of self knowledge? Maybe it was the knowledge about level headedness, courage, patience and perseverance that pushed us up those granite walls? I think that most of all, I learned there is a way out of any situation no matter how tough it seems at the time. Trouble will come and it will pass.

May 6, 1994

Well, I'm into my fourth day in the hole.

I was busted with a small quantity of liquor and then, when they locked me up, as they were packing up my stuff, they found some money.

I got two shots for this, a 222 and a 303. I was popped on Wednesday and today is Saturday. I won't see the DHO until Monday, and God knows how much time I am going to have to do in this shit hole. I get a shower three times a week. I can use the phone once a week until I'm sentenced, then it goes down to once a month.

I've only been here two and a half months and couldn't even make it until August without getting into trouble. I have yet to be rated for points. I am disappointed that I've not been able to control myself until my first Team meeting. Sometimes I'm such a dope. All my friends are here: Randy, Shooter, Slate, Moe, Kicker, Eddie the Barber, Bottom Line, Winebucket . . . those guys are just the ones from my Unit 4B or, Las Vegas. Johnny and Elvis (Aaron) are across from me. They stuck me in with some P.C., but I got that changed quickly.

I'm starting to forget the names of my friends, so I'm going to write them down before I forget. Pete, Amy, Ron, Shannon (hates me), Laura, Dave, Jimmy, Chuck. I try to remember the rocker dude and his woman or Dave's girlfriend who I used to have a crush on and who had a crush on me. Neither of us said anything, though, until after she and Dave were together for a while. And Pam who was Pete's roommate. And little Jimmy. I remember them all like they were family. I was never closer to a group of people. Someone was always there when one of us were down.

The drugs and booze were non-stop. It was awesome. There were times when life was just so damned funny you knew everything was going to be alright. But there were other times when we knew we were pushing things to the limits.

You know when you walk that ledge, when you push the edge. You search yourself and sometimes you don't like what you find.

May 7, 1994

I've got so much time to write I don't know where to start. I slept all morning missing breakfast and getting up for lunch. I called Diane last night and, amazingly, they let me call her again this morning. What a waste of a call. I hate loving that girl. I hate loving any girl. Its too bad that love couldn't just be sex, then everyone could run around and screw anybody and no one's feelings would get hurt. But there's gotta be all these feelings and emotions. Its so bogus. You love her, she loves him, he loves somebody else who could care less.

I think about my release date like nothing else in the world matters. Florida could fall into the ocean and I wouldn't care. They could nuke New York and as long as the wind blew the fallout the other way, I wouldn't care. Just don't screw up my release date, that's all.

I've got to write my daughter a letter but I've got to write in pencil because I'm in the hole. I hope I get her address with all my stuff. By all my stuff I mean my soap dish, my toothbrush and my shampoo. They actually allowed me to buy things in commissary last Friday.

Cigarettes are not allowed on SHU, but you can buy two for a book of stamps which is $5.80. So, I bought a couple of books of stamps, a bar of Irish Spring, some shampoo and toothpaste. Who knows when I'll see the rest of my stuff.

More good news. I found out my counselor makes the recommendation for time and of course he hates me. I'm not sure but today has to be Sunday so I'll see the DHO tomorrow. I haven't had a shower since Friday night and can't take another until Monday night. So, I get to see them looking like a scrub. Oh, joy.

I spend a lot of time wondering about what's going on in the outside. What are people doing? Does anyone remember me? That kind of stuff. I know everything is going to be so different when I get out. Four years without me around and things are bound to change. My worst fear is getting out and being labeled some kind of scum-bag. Maybe they called me a scum-bag before but now I'm an official scum-bag.

"Pssst, there goes what's his name, did four years in prison."

I can see myself labeled by society as a hopeless loss, a stark raving mad non-conformist. But then again, I've always been a non-conformist. I'm becoming harder every day but I also see things changing all about me. I have a lot of respect in here because there is no bullshit with me. The things I do and say are from the heart. A lot of guys have told me that there are so many guys running around pretending they are killers, this or that.

I was drinking with this guy.

"Man, I'm no killer," I told him straight out.

He was doing thirty-five years and I'll never forget what he told me.

"Sean, you'd better be a killer," he said, "because what are you going to do if some guy comes after you and he's gonna kill you? Huh? What are you gonna do? Are you gonna let him kill you?"

Some words of wisdom. A wake up call for sure.

The other night some friends got drunk. Two of them got into an argument and one got beat up pretty good. One of the guys filled up a pot with boiling baby-oil and dumped it on another guy. Then he ripped a phone out of the wall and beat him with it. Meanwhile, another was jumping around with a razor, slicing him up. These are my friends! I went to sleep before everything really got out of hand. God, please let me make it at least halfway through my bid.

May 8, 1994

I woke up at dinner time. We had roast beast and a bunch of other stuff. I didn't bother to eat. There's not much to do so I try not to eat too much. It's not like I'm burning up mega-calories in here.

I am beginning to dislike my cellmate more and more every day. Unless you are from where he's from, you're inferior. This one's a Dago. This one's a nigger. He really hates blacks. He's pathetic. I think he's got an IQ of about fifty but he's down in the law library all the time like some kind of Perry Mason. He claims no one here has any respect, that we are all "kids." He calls me "Sonny" and "Slim." That will change soon. The blacks over in 4A burnt him out so he checked in here. Damned pussy. He raves about the blacks being niggers and all this shit while he exploits his white brothers by charging them big bucks for cigarettes.

When I confronted him about exploiting the white guys (after one of his particularly nauseating "nigger speeches") for money, you know what he told me?

"Well, I didn't come in here with any of these guys," he said.

What a bunch of bullshit. I really want to kick the shit out of him but he's so stupid I might knock out the last of his brains and leave him a complete idiot the rest of his life. When he was on the phone yesterday he mentioned something about being on the "Most wanted" list and something about "killing a Marshall." Big deal. He probably threatened to kill a Marshall. Even if he did, I still think he's a pussy. Anybody can pull a trigger and kill somebody. The tough part is not letting it eat at your conscience.

May 10, 1994

I saw the UDC, or Unit Disciplinary Committee. It was actually nothing more than my Unit Counselor, Mr.Thornton. I was found guilty of the lesser charge, the 303 possession of currency. My penalty was confiscation of funds. The 222 shot was a little more serious. Mr. Thornton, the UDC, or whoever, recommends the standard thirty days in the hole. Both shots will go on my record and add at least five points. This may push me up to the penitentiary level. I'm lucky, though, because all the U.S.P.s are presently full.

As a matter of fact, I have yet to be awarded points. You have to be here six months before they score you and decide what level you will be at. I was told that the one shot, the 222, would be damaging but that the two of them would definitely make it worse.

Anyway, screw it. At least they aren't going to take any of my good time because its my first offense. The UDC has authority to rule and punish on lesser charges. But serious charges, such as Disciplinary Segregation (D.S. or the hole), are delegated to a higher authority. It is my first offense and they will most likely suspend 15 of the 30 days leaving 15 days. Of those 15 days they may credit me with 7 days served, even though it may take two or three weeks to see them. So, I figure 7 or 8 days from whenever I see them which, if I'm lucky, will be next week.

They transferred Aaron today, otherwise known as Elvis. He's been here at SHU since the first week of March or around 72 days.

Tomorrow, at about 2:00 PM, will mark my first week in here, my first 168 hours. Oh joy. For some reason this does not really bother me like it's supposed to. I sleep all day, which is cool. I get my meals brought to me, which is even cooler. I'm supposed to only get one phone call a week. I've made about six. I haven't even attempted to go out to what they call "Rec" which is on Tuesday, Thursday and Sunday. They let you out for an hour into this little fenced in basketball court.

I've missed Rec because I've been so busy sleeping my days away. At night I read or write on these pages. My cellie has turned out to be a jail house attorney of sorts and has convinced me that I can go back and overturn the state conviction that added time to my sentence. I am going to try to do it myself I guess. I'm sure it's another legal dream but probably worth pursuing. Like any dream.

Speaking of dreams, I've been having some pretty vivid ones lately. In the most vivid one I was with a group of people at an airport by the sea. My mother was one of the people there with me. All of the sudden this plane came up behind us. It was a big 747. It looked like it caught on fire and exploded in the air. There were pieces missing and the plane was flaming and smoking.

"Look at that!" I yelled. "Holy shit, look at that!"

The plane passed over the airport and almost crashed in the sea. At the last second, the pilot pulled it up and banked back towards the airport. The plane was messed up and many pieces were missing. I could see the people inside. It was packed with people. It was obviously beyond control but the pilot circled back to the airport. I thought, "My God, this can't be happening."

The smoking wreckage began a series of tight circles and almost looked as if it was going to land. The circles were so tight, though, and so fast it looked as if the plane was falling straight down. I thought the pilot must be getting dizzy. Then, the plane just dropped, hit the tarmac and exploded. There was nothing left. It was the most tragic struggle for survival I have ever witnessed. I really thought they were going to make it, but everybody died.

I ran over to the wreckage with the emergency crews to an area where there were a lot of pines. That's where most of the bodies were. There was wreckage everywhere. Then, a few very strange things happened. One was that I saw a leg sticking out of a tree. The bones had been stuck directly into the tree trunk and a shoe was still on it. It was white. The other weird thing was that I saw jewelry everywhere on the ground: diamonds, emeralds, watches of gold. I started stuffing my pockets. It was the damnedest thing.

I woke up remembering that my mother was flying back to San Diego today. Actually at that very moment.

It was very freaky.

May 16, 1994

Today marks my 13th day in the hole. I still haven't seen the DHO.

There are two kinds of days in the hole. Either it's is a shower day or it's not a shower day. Saturday and Sunday are not shower days, but today, Monday, is. After the four o'clock count, they feed us, then come back to get the trays and start the showers. I have yet to receive any of my property.

I bought shampoo and soap and toothpaste again. The toothbrush they gave me has the handle cut off of it. Its about 2 1/2" to 3" long. They take the handles off so you can't make a shank by melting a razor into the plastic of the toothbrush handle.

Today, they moved me into a cell by myself. I was up until 4:00 AM last night. My cellmate is an orderly. He is a dim-witted, prejudiced idiot who I can't stand. This morning around 8:00 AM he was yelling at me to wake up and clean the cell. I am not a morning person. I told him to shut up and that if I had to get up out of my bunk, I'd break his jaw. The little P.C. punk ran right out of the room and down to the Captain's office. He was crying like a baby. After this incident they moved me to my own cell with no cellmate. Most of the guys on my tier have doubled up rooms.

I guess that once again I am a problem child. It didn't help that when I told the kid I was going to break his jaw there was a screw standing right there. Life goes on in the hole. I am rather enjoying my own cell here. The privacy is excellent after being doubled up for the past three and a half months.

My mother got to see Stephanie, my daughter, when she went back to Massachusetts. She took her shopping, I guess. I had a silver cross and a chain that I gave to my mom when she came here to visit. She gave me a gold one. Then she gave my silver one to Stephanie. She took pictures and Stephanie talked about me like she adored me.

God, I miss that kid. I wish her mother was a little more lenient and let me call her just once. I haven't spoken to Stephanie since the Christmas of 1992, but I still write her a lot. Her grandmother is stashing the letters away for her. I actually wrote Samantha another letter and enclosed a letter to Stephanie too. I've written Samantha three or four letters begging her to just let me talk to Stephanie or let her talk to me. As parents we have a responsibility to act as parents but she is behaving like a child.

May 18, 1994

Today is Wednesday morning. It marks my fifteenth day in captivity. I have had my own cell now for the past three days, ever since I threatened to break my cellmate's jaw.

This cell is probably the worst on the tier. It is in dire need of a paint job. Graffiti is everywhere and, of course, I didn't hesitate to add my own. There are slash marks everywhere made by guys counting their days. Four vertical lines crossed by the single diagonal. I have my own set of slash marks and have just chalked up my 15th line.

Tonight is not a shower night but I have developed a method for washing my hair on off days. I save the milk cartons from breakfast. They are the half pint ones like you used to get in school. I open them up and run the water until its hot. You have to keep your finger on the button or the water will shut off. I fill up my "cups" and wet my hair. Then I fill them up again and shampoo my hair. I rinse and then repeat the process. The last time I used four of the containers to make sure I rinsed all the shampoo out. Then I washed my face and beard.

I haven't received any mail except for the first day I got here. I've just about written off Diane and Suzy Q. They ratted me out to my mom. I think they both told her I'd been drinking. Women are so unreliable.

May 21, 1994

Early Saturday morning.

I finally saw the DHO two days ago. It took him sixteen days to see me, then he gave me another 15 days of hole time. He also took 14 days of my good time that hadn't even been awarded yet. So much for my release date of August 16th.

Today I slept late and missed breakfast and lunch. The thought of food actually makes me sick and I wonder if I should skip dinner also or if I'll be ravenously hungry at midnight. I've developed a set of exercises I've been doing daily. They're nothing elaborate but enough to keep me from turning into total mush. I can easily handle a couple more weeks of this, but it is beginning to bore me. I would sleep twenty hours a day if I could.

I hear the food cart on the tier below me. It has one squeaky wheel that hasn't been greased in a long time. They leave it that way because you can hear it as soon as they open the door to your tier. Operant conditioning. Squeaky wheel, inmates salivate. The thought of food is really making me nauseous.

I'm having difficulty concentrating on reading. That has never been a problem for me. It must stem from doing nothing but reading for the past two weeks. I thought today about doing these thirty-one days as I scratched out my eighteenth pencil mark on the wall. It's the most realistic sentence I've had, so much easier for me to comprehend. Three more days will leave me with ten more. Piece of cake.

The entire month of May is almost gone for me, spent in an 8 x 12 room. I haven't gotten any mail in three weeks. I sent out a few letters but haven't gotten any replies. Maybe I'll write Ruth Ann in New York. Maybe she'll write me. Tomorrow, I'll write letters, work more on my journal and starve myself. I've always had a good appetite but I'll have to find something else to occupy my time. It is far too easy to eat excessively when there is nothing else to do.

May 24, 1994

I've been transferred to Cell 103 on D range. The famous Winebucket is my cellmate. Both of us have been in cells by ourselves and deprived of human contact for the past week and a half.

We stayed up until breakfast talking.

Winebucket is an old style convict. His name is derived from the fact that he is a major brewer, sometimes making up to twenty gallons of wine at a time. He is a master of the art. He is also intelligent, easy to get along with and has a good sense of humor. His record shows three murder charges with two convictions and countless crimes. He is a career offender. He has been to Marion, Clayton and the dreaded Florida State Prison system. Although I can't remember all we said, the conversation last night went something like the following:

"Hell, I've been doing armed robberies since I was thirteen years old," Winebucket said. "Had a job once washing trucks for about a dollar a day. This was a long time ago. Anyway, I remember I had just turned thirteen and I'd seen a lot of these guys paying with cash. Well, I was in the office snooping through the boss's desk and I found a pint of Old Mr. Boston Sloe Gin. So, I was nipping on that and I got to rooting around a little more and I found a little .32 revolver. Well, I put that in my pocket. A little later, the boss came into the office and was sitting at his desk. I pulled out the gun and pulled the hammer back and told him to come across with the cash. Now this guy, he was a big mother, and he wasn't gonna hear none of this. Here's this little 13 year old kid threatening this big guy. He wasn't agreeable to turning over the money. 'Bout then, I put a bullet in his desk 'bout six inches in front of him. Then he started to cooperate a little. So I tied him up and stole his car. He had this big ol' station wagon. Power steering. Power brakes. I was just a kid and I remember I barely got that car out of the parking lot. I was bouncing off trailers and finally hit the road. Picked up a wino hitchhiking. Almost clipped him too. I still had the Mr. Boston. I took that too. After a while, I told him I stole the car. He didn't care. I reached down to peel off some money for him. You know, I was looking for a ten or a twenty. Damned if I didn't peel off a hundred dollar bill. Had him drop me off. I had thirty-six hundred dollars. Bought me a car. Back then, you didn't need no insurance and all that crap. If you had money, you bought a car and got a plate."

After his story, I told Winebucket about my first job and a couple other ones I'd done. The discussion was crime of course and I, as a novice, listened intently into the night to the words of a wise, older convict.

"Down in Florida," Winebucket continued, "was where I met Bundy. I was the orderly for Death Row. I brought them newspapers, books, all that stuff. I knew Bundy, Williams, all those guys. Now Bundy, he was smart, a real smart guy. Kept admitting to other killings so as to keep his case going. He didn't want to die, no sir. Yeah, he was smart. Williams, now they did that man wrong. See, a lot of people think that once they take you up to the chair and juice you, that's it. Well, the truth is, it takes nine minutes. They hit you three times. It's a long nine minutes. They put a wet sponge on your head before they put that headband on. That's what is supposed to knock you out. Then, they juice you the first time. That breaks the bones in the arms and legs from the convulsions. Supposed to knock you out too. Three minutes. The second time, it'll start cookin' your insides, your liver, your guts start steaming. Then the third time finishes you off. Well, they put Williams in the chair and put that sponge on his head. It had hardly a drop of water in it. Technically, if you live through this, they can't do it again. They've gotta let you go. Ol' Williams lived. After the third time he was still alive. So they hit him three more times. Old Sparky prevailed and Williams was executed."

Winebucket's stories continued into the night.

"Wasn't long after that they stuck me in the place for the criminally insane. I'd been charged with three murders. The last one, I stabbed a guy twenty seven times. They told me I overdid it and sent me to Chatahouchee. They asked me why I stabbed him so many times and I told 'em the truth. Told 'em I was scared shitless. The guy was a monster. Had more muscles than you ever seen. Been lifting weights for twenty years. I was petrified. I came up on him and stuck him in the kidney. Nailed him eight times there and it should have finished him. Hell, all he did was drop to his knees. I said, 'uh-oh.' So I stuck him some more. It was like riding a bull. The guy had so many muscles he just wouldn't quit struggling. Finally, he was dead after I stuck him twenty seven times."

Winebucket shrugged.

"At the place for the criminally insane I remember this one guy, Todd. This place was goddamned crazy. I mean absolutely crazy. More nut cases than you ever seen. This guy, Todd, would run up to you and say 'I don't know what I'm doing. Do you?' And before you could answer, off he'd go running to someone else. But Todd, he knew what he was doing. He'd wait 'til he caught you with your guard down, then he'd latch onto your neck with his teeth and he'd hang on your neck like a turtle. Couldn't get him off. I imagine its hard trying to get somebody off your neck. Kind of like punching yourself in the face. The orderlies would come. That was another thing I remember. Every single person that worked there had to weigh over three hundred pounds and be over six feet tall. They had these big, big sticks that looked like baseball bats. Anyway, they would come over and hit Todd with the Thorazine and they'd pull him off and there'd be a big hole in the guy's neck. They'd start beating on Todd with the sticks. Then they'd throw him in a rubber room for a few days. I went to get a drink from the fountain and had a little guy jump me from behind. Got his arms across my throat. I just couldn't get him off. I'm hitting the guy in the ribs with my elbows. I can hear 'em crack. He's hanging on me. I start bashing his head against the wall and he still wouldn't let go. Here comes the orderlies. They hit us both with Thorazine and threw us in the rubber room. In there, they don't care who starts what, who's guilty of what. If you're involved, you go into the rubber room. Once they hit you with the Thorazine, you're gone. A couple of days at least. You wake up and your ass hurts like hell from where they hit you with the needle. Most likely, you're lying in your own shit and rolling around in your own piss. It'll be a while before you can stand up. When they see you standing, which takes about three days, then they'll let you out to take a shower and get cleaned up."

Winebucket talked about penitentiaries.

"I've done my share of penitentiary time. Don't really want to go back there. Would if I had to, but don't really want to. You walk on eggshells all the time. You've got to be real lucky. Bump into somebody that got a 'Dear John' letter, you're stuck. Someone don't like the looks of you, you're stuck. Owe somebody five dollars and they even think you're gonna run, you're stuck. Fart in the chow line, you're stuck. Walking on eggshells all the time. You gotta remember that a lot of these guys are doing all day. They ain't coming out ever. These guys are already dead. They've got nothing better to do. It's a whole different world. It's a whole different attitude, a different lifestyle. Survival is all that counts."

May 29, 1994

It's early Sunday morning.

Four more days to go in the hole. I can't sleep and decided to write a poem.

> For every cop, there's a gun.
> For every criminal a law undone.
> For every victim, pain and rage,
> For each intruder there is a cage.

For each attorney there is a court,
For every mother's children to support.
For every court there is a judge,
From federal guidelines he won't budge.
For every child, there is a space,
Unless some new daddy takes his place.
For every con, a heavy heart,
That counts the days his family's apart.
For every month grows more gray hair,
As all the days turn into years.
For every drug and every drink,
There was one moment we didn't think.
For every night we sleep alone,
For every night we think of home.
For every con that dies in here,
No one else will shed a tear.
For as I sit and look behind,
I wish I could go back in time.
For as I write I slowly die,
And as I do, I wonder why.

It's only 3:00 AM and it looks like I'll be up until 6:00 AM at least.

Winebucket and me couldn't resist and whipped up a gallon of wine. It is kind of hard to do in the hole but its coming out nicely. It started to turn, but that was because it was too cold in the cell. I've now got the bag next to my body and the heat has activated it and it's cooking very well. I'm afraid of rolling over on the bag while I'm sleeping but, as Winebucket says, I'll only have to worry about this once.

Someone kicked the sprinkler off the wall and flooded the tier the other night. My boss, the plumber, got called in to replace it. I saw him in the hall.

"You dry out yet?" he asked me.

"Yeah, yeah, sure." I said, laughing to myself and thinking of the gallon that's brewing. The idiot wouldn't give me a cigarette either.

I just found out that a guy I owe a hundred dollars stabbed someone last February. That's just great. I was supposed to pay him over a month ago so he'll probably kill me when I get out. Christ, I've gotta make a shank and all that shit. If I know I'll have to knife fight him, then I'll have to tape some National Geographics to my body.

How I ever got into this damned mess I'll never know. I am putting in for a transfer to Terminal Island or Lompoc F.C.I. Both places are in California. Screw all this cold weather. I can live at either Terminal Island or Lompoc and am not sure which one I prefer.

I guess it's been so long since I've had any kind of structure it's taken its toll. I've always been able to run though, always been able to hide. No more. You can always "check in" or P.C. (place yourself in protective custody) and then get transferred. But not me. I don't know why. I don't understand the reasons or the politics of it. I only know that I can't run from another man. I can run from myself. I can run from a woman. I can run like hell. But I can't run from a man. And I'll be the first to admit that I'm no tough guy. I'm no panty waist either.

It's been said that if a dog runs with wolves long enough, he will begin to believe he is a wolf. However, in a fight, he would not be as strong. His endurance is not as good and he would starve to death faster than a wolf. Of course, he would be some bad-ass dog. Better to be a dog among wolves than a sheep.

Memories are what keeps me going. Memories and projections of the future. I keep remembering my friends in California, even Shannon who hated me. I try to guess how much things will be changed when I get out. Will the same people even be around? I don't want things to have changed too much. I know the sun will still set over the water. I know it will still be cloudy in June. I know Mexico is only 15 minutes away. I know the beach at night is nice and I see me sitting in the sand playing guitar. Just me and my guitar. I can hear the waves.

May 31, 1994

The 12:30 count is soon coming and this marks my last day in solitary. Bucket and I both get out after almost thirty days.

It's raining, really pouring. It's an electrical storm and set off fire alarms earlier leaving me in the shower for about 45 minutes. One more full day, that being Wednesday the first, and I'm out on the morning of the second. Back on the pound. Back to playing guitar and raising hell.

There are a few disadvantages to being in the hole. One is that you lose your cell and have to go back to the common area. The worst part must be people worrying if you "checked in" owing them money. Rumors start and are perpetuated. If someone else goes down they might speculate, "He must have said something."

When you get out of the hole you have to deal with all of this bullshit. Like Bucket says, "You need to realize you're not dealing with the highest mentality. Most of them are pretty dumb." Of course, I say that sitting here in the hole, in prison. I don't think you can get much lower in the eyes of society.

Bucket tells me it can get a lot worse. He just told me about "the box" in the Florida State Prison. It is a hole about 4 feet by 5 feet. You can never stretch out in it. The most you can stretch is from corner to corner. They throw you in the "box" with just your underwear. No blanket, no toilet paper, none of that. There is a hole in the middle of the floor that flushes about once an hour by itself. There is no light. They feed you once a day and all you get are two pieces of bread and a little Dixie cup with vegetables in it. You get a quart of water. Once a day. You'd better get ready for the "beanhole" to open too, because it comes through express and if you drop it, you're screwed. A beanhole is a little trap door built in the door that your beans come in. The rats come up through the hole. The worst are the cockroaches. You learn to sleep with your fingers in your ears because the roaches crawl in your ears and die. You get one hell of a headache. They send you in with underwear but you don't come out with any. You have to tear it into little pieces to use as toilet paper. By the time you come out you are naked.

So, yeah, it gets worse I guess. It gets a lot worse. On the other hand, its not too great in here either. I had the opportunity to use the phone the other day. I called my brother in San Diego. I told him I was doing thirty days in the hole.

"Yeah," he said, "you've probably got a sauna and hot tub and . . . "

I interrupted him by flushing the toilet with the receiver dangling in the bowl.

"What the hell was that?" he asked.

"My sauna," I said.

There are too many people on the outside who see us federal inmates as playing nine holes of golf every day. It's just not that way.

It's now the first of June. My last day in the hole. It hasn't seemed like a long thirty days, but its only about about 1:00 AM. The day will drag, I'm sure. That's why I'll stay up until two or three and sleep until dinner today. Then it'll be a coast, fifteen or sixteen hours.

June 3, 1994

I play bass in my friend Jimmy's band and he plays guitar in mine. Two sides of Jimmy's head are shaved and he has a tattoo of a music note with a lightning bolt going through it. Jimmy, like Winebucket and me, is in for bank robbery. He's got one hell of a singing voice and writes some good stuff. We are creatures of a similar mind. But Jimmy has done a lot more time than me, starting with a correctional home for boys. I forget the name of it.

Jimmy told me the following in the yard.

"The first time I ever shot a pistol I shot somebody. I was twelve years old. It was a neighborhood bully. Me and my friend went over to his house. His dad had lots of guns lying around. I saw this little automatic and swiped it. After we left I told my friend 'Come on, let's go down to the playground. I wanna find the kid.' When we found him, I pulled out the gun and made him get on his knees. I guess some people saw us and heard me yelling at him. I was pissed. I threatened the kid. The people around heard me threaten him. All I wanted to do was scare him, but the goddamned gun went off and I shot him in the jaw. They sent me to the school for boys. I remember when I first got there, I went in to take a piss. I heard this grunting and looked around. I saw these two black guys. One of them was screwing this Indian. They told me to mind my own business and I did. You know I saw that Indian years later in prison, only he was doing the screwing then. You're gonna see a lot of guys here that act like real tough convicts. You'll see them treating other people like shit. I'll tell you this Sean. I've been in the system a long time and most of these guys, the way they treat other people, is the way they've been treated themselves. Take Hank. He's a real piece of shit, treats his cellie like a real piece of shit, too. I had an altercation with him and he ain't shit. He's all talk. You know, I had this device that I was gonna come up behind him with, like a coward or whatever, and do him. But you know what? I overheard him telling someone that he was going to stick somebody and I knew right there. I knew he wasn't shit because you don't go telling somebody what you're gonna do. You just do it. When I was seventeen I went to Florida State Prison. It's a very, very bad place. I did three and a half years there. After three and a half years I got out and I remember thinking to myself, 'Man, that's all they can do to you? You can rob, steal, rape, kill and all they can do is put you in prison?' I got out and after all that time, I still wasn't twenty-one. Went right to a titty bar with a friend of mine and they gave me a hard time about getting in. Finally, I showed a piece of paper that showed I had just done three and a half years and they let me in. One of the girls took me home and the next day I went up to a few houses and broke in. I got lucky. The guy was my size."

June 5, 1994

Time is passing quickly since I've been out of the hole. I had it out with my boss at the plumbing shop and quit. I acquired a job at the music room in the Rec Department, which is where my heart is anyway.

Days turn into night and nights turn into days. The carousel goes round and round. It seems I feel much better when I take a drink now and then. It relieves the stress extraordinarily. My parents just wouldn't understand. I try to alienate myself from family and friends. I still call and write, but I expect no answers.

I am alone.

Again.

I called Diane, the love of my life, last night to try to get rid of her. What started out to be a tactful, sensitive cutting of losses, turned into tears and heartache.

"Why are you so easy to love and so hard to leave?" she asked me.

I said mean things trying to let go while inside I was hurting. She's holding on and I'm out on the ledge, pushed to the edge.

Too many nights I ponder my stupidity. Too many dreams I wash away with confusion. My associates are criminals. My best friend a killer. Life is a kaleidoscope. Where is everybody? Such a waste, the things that come to pass. I become familiar with the dark side of human nature in its crudest form, that of the prison system. My mind becomes bent, my visions become dim and the pessimism is a knife that sticks to my guts. So sharp and demanding. Misery forever? Forever misery.

To die would be much too easy. To suffer through two and a half years with no love seems the ultimate test of will. The worst is just imagining what's going on in the real world. It's such a tremendous kick in the groin. I remember I used to get so high I wished I was dead, wished I could fly away and just drift off like a leaf in the wind. Fantasies of cryogenic bliss. Put me in a coma, let me wake in a few years to see something else.

I remember running free on the full moon, wild with the blood coursing through my veins, wired on alcohol, armed with dangerous weapons of death, daring life to challenge me.

So many things I did right, too few things I did wrong. I've broken hearts, yet I've loved so hard. I gave my all and I tasted the sweet kiss of a true lover. I laughed, I cursed, I lived lonely on the night. I prowled, I caroused, I took by force and was taken up by the breath of freedom. All the sunsets that led to starry nights. All the rivers that eventually led to the sea.

And still, I find someone loving me. Just a little more space? Just push me into the corner a little more. Save my dreams. Leave my memories. I have seen too many empty husks of men. Don't leave me shattered. I plead innocence and ignorance. My mind may be sharp enough to cry for you, but my fate has left me searching until death. Like all others.

So come now, all of you sages, all you speakers of wisdom, all you seekers of truth, and the rest. Come now and speak to me. Explain the whyness of things, and I shall listen.

To me, it is nothing.

June 10, 1994

Back on the pound. Back on the attack.

After quitting my job in the plumbing shop I roll into work about 12:30 and play guitar all day. The hell with getting up at 7:30 AM. I figured today that I might be the most underpaid guitarist of the year. But the government is really paying for it, so I guess it's all right.

The Spartanville Bike Show is coming up and my band is playing at it. Now days I immerse myself in the guitar. It seems my soul is seeking a vent to air its frustrations. My new job seems an excellent thing to have stumbled into. There is not much to do. The music room is located right next to the yard and the weight pile is right outside the door.

I am back in my cell with the famous Kicka, another bank robber. We argue all the time because we get along so well. Matter of fact, he just came in and told me to write more about him.

"Tell 'em how tough I am," he tells me.

July 3, 1994

I've been back in the hole for almost a week. I'm in for thirty days, so it looks like most of my summer will be spent in a box.

Today I finally got a pencil.

Last Sunday I drank a gallon of wine and smoked a bunch of pot. I was totally trashed at 3:30 in the morning and tried to get hold of my little brother but ended up talking to his roommate, Rob. The next thing I remember was sitting on the steps in front of the office. There wasn't even one cop in my unit, but when I looked up, I saw three of them.

"You're in an unauthorized area," one of them said to me.

I managed to get up and began to stagger away.

"Get back here!" one of them ordered.

They wanted my mug. It was a big mug and held a whole quart but now it was almost empty. The cop still wanted it. I wasn't giving it up.

"I'm drinking this," I slurred.

Next came the handcuffs, the breathalyzer and the walk to SHU. It was around 4:00 AM and we walked all the way across the compound. My second breathalyzer was a 1.50. With the weed, I was gonzo. I have to get that way about once a month. If I didn't, I'd just go nuts and probably end up either in a penitentiary, doing another bid, or dead.

I saw Mr. Brofly who gave me thirty days, like it's an ice cream on a hot day.

"I won't take any good time," he tells me, "and I'll put 15 up on the shelf for you."

Oh boy, I thought. Probably a disciplinary transfer.

Am I daunted or depressed? No. Inside I am cackling with glee and have a half gallon of primo nectarine wine brewing as I write. Taught by the famous Winebucket how to brew in the hole. I expect this to be a killer batch. As long as it doesn't get found. It's been a little chilly, about 65 degrees. Let me see. I put it up Friday night when I got my cell. It should be cooking good by tomorrow and ready by Friday. A seven day batch.

I am going to try like hell to get to Phoenix, Arizona and closer to home. I'm going to try and shuffle my way across the continent.

I slept for most of the day and then woke up to the obnoxious sound of a P.R. kicking the shit out of his cell door and yelling, "Bullshit, bullshit." I almost started slinging a few epitaphs of my own. The guards are gone. I've got to check the wine now. It's still not really cooking like it should be. It is a little cool and today is only the second day.

Eating an apple reminds me of home. The part of western Massachusetts that I'm from has many apple orchards. They grow the best apples I've ever eaten. Macintosh apples. They're absolutely the best. I heated up the wine a little to see if an increase in temperature will help it start to cook. I sure could use a joint right about now. Used to grow some pretty good pot back in Massachusetts, too. After July I will only have 24 months left. Almost halfway. Suzy wrote me a good-bye letter and Diane is no longer accepting my phone calls.

It sucks to be me.

July 4, 1994

They just finished midnight count and I'm lying here waiting to get tired. It occupies a lot of my time. I read a 274 page novel today called *The Concrete Boat* by Kenneth Joyce. It's OK. I have read much in the past 17 months and will undoubtedly read much more.

Outside of music theory and music history, my interests are beginning to wane. I spend a bit of time hiding behind the burnt out surfer image. It suits me and it's a great image to project. I keep my hair long, although it needs to be cut. I have a beard, but instead of being all scraggly and uneven, I keep it trimmed. I like it. My mom hates it. She wants me to be a kid forever. Hell, I want to be a kid forever. Isn't it everybody's greatest fear to grow old? To grow old and find yourself alone. That would be bogus.

After Samantha, I swore that there would never be another like her. But fate had other plans and I fell hard for Diane.

Then I came to jail. Extremely bad timing on my part. What could I do? I set Diane free. Told her to get lost basically. I couldn't get rid of her if I tried. For a year, she wrote me every day, came to see me every week. I called her every day. Sometimes several times a day. Not once did she ever not accept my collect call. I tried to be gruff. Tried to be tough and to end it early. The inevitable was coming. I knew it. She gave me unconditional love and never asked for anything.

When I first met her I was playing in a band called Breakaway. I kind of stumbled across her. Three months later I was a prospect for a motorcycle gang called the Devil's Disciples. I carried a gun. Sometimes more than one gun. Always at least two knives.

I remember Diane lived with her sister, who didn't like me too much. I would sneak into the house late at night. One night coming back from a club meeting/project, it was very late and I was very drunk. I snuck into her house, got in her room and it took me twenty minutes to unstrap (mostly because I was drunk). I had a sawed-off shotgun, pockets full of shotgun shells, a .380 semi-auto and a Colt Model 1911A1 .45 caliber semi-auto, both pistols. I had three spare clips for each. I had a K-Bar trench knife in a sheath in the small of my back. I had a 9 inch boot knife that was balanced for throwing and a set of leather fisticuffs to which I could attach small daggers.

This was in Greenfield, Massachusetts. People were petrified of me.

Diane wasn't though.

Enough of this subject.

July 5, 1994

I believe the pressure of prison is beginning to take its toll. Maybe it's a combination of being in the hole again after only 19 days out.

My friend Mitch hung himself yesterday. Or was it the day before? Mitch is a character like myself who also frequents the hole. His two favorite sayings are "Wow" and "Heavy." We are separated by two cells and we bring out the insanity in each other. It helps to keep us sane. Mitch gets the paper *U.S.A. Today* every day and lets me read it.

The cells in the hole are all on one side of the corridor. The only thing visible is a wall and a light. You can hold a conversation if you lay on the floor and speak under the door. Mitch was telling me how he was looking forward to going to Clayton. He was always a little unstable. The hole is an unstable place.

Mitch has hung himself probably eight times since I've known him. It's the only way he can get a cigarette. Plus, it's a break in the boredom. He really goes all out with his grandstanding. Even when they leave him with only what he calls "underwears" he has plenty to work with.

"Sean, Sean," Mitch screams.

The hanging episodes usually begin with him calling for me like this.

"What?" I yell back.

"I'm gonna hang it up, Sean," Mitch yells. "I can't stand it anymore."

He yells loudly so that the whole tier can hear.

Immediately a cry goes up from the tier. It is almost like a chant or cheer along the sideline in a football game.

"Do it Mitch! Do it!" the tier chants at Mitch. "Cut your wrist, Mitch!"

Mitch is a kind of celebrity.

I am the only one who doesn't encourage Mitch.

"Don't do it, Mitch," I proclaim loudly. "Don't do it."

But I have to smile when I say this. It is all a hoax, a sham, though a serious one. He must rip his "underwears" into a noose and as soon as a guard comes by, he begins his act.

"What are you doing, Mitch?" asks the guard.

"I'm hanging it up man," Mitch says to the guard. "I can't take it no more."

In no time, a whole gaggle of coppers are in the hallway. It is quite a fiasco. All this for a lousy Marlboro. At first he won't cuff up. He won't come out and they can't go in unless he cuffs up first. He stands there and wails, butt naked with his "underwears" in a noose, tied to the window and then around his neck. They won't take Mitch to suicide watch anymore, except when he actually hangs himself. You can catch a smoke in suicide watch. Mitch tells me of how they had him four pointed one time. That's when they tie you up. He escaped, knocked the sprinkler head off and flooded the tier.

"Wow," I said.

"Heavy," agrees Mitch.

We chuckle.

I am lying on the floor talking to Mitch under the door.

"Mitch," I say, "this has got to be like some cosmic joke."

"Wow," says Mitch.

"Heavy," I agree.

We are both losing it, I think.

I put up my second batch of wine today. The first should be ready by Friday. I used a lot of fruit in this second batch. I hope it comes out good. I need sugar badly. I used the last of what I had to dump in batch number one. Batch number one is nectarines and an orange. It contains hand-picked raisins from Raisin Bran. The raisins have a natural yeast in them. Batch number two is nectarines and some canned plums we had today. I also peeled and deseeded an apple and tossed it in. I am letting the pulp sit for a couple days until I get more sugar and the raisins from batch number one.

Life in the hole goes on.

Tomorrow I see the shrink about getting some dope to sleep at night. I can't sleep. I find myself laughing out loud in my dreams.

Like a madman.

July 7, 1994

Cameron flooded his cell next door. He knocked the sprinkler head off the wall. Man what a mess. Mitch also flooded his cell right after Cameron. Lt. Hackett, the one who escorted me down here June 26th, took Cameron to a shower cell.

I broke into the first batch of wine. It could have used a couple more days but what the hell. My second batch is going to be phenomenal. Straight juice, just pulp, it's cooking after one day by itself. I added the remnants of batch one to it.

I called Diane last weekend and she didn't accept my call. Am I to be finally rid of her? Maybe my heart can't get anymore broken over her. I guess its kind of a relief.

In a way, I wish everybody would just piss off and die. When I call it's always, "Oh yes, we miss you terribly." But then nobody writes to me. Not any of my girlfriends, not my friends, my brothers, my father or mother. Only Suzy writes. And she wrote me a "Sorry, can't write or accept calls no more because you're still drinking" letter.

I can count the mail I've received in the past three months on one hand. A letter from Suzy on May 2nd when it was my first day in the hole. A money receipt and pictures from Mom. On June 27th, my first mail day in the hole, the letter of resignation from Suzy. A receipt for money from Mom. No mail at all in the month of June. Today I got a surprise package from Suzy. That's five pieces of mail and that's a wrap. At least I got mail for my first year.

I can't wait for August 17th to get here. It will mean only two years left. Twenty-four months, a paltry seven hundred and twelve days. I really feel it when I scratch it out on paper and exactly figure out the days.

I miss my daughter the most. I think of her a lot. When I see little babies in movies I feel a real ache inside, a real sense of loss of not being able to be there to see my little girl grow up and not being able to give her the things she wants.

July 14, 1994

On July 7th I was stupid enough to take a shower and let them search my cell. I was busted again for another 222. I still haven't seen DHO Usually I see him on Thursday. But if they came for me today I would refuse to cuff up because I have another half gallon brewing.

On July 9th I saw the UDC and they are recommending a disciplinary transfer. Yesterday I saw the psychiatrist and he prescribed something I can't pronounce. I'm now taking psychotropic drugs for my depression. I had to sign a release form. I was hoping they'd just give me sleeping pills, some kind of brake fluid. But he didn't. I'm not too sure about this psychotropic business.

My mom wrote a letter about transferring me to Phoenix to my case manager, the Bureau of Prisons and my psychologist. Mitch is going to a loony ward in Springfield, Missouri. He seems very happy. He has been there twice before. I like Mitch even though he's a little nuts. Twice when he was flipping out I hollered at him to chill out and hand over the razor blade or whatever.

Mr. Winefoot came to see me twice.

"I really want to thank you for helping with Mitch," he said to me. "I realize you could of done the opposite and got him going and I appreciate what you did. Really, I won't forget it."

The second time it happened with Mitch he said, "You are consistently being of great assistance and once again, I will not forget it."

Yeah, right. Mitch is my friend, that's all. I just didn't want to see him four-pointed in a dry-cell somewhere.

I'm two weeks into my thirty days of ice and already sick of reading. I have my cell set up just how I want it. Eighteen pictures of my family and daughter hang on the wall. The pictures are just out of view of the guards. If you look in the door from the outside you can't see them. But on the inside, sitting at my desk, they are right in front of me.

The top of my desk is cluttered with envelopes, shampoo, a soap dish and cups with salt and pepper in them. When they deliver the food, the salt and pepper has usually solidified in the packages. I take them out, put them in one cup and take packages from the other cup which has dried out. A couple of old letters from Diane are also on my desk. I like to read them every once in a while. There is an almost gone roll of toilet paper on the desk and my foot cream for athlete's foot. There is aspirin and Tylenol and a tube of Chapstick I've had forever. There is a drawing that Blaze, my old singer, drew for me. It must have gotten slipped in my property with all my files and folders. There is an empty milk carton, a thin strip of sheet, a small plastic bag and a cup of hair conditioner.

The cup is used to hold my conditioner because I use the conditioner bottle to hold the fruit for the wine in. My peaches were starting to go so I had to peel them and put them in the conditioner bottle. The bottle has a cap and when I go to take a shower, I place the bottle in the mattress. I made a rip in the corner of the mattress and the bottle fits perfectly. You can't tell it's there.

I use the bottle because I don't have a bag to make wine. A clear plastic trash can liner with no holes in it is the ideal type of bag. It will easily hold a gallon, through I have not yet brewed that much in here. Without a bag, though, the fruit was going so I had to do something.

It takes time to acquire enough fruit to start a batch. When I get enough fruit, I stick it in the bottle and let it ferment for a few days. This also allows me to take my last shower on Wednesday. I put it up on Monday or Tuesday night and let the fluid ferment. I hide it for the shower on Wednesday. On Friday I skip the shower. There are no showers on Saturday or Sunday. It should be ready by Monday. Easy. The only thing that can screw things up is if they call me to see the DHO. If they do, I'll refuse and get another shot. But screw it. I'll get a buzz on too.

The thin strip of sheet on my desk comes from a long coil of it called a line. Most of the doors have at least an inch of clearance. You take your line and attach a weight to the end of it. A book serves well. Then you heave it under the door. Your accomplice does the same with his line and if you are close enough you can usually connect lines. Then you can pass whatever between the two of you: cigarettes, matches, notes, razors, weed, whatever.

My door has a metal plate welded to the front with only a quarter inch under it. Therefore I have to use a very thin line with no knots in it. Even a small knot hinders the line's flow when I leave it out. At the end of my line is a piece of tile. It just skims under a certain part of the door because the welding job was sloppy. The knot that I had to tie on the piece of tile is tied so the knot rests on the edge of the piece of tile. It is a very exact thing.

Mitch and I play with our lines a lot. We play with them whatever chance we get. It helps alleviate boredom. There's plenty of that to go around.

July 22, 1994

Day twenty-two of my isolation.

Tonight is a shower night.

I'm back from suicide watch and into the swing of things again. I went to suicide watch on Sunday the 17th because I had a little to drink and wanted a phone call. One phone call a month is exceedingly trying on one. I got an hour long phone call and talked to Diane. I guess she loves me still. She wrote a fourteen page letter while I was on suicide watch.

The day I went on suicide watch began innocently enough. I'd been prescribed a psychotropic drug for my depressions. It didn't seem to work and after a few days I decided to stop taking it. I only wanted something to help me to sleep. During this time I had an excellent batch of wine brewing. It was the best I've ever made and I drank it on Sunday afternoon. I kept telling them I wanted a phone call and if I didn't get it I would hang myself.

No phone though.

I had a noose hanging from my windowsill for about two weeks. It is kind of difficult for them to see into my cell so I brought it to their attention.

Still no phone.

I wrote out my last will and testament and stuck it under the door.

Still no phone, but this time they did put a guard in a chair outside my door.

Finally, in exasperation, I wrote a little suicide note to the regional HQ of the Bureau of Prisons. Suddenly, the Lieutenant and the psychologist appeared. Everyone seemed genuinely concerned. I spoke with the Lieutenant. He was reasonable and we came to an agreement. Two cigarettes would be sacrificed to appease me. In exchange for these, I would tear up my suicide message instead of sending it to Regional and go back to my cell.

Suddenly, Mr. Winefoot appeared and the real show began.

I've dealt with my share of psychologists and found most of them to be disturbed individuals. Mr. Winefoot was no exception. He was middle-aged, balding and overweight. On previous occasions I came to the conclusion that he was definitely "on" something.

Mr. Winefoot took me to the law library and in the presence of Lt. Smith began his systematic questioning. I found this very boring and decided to have a little fun with him when he started twisting my responses to meet his requirements. I am pretty good at toying around with words. It's done by making a statement that invites a speculation or assumption.

After eliciting several satisfactory responses, he launched into his interpretation of my life. This is something I can't stand. I began to point out all of his assumptions and miscalculations, to the delight of the Lieutenant who could hardly keep from laughing.

Things began to heat up. Within 45 minutes, Mr. Winefoot was reduced to a blabbering idiot and was frothing at the mouth.

"You loser," he yelled at me. "There's a 99.9% chance you will be in prison the rest of your life. You are nothing but a loser and a career criminal."

He went on and on.

He was panting and out of breath at the end of his tirade.

He glared at me.

"And, you used to abuse animals, too, didn't you?" he said.

I laughed out loud. I had been tearing him up for a reason. He had provoked me with sheer stupidity and accusations and he wanted me angry and pissed off. The longer I sat there with a silly grin the madder he became. Once I realized that he was trying to force me into angrily defending myself, I clammed up entirely. All psychologists are nothing but verbal battlers anyway. He knew this and threw me in suicide watch, even though I repeatedly assured him I was not suicidal.

Suicide watch is a cell with a large mesh door plated with Plexiglas. The "beanhole" is always open and large enough to crawl through. Inmates watch you around the clock. They come in three hour shifts from 6:00 AM to 3:00 PM and then four hour shifts. Inside the cell there is a big cement "bed" with iron handles built into it. The mattress that lies on top of it was soaking wet and ripped its full length. It was stained with piss, shit and blood. I threw it on the floor and slept on the bare cement for three nights. Actually, I only slept a few hours the whole time I was there. The cell was disgusting.

July 24, 1994

Mitch is hanging himself again and the Lieutenant is up here with a bunch of officers. I'm sitting here writing and smoking cigarettes wrapped in a fine tissue paper. It is the same paper wrapped around the toilet paper rolls they give us.

Mitch told me he sliced his arm 79 times. They took his commissary away for a month. All he wants to do is smoke. I help him out and give him what I can. I just smoked my last cigarette. I've started a new batch. This time I don't have a bag to put it in, so I've divided the mixture into three milk containers. I don't know if it will work.

Mitch has been giving me a steady supply of Thorazine. Two hundred milligrams a day. I traded a couple of these for some Vistoril and sleep most of the time. I've been taking only 100 milligrams at a time, but lately it doesn't do the trick, so I take a higher dosage to sleep. I try to justify the medications by telling myself that the medical professions here will not help me. The bottom line is they won't give me the straight sleeping pills I want.

I guess when it all comes down to it, nothing has changed. I still drink and do pills and get high and struggle to justify it all. I remind myself I'm in prison. It's hard. I tell myself I'm in isolation and it's rough. Tell myself I'm miles away from family and friends. Tell myself I'm a failure as a father and that nobody writes anymore. I tell myself that it's so damned hard being alone. It seems like the whole world has forgotten me. Does anybody remember any of the good things I've done? Have I ever done anything good?

They've got a camcorder in the hallway and they are taping Mitch.

"I'm gonna die today, I'm gonna die today!" he chants.

Heavy.

I am starving and its not even 4:00 PM yet. I can't wait to eat so I can just doze off to sleep. I wait for my wine to come around. It is five more days until I finish my first 30 days.

Of course tomorrow I'll go to the DHO and get another 30. Maybe even 45 or so. Who knows? Who cares?

I just want to get to Phoenix.

I just want to go home.

I swear I won't rob any more banks for ever and ever.

July 27, 1994

A few days ago I took in a new cellie named White. We get along good enough. They didn't even ask me to cuff up. They just threw him in my cell. I had received another shot for refusing a cellmate. That makes eight.

Looking back at my calendar, I see that Mitch flipped out again last Saturday. This time he was trying to drop kick the sprinkler head. They stormed him and messed him up pretty good. They broke his nose and gave him black eyes. His face looked like an overripe pear.

White used to be an orderly, so we've got the tobacco situation under control. The wine situation is also going well. We smuggled in five pounds of sugar into the cell. It beats hoarding it piecemeal from breakfast. I've got six boxes of raisins and a couple oranges. I've got a gallon up now and it's probably coming down tonight. Tomorrow at the latest. Plenty of tobacco. We've got cards and gamble for stamps. They took my commissary away for 30 days yesterday. Life isn't all bad though. I can appeal the 30 day commissary loss. They got my number wrong again on the shot.

Yesterday, they moved us downstairs. White panicked because he had an ounce of tobacco and I panicked because I had a gallon of wine. I bled off the bag, packed it up in my bedroll and made the transition smoothly. After they told us to pack we had to wait for three hours. I was pissed because the wine was packed up in bags. I had to keep unpacking it and bleeding it off. White kept pacing the room and changing hiding places for the tobacco.

"Sean," he said to me, "I'll put it under my foot."

"You're too paranoid," I said.

"No way, man. I ain't paranoid."

"I'll wrap it up in a towel, put it around my neck."

"Dude, chill out," I told White.

There was silence.

"Screw it, I'll leave it in my underwear," White said.

"Christ."

"Dude, this is a trick man. I got 'em shaking us down bro. We're hot. I don't want to lose my tobacco. You know what I'm saying?"

"Man, I'll take all the shots," I tell him. "You know I don't care."

"I know, Sean," White says.

"You want me to carry the damn tobacco?" I ask White.

"No man," he says. "I'm straight."

Silence again.

"Maybe I'll stash it in our roll of toilet paper," White says.

It went like this until they moved us.

When they finally moved us there was a moment of panic. Between floors they pulled me aside in handcuffs to see the UDC about my shot for refusing a cellmate. I saw the guard carrying my bedroll of carefully wrapped and concealed hooch and stifled a whimper. I could see the 222 shot already written. Certainly they will shake us down with only White down there in handcuffs. They usually shake you down when you go to the showers.

The procedure for removing a prisoner is to handcuff both cell-mates, remove the handcuffed one, lock the door and uncuff the other through the beanhole. While they have you both handcuffed you are totally at their mercy. They can ransack your stuff. The trick is to have one guy pretend he's sleeping. Therefore he's harmless. By never allowing the two of you to be handcuffed simultaneously, you avoid the possibility of a "visual" search which might turn up contraband.

July 30, 1994

Last night I dreamed I saw the Grim Reaper. I was ascending a mountain trail by a stream and he peeked at me from behind a tree.

I am getting tired of dreaming.

I finished up my 30 days D.S. time and caught a fresh 30 all the same day. And, the day before that, they again found a gallon of wine in my cell.

When I saw Mr. Brophy, the DHO, he told me, "You can stop making wine now."

"OK," I said.

But can I?

I wonder.

Mitch clued me in on suicide watch. When you go there it's inmates that watch you. You can smoke because they'll slip you cigarettes. Anyone can go back there and slip you anything. A friend came down and threw me a pack of cigarettes. Someone else gave me two packs. I had more cigarettes than I knew what to do with. I carefully tore the lining on my jumpsuit and squeezed in a few packs and matches. They found them though.

Another shot.

Two days ago they put Mitch in the shower and he had his line with him. He saw the guard bend over around the corner to get his soap so he knew the razor blades were there. He snagged the box with his line and got four razors. He started right away.

"I'm cutting up, I'm cutting up," he yelled.

The officer came down. He was mortified. They had been warned about Mitch and no razors were to be left in the hall anymore.

"I've got four razors," Mitch said, "and I want four cigarettes or I'm cutting up right now."

Mitchell started to cut himself up. He would cut himself in a second to get a cigarette. Sure enough, they gave him four cigarettes. As he walked by my door he was puffing on a Marlboro the way George Burns puffs on cigars. He was holding three more in his hand and was not wearing any handcuffs. I couldn't believe it. Everybody gets cuffed to go to and from the showers. I was sitting on my bed when I heard the unmistakable toss and retrieve of the line. So, I was yelling to Mitch the whole time. My cellie and I were both jonesing for a cigarette. When Mitch came back I threw out my line and he gave us a cigarette.

That was two nights ago. Since then, he's been on the Thorazine train and taking 400 milligrams a day. I haven't heard two words from him. He told me he doesn't want to get four-pointed again. They really beat the shit out of him the last time.

The D.H.O. told me he was going to transfer me. I guess I should write some letters and request to be closer to home. I'll try to get to Phoenix or Stafford, Arizona.

I've been getting Thorazine from Mitch. At first I was just taking 100 milligrams to sleep. Now I've got to take 200 milligrams to sleep or I'm up. Like now. I've been up since breakfast and wrote a couple of letters. I gave White 100 milligrams and he's still sleeping. He slept through breakfast and brunch.

It's twenty to one on a Saturday afternoon and I'm sitting in my underwear writing. White had some tobacco that lasted a few days. Stevens, the guy who busted me for the wine, has been giving me tobacco right along. He doesn't know it though. It gets passed to me in the newspaper Stevens brings me. Guys I know tape a little brown bag between the pages in the newspaper. Sometimes it comes in a book, tucked into the library card flap. Stevens would be pissed if he knew he was delivering my smokes.

August 3, 1994

I am constantly at battle with myself. With nothing to do but ask myself questions and answer them, I guess I am finding out a lot about myself. I send letters to my cousin Sarah and I rant and rave about self appreciation and the art of psychologically, accepting and understanding one's self.

While I still have some doubts and questions I find myself more self-assured every day. I know what I want. I know who I am. I am becoming comfortable in my own skin. I am accepting. Yet at times I still feel lost or in a daze.

With a pencil or pen my mind seems to work clearly. However, when I'm having a conversation I forget the simplest words. I've forgotten the names of many friends and girls I've slept with. Then, I will remember the name, address and even phone number of somebody I haven't spoken to in a year. Is it all this hole time?

They came and four-pointed Mitch a couple of days ago. He flipped out and flooded his cell, smashed out the glass in his door and cut himself up. Will that be me some day soon?

Maybe I feel this way because I miss life's unpredictability the most. Day to day I simply stagger on. Writing letters and never getting responses. Eating, sleeping and doing hole time. Three out of six months in the hole. Half my time here.

My intellectual stimulation is limited to what I can produce myself. I'm not sure about what I write on the pages of this journal. Properly edited, out of the almost two hundred pages, maybe ten of them really say something. The rest is just globber. Because nothing really happens. It's the same shit day in and day out. Except my mind is changing. Maybe I'm going crazy. Maybe I'm becoming sane. My God. After all these years a clear head prevails? Why, then, do I seem to have a random access memory?

It's true I take some comfort in writing. Every now and then I'll hear a song in my head and I sit down and it's suddenly there. Heavy. I burn through novels with the hunger of a midwestern housewife watching her soap operas. Four to five hundred pages in twenty-four hours. I write letters to everybody: the Bureau of Prisons, my mom, my counselor. Get me outta here. Send me closer to home so I can see my mom more than once a year. If I don't get some emotional fulfillment in here, I might just crack and cut everybody off.

I'm doing my time, though, and will do it how I please. Drug program this and school that and A.A. this. That all sounds fine and dandy from out there. But the truth is that I'm too damned alone to take anybody else's advice. I know what is best for me because I live with myself. Right now, I'm my best friend. At times it seems I'm my only friend.

But I will make it.

I am going to come out of this one strong.

And probably with an attitude.

August 11, 1994

The alarm goes off.

Somebody has flooded the tier again by knocking the sprinkler off the wall.

Today is my forty-seventh day in the hole. It is also my daughter's birthday. She turned seven today and will be starting the second grade this fall. I wrote Samantha and told her I would call today. Surprisingly, she accepted the call. I spoke with my daughter for the first time in a year and a half. Although she didn't have much to say, it was a great just letting her know I often think of her. Oh man, I can't wait to get out of here.

Samantha seemed disturbed. She was bitter and extremely cynical. I hope she is alright but she sounds depressed. I told her that it was OK, that it would pass.

This morning my cellie Mike left to go home. When he left the cell he was a free man. He is on his way to Waterbury, Connecticut. He had been to a halfway house where he screwed up and was shipped back. Now he is free after six years of bullshit, one half incarcerated and one half under supervision. No paper on him or nothing. I got excited on his last night here. It's always good to see someone get out. In a way, it is like I was getting out too.

We talked about stuff everyone takes for granted: eating at McDonald's, pizza and good junk food. Buying that first bottle. Smoking that first big joint. Free stuff. I realized how much I miss a friggin' Big Mac and Pizza Hut pizza. How much I miss Jack Daniel's and Budweiser. How much I miss my friends.

Mike had been to Massachusetts and gone to some of the same towns, pizza joints and stores as me. Small world. Right now he's held over in New York City until 6:00 AM. He's probably sitting in a bar somewhere having a beer. Late last night I made us coffee with the hot tap water and we toasted his last night in prison. It was something. I realized how much time had passed. Almost a year and a half. My God, I might just make it out sane after all.

Mike left this morning. Cameron leaves tomorrow. He's been here since May 4th. I have a little over a month left to do for my D.S. time. I'll be alright. Mom's sending me in a Bible and some AA books. I've been pretty good for the last couple of weeks, although tomorrow someone is sending me down a half gallon.

Today I was really mellow. Usually I scream and curse at the guards all day and night. Especially when they count. But I was doing a lot of thinking and didn't speak to them at all. They figured something was wrong and sent down a cop to give me a breathalyzer. Of course, the breathalyzer was triple zeros.

I'm seriously thinking of refusing a cellmate again. Although I don't need this shot, I'm in the dark while waiting to hear about my transfer. While I'm waiting to hear, they want to use my cell like a hotel room.

I've had enough. I'm doing some serious D.S. time and I am beginning to have a problem with my anger. I hope that receiving my Bible will help a little.

I have only myself to seek comfort from now.

Only my pencil to keep me company.

But what the hell.

At least my pencil won't talk back.

August 17, 1994

I remember when I left my family that fall of 1989.

My little girl Stephanie had just turned two. I bought her a red tricycle for her birthday. I looked like hell. I had been partying all night at the house of my older brother Tony.

The next day I tracked him down my younger brother James. I call him The Little Puke. Turners Falls is a small town and I figured any kid would know where he was. I staggered around town until I found a little brat and terrorized him into telling me where James was. I was drunk as blazes at nine in the morning. I must have been a sight.

I found him in bed with some wench and practically kicked in the door. I don't know why it was so important to have my little brother with me. He was always extremely important to me though. We bought the red tricycle and I brought it to Stephanie. She was so young.

Things had come to a head in Montague. Samantha wanted absolutely nothing to do with me. I'm not sure why I still loved her so much. I wanted things to work out so badly. I could not fathom losing my family. But it was gone and no amount of talking or drinking was going to bring it back. Oh man, did I try to drink it back. I drank and drank, certain that my drinking would somehow bring her to her senses.

It never did bring her to her senses. But it did make me an absolute wreck. I'm not surprised that she felt nothing but pity on me. I was lost. Sometimes, though, I could look into her eyes and see how she really felt. There was that questioning look, that flicker of doubt. That was all I needed to see. Only years later could I look back and see that look. I knew then, could see deep down inside, she still loved me. I knew she always would. It took me some time to piece it together though.

I try to remember that exact day I left for California but only Stephanie's birthday stands out in my memory. Sometimes I called her from California and she'd yell and scream how she hated me. That would happen nine times out of ten. But the tenth time she would laugh and reminisce and then burst into tears.

"Whatever happened to us?" she would cry.

And her tears would melt my heart no matter how hardened I was in those days. But I came to realize there was nothing I could do. I had to give it to her the way she wanted it.

Soon, my little girl was running around and calling another man Daddy and I was just another picture in the photo album. You must understand that before Jim moved in with Samantha, he acted like my best friend. We went out drinking and to the beach together. It seems that a man's true feelings come out during heavy-duty drinking. I thought we were becoming great friends. We weren't the only ones becoming friends.

Things were tough in the fall of 1989. I lost both my family and a good friend. They were going to get much better and then they were going to sour again.

Looking back, I learned a lot that fall. It was a good, hard lesson that was well learned. It would be a long time before I realized the full implications of what had happened and how it would alter several lives forever.

September 1, 1994

The federal system in its infinite wisdom has raised my security level to a "high." One of the guards said I drank my way to a penitentiary.

So be it.

I've been moved to a shower cell since I last wrote and have had two cellies. First, there was Danny who used to get pissed off and mutter things like "wonder what his mother'd look like with her eyeball poked out of her head, dangling down by her neck." But overall, Danny was a good kid and taught me a new card trick. My new cellie, Jenson "The Joker," has a thing about bombs and likes to blow things up. He blew up his brother in his car, but says he didn't kill him.

My new cell has a view of the woods. I can even see the sunset. The other night two skunks came within ten feet of my window. Two spiders live in the window which is grated, barred and recessed. They have their own little cell too. Spiderdude and Ultraman.

I spoke with my daughter on her birthday. It was the first time I spoke with her in a year and a half. She didn't say much but I didn't care. It took a year and a half to catch Samantha in a good mood.

I got a letter from my friend Dano and a letter from Diane. That girl. She puts perfume on her letters and I put them on my pillow so I can smell her when I dream.

I have less than two years left now. One day less than two years. Like a Timex, still ticking.

Tulsa, Oklahoma is flat and boring. I lived there for some time when I was a little kid. I remember the house we lived in on East Newton Place. I remember the address was 11425 E. Newton Place. Do you know how I remember? Because after that we moved to 13 Marshall Street in Turners Falls, Massachusetts. And after that to 94 James Street in Greenfield, Massachusetts. Nine and four is thirteen. So is 1-1-4-2-5. Pretty heavy, huh?

The house on East Newton Place was at the end of a dead end street. Beyond the street was a huge cow pasture. It must have been about five square miles. There was an oil well in view of the house. A quarter mile from the old rusty barbed wire fence behind our house was a single oak tree out in the field. From the tree you could see a little pond nestled in a dip in the field. My brother Tony and I had many excellent adventures in the field and particularly at the pond.

I've loved to fish since I was young. I remember getting my first fishing pole. I came home from school and it was behind the door. My own fishing pole. I immediately raced to the pond with some worms and proceeded to catch fish. It was amazing to me that there were even fish in this pond which served mostly to water a very large herd of cattle.

It gets hot and dry in Oklahoma and I'd seen that pond dried up entirely, down to a tire in the middle. There were also a lot of water moccasins around. Although they can be aggressive, I wasn't scared. There are snakes everywhere in Oklahoma. Many nights Momma would have to walk out to the pond and fetch me for dinner. It seems I developed a hearing loss when I got near the pond and could never hear her calling me for dinner.

One evening my mom walked out to the pond to get me. My grandpa Fred sent me a couple lures from Massachusetts. I was working the pond with one of them. Mom watched me for a couple of minutes then said, "Let's go, honey." I said, "One more cast." I threw Grandpa's lure out there and wham! My pole bent violently, almost breaking, and I caught the biggest bass I had ever seen. I never saw my mom get so excited.

I landed the big bass and took him home to scale, gut and eat. He was a trophy. I was a King. A King Fisher.

On another occasion I had gotten to the tree and looked down to see what I estimated to be about a thousand cows. When they saw me, they thought I was there to feed them and stampeded right at me. Until that day, I had not been able to reach the lowest branch of that big oak tree. That day I almost jumped clear over the branch. The cows surrounded the tree and mooed hungrily. I yelled and soon half the neighborhood was lined up at the old barbed wire fence. Everybody had a good laugh. It was the first, but not the last time I got treed by cows. I won't mention the other time though, because no one knows what happened that day but me.

I had other adventures at that pond. One day my brother Tony stepped onto what he thought was a big rock. I was looking right at him when he started moving backwards. He stepped on the back of a giant turtle. We chased it but it disappeared.

The day that sticks in my mind is the day my brother and I killed the snake. It was a hot day in the summer. I had my fishing pole and went out to the pond with my brother. Looking down into the water off the bank, I saw the back of a water moccasin draped over a branch. The branch was level with the top of the water, so I only saw a piece of his back. After some speculation, we figured the snake was dead and I lowered my hook down and snagged him.

What came up out of the water was our worst nightmare. It was four feet of gray-black, pissed-off cotton mouth. I didn't know how to get out of the situation. The snake would lunge at me, fangs barred, only to be brought up short. I held my fishing pole straight out. My arms extended as far as they would go. The snake was really upset.

My older brother came to my rescue. He squished the snake's head with a big rock after a couple of misses. He probably saved my life. I figure that snake was hunting food and probably had a good load of venom in him. Being as small as I was, I probably would have been pretty messed up. I carried the snake home to mom. It was a while before we went back out to the pond again.

I look out my window, through the thick steel mesh and thick bars and out beyond the double fences lined with razor wire from top to bottom. Out past all of this, over the trees, the sun is setting. The Pennsylvania sunset might not be as grand as the San Diego sunset, or as memorable as the western Massachusetts sunsets I spent so much times watching, but it is colorful and symbolic of freedom to me.

Two months now of solitary. Within three days I received two letters and somehow pulled off two phone calls. I was due one as part of my once a month call. The other was given to me by a guard who looked the other way. My mother, eternally convinced that my little brother is using hard drugs, has listed him as missing in action. My older brother's first marriage has ended in a tragedy. He came home from work to an empty house. His wife packed up the kids and flew back to Massachusetts from San Diego. What a drag.

I bought ten cigarettes today for $17.40, or three books of stamps. That's the limit you can buy in the commissary. I've learned to buy them when they're around. Tobacco is a hard commodity to come by in here.

I saw my counselor today. He said they might ship me out west.

Mitch told me today that he is dying of AIDS.

The light of another day slowly fades. I sigh and let my thoughts wander to past and future days. There is now less than two years before the nightmare comes to an end. Time is passing and each day I become a little wiser in my quest for serenity.

September 24, 1994

Well, it's finally happened. I've been moved to the second most secure institution in the country. The United States Penitentiary Eagleview. It has a security level of 5 and security levels only go to 6. The next highest prison is Marion, Illinois. I guess I really pissed them off at Spartanville.

Yesterday, while leaving the chow hall, I ran into the Captain and the Assistant Warden.

"Aren't you Legacy?"

"Yeah."

"You're the one that was making all the wine at Spartanville?"

"Well, yeah."

My reputation follows me to the penitentiary. But there is no place to make wine in here. It's very tight with no blind spots, no places to hide the wine. Eagleview just opened in February and is brand spanking new. It is a great round wall, a large circular complex entirely connected and totally enclosed. When the fog is too heavy to see, they close the compound and access to the mess hall is by walking all the way around the complex through the "tunnel." Outside the walls is double fence thickly laced with razor wire. It is the real razor wire and not the stuff with nasty looking "false" razors.

I've been here before. It was in February while coming from Johnsville. After stopping at Clayton for a week, we dropped a guy off here. It took about 45 minutes to clear Sallyport and just get the bus into the compound. I remember joking about it, while at the same time thinking, "Thank God I'll never go to a place like this."

Well, here I am.

For a while, I convinced myself they would not put me in a penitentiary. It's the worst time you can possibly do. The pen is hard time. In the Federal system there is the camp, the low, the F.C.I (medium security) and the U.S.P. (high security). A lot of guys here are here from Clayton. Most inmates here have at least 10 years and a large number have twenty to thirty years and life.

The tension is distinctly audible through the silence. There is much more respect between the convicts here. No petty bullshit guys sticking their noses in your business or talking shit. That's all gone. Here there are a lot more serious attitudes.

I think I actually like it more. Time seems to be moving much faster. From the inside looking out I can read the paper and catch the news. I watch the world go round like this, like I'm reading a book or watching a movie. It's strange.

You must be selective, though, about who you hang out with. It is best to hang out with a small group of people. The more people you hang out with, the bigger your chance of catching a beef with somebody. Be polite at all times and show respect to other guys and they will respect you.

There are three or four guys here from Spartanville, but I haven't been here long enough to hang out with any group. I became a minor celebrity in the music room which led to meeting a lot of fellow convicts. I hit it off with one guy in particular, named Todd. He is learning to play guitar and is the proud owner of a beautiful Jackson Fusion electric guitar along with various effects and "gadgets." Todd loves gadgets. He works in the music room where I concentrated my efforts to gain employment.

Because this is a new institution, the music department is an unorganized mess. For two days, I worked to write up an evaluation proposal to organize the system. I did a damn fine job if I do say so myself. I'm not even sure I'm technically hired yet, but once they see my write-up they should put me right in charge. I would like nothing better. The hours are splendid, from twelve-thirty in the afternoon until recall at 8:30 PM.

At this point I would like to describe how actual the violence is in the penitentiary. Eagleview is brand new and there is yet to be a killing. But that day will soon come. Todd and a few others I talk to came from Clayton. Other noteworthy pens are Terre Haute (the Hut) and Leavenworth.

These are some of the random stories I've heard.

"Hey, whatever happened to Hank?"

"He didn't like his cellie too much and put a pool ball in a sock and beat that big Puerto Rican half to death."

"Oh yeah?"

"Yeah. Then he grabbed a mop handle, snapped it in half and started sticking the guy with the sharp end while he was on the floor. Don't know where he is now."

Todd talked about Clayton.

"The first stabbing I saw was a guy walking down the hall holding his guts in his hands. The second one I saw was a guy holding his neck while blood was shooting out of it like a damn hose."

In a cell, talking to a guy.

"I remember I'll never forget when they stabbed the 19 year old kid in front of me. They stabbed him in the neck and in the lungs. He was dead before he hit the floor."

Talking to my neighbor.

"At the hut," he said, "the guards are a lot different. I came out of my cell one afternoon. There were two guys sticking each other right in front of the guard."

"No, no man, not on my shift, please," the guard was pleading. "Come on guys, take it in a cell, take it in a cell. Someone mop up this blood. I don't need all the goddamn paperwork."

September 25, 1994

I'm not sure but I think a dude got stuck last night. I saw a guard running a guy across the compound. The guy was holding his stomach. George and Todd, being more experienced in such matters, speculated that he was probably stuck and holding his guts in. However, closer investigation revealed no blood on the sidewalk where he was seen.

I drank some wine today. It sucked. Too expensive and poor quality. I'm probably not going to mess with it any more. I'll certainly be watched for a while. Unable to do anything myself, I refuse to place myself at the mercy of others. As with anything else, I would rather listen to a good country and western song than a shitty rock song. Better to not drink at all and deal with all the bullshit than to chase a lousy buzz.

If only I possessed such wisdom a couple years ago.

I slept and missed dinner. Then I went to the music room and griped about not having a band slot. I'd spent a couple days on that damn proposal to revamp the system to where it needed to be. It would only involve spending a minimum amount of money. Dealing with the staff is pretty screwed up. I feel I'm doing their jobs for them without any reciprocation. All I get in return is idiotic statements and looks. They know that they don't know what they are doing, but God forbid a convict know more than a C.O. They want to make it plain that they are the bosses around here, like it or not.

Increasingly, I am becoming aware that politics play an important part in getting anything done in the penitentiary.

And I hate politics.

September 26, 1994

Today started out lousy but ended alright.

I talked to Samantha. She was in a lousy mood. I guess we had words. I've made the big decision to just give up. After almost two years of heartache and bullshit, I just plain give up. I've got plenty of other shit to deal with.

It really hurts to have to forget her altogether. I really wanted to maintain some kind of decent relationship. But hell, I couldn't even get a relationship started in the first place. Not that I didn't try. It is so hard for me. I will still continue to write my daughter at her grandmother's. I will always love her, only now I am extremely restrained and limited in communications. But then, it's been that way for almost two years now.

Sometimes it gets very difficult. You lose all your friends and family. There's no other way to put it. All of the sudden they are not there. Sure they are there, but in another place, another time. Almost like another dimension.

You realize that everybody is getting used to you not being around. I am bad. I am sad. I am alone. I am angry. I hate. I envy. I despise. I cannot cry. I cannot be with the ones I love. I can't be touched. I can't be held. I am pain. I am rage.

I am the prisoner.

I wait.

Wait to taste my freedom again.

Taste it like a tall cool glass of iced spring water on a hot day.

October 1, 1994

Today we watched the movie *The Fugitive*. Everyone cheered when Harrison Ford made his exceptionally close getaways. They were especially excited when the cop shot at him through the bullet proof glass.

October is here and there is a chill in the air.

Today I saw a flock of geese heading south for the winter.

Smart birds.

It reminded me of the first year I got my waterfowl stamp in Massachusetts. You need this stamp to hunt geese and ducks. Of course, they all seemed to disappear the day I walked into the sporting goods store. My two hunting partners, Danny and Steve, loaded up on steel shot and we headed up to the cornfields of Gill. This was one of my favorite hunting grounds.

After sitting in a blind for a couple of hours, I decided I didn't like duck and goose hunting very much. Not even one pigeon flew by. We resorted to testing our duck calls by using our vocal chords. The situation rapidly became humorous.

We ended up leaving early and heading back to Montague.

It was dusk when we spotted the flock of ducks. We were driving on a back road through farm country. It was the largest flock of ducks I had ever seen. They were migrating, legal ducks and it was the very last day of duck season. They all dove down behind some trees to roost for the night.

Steve was tired and seemed unenthused but Danny and I got excited and set out to find the ducks. We went through a cow pasture and across a creek. I was pretty nervous about the cows. Slowly, we crept up on the flock. There were a couple hundred ducks just quacking away.

"OK Danny," I said, "at my signal, we stand up and nail them."

When I gave the signal we stood up and raised our shotguns. There was a thunderous flapping of wings and the flock of ducks took to the air. Our flock of ducks had stopped to party with another big flock and now they all took off at one time. The sky was so thick with ducks you couldn't see through them.

But neither of us fired a shot as we watched the ducks fly away. We mumbled to ourselves, inventing excuses. It was too dark. Maybe there was a house behind the flock. But it wasn't too dark and there was no house behind the flock. I think we both remembered a film on illegal goose hunting we had seen a month before. It was about baiting and slaughtering and was pretty sick. Everything was caught on film.

We trudged back across the pasture full of cows.

Steve was waiting for us.

"What happened?" he asked.

I looked at Dan and he looked at me.

"They spooked on us," I said.

As one hunter to another, that was all that needed to be said.

I guess I should have been as moral and ethical in my later life as I was that day in those woods. The rules are simple in the woods. Don't trash anything. Use common sense. Be courteous. If you are hunting, be cautious. Safety is the first rule.

October 5, 1994

It all started when I met an ex-CIA courier named George Green who was stationed in Manila. Although George was not a CIA agent, he handled information that was to be given to certain individuals.

One particular document contained a statement regarding a new type of plastic explosive that could be molded to the shape of anything. Particularly, in this case, suitcases and briefcases. The document also contained information about a guerrilla training camp. It noted the location of the camp and the name of the contact.

George Green was told to pass the document on to the Department of Tourism. Before he received this document, a similar one was disclosed to all international airports in the Philippines. Green felt the information about the guerrilla training camp was irrelevant. He tore that part off, burned it and flushed it down a toilet. Two days later, a briefcase bomb was exploded in downtown Manila.

Shortly thereafter, Green was lured to the United States under the guise of a job offer. His CIA contact informed him that the CIA was looking at him to be Head Instructor teaching martial arts to field agents. This seemed a reasonable job for him. He was an expert instructor and had devoted his entire life to the arts and instructed silver and bronze medalists.

But upon arrival in the United States, he was immediately arrested and charged with two counts of espionage. The whole thing stank. Green eventually pleaded guilty to a reduced charge of obtaining information but only after his wife and family were threatened.

Once in conversation with me, Green brought up the New World Policy. This is a secret political group run by a handful of people seeking to control the world. A number of them are famous and well-known. They plan on utilizing the government of the United States as a mere puppet. The group has gained a horrifying amount of control over the future of the world. They have all the money, all the power. I was told about computer chips injected into children's hands. This would enable a satellite to track an individual anywhere on the planet.

I told George that all this would never happen. He told me that it already is happening, that the New World Policy unites every nation. Those who reject the policy will be totally shut off. There is talk of a Global Police with an Overall Court in Switzerland.

When you hear all of this and you reflect on recent developments, you see some things in a different light. Gradually, our Constitution has become more restricted. They pretty much rewrote the whole thing to suit their own purposes. Our freedoms have become so limited soon half the population will be in prison. Everybody must be submissive. Crack and alcohol are rampant and are disabling most that aren't in prisons.

This is when I discovered the Anarchist Movement.

October 7, 1994

Today is Friday.

The week flew by. I spent it practicing music all day every day. I woke up around 10:00 AM. Screw breakfast. The food here gets pretty gruesome after the first few weeks. I spent the morning showering, shaving, doing laundry and drinking my coffee. I swore I'd never drink coffee and smoke cigarettes every day. But hell . . . when in Rome.

Some mornings the compound gets so fogged in you can't see anything out the window. On the rare occasion I make it to breakfast I grab a TV room when I come back. This is the only time I watch television and I watch Rude Awakening and the lovely Idalis on MTV. Once in a while I watch a movie but I usually avoid television. It seems a waste of time when I could be playing my guitar.

After my MTV fix I fall back to sleep. If I feel unusually motivated I try to clean up the room, particularly the colossal pile of papers, books and stuff on top of my locker. Sometimes the junk gets stacked so high its like a miniature, precariously built, pyramid. The removal of a single ink pen could spell disaster for the unwary. Recently, though, I actually got organized. Usually A.C. stops by and we talk. He is my blues teacher, friend and mentor.

When lunch is over I run back to my unit to grab whatever music I happen to be working on that day. Whether it is scales, theory or songs. Then I'm off to Rec where I'm supposed to be working. I grab a guitar, an amp and a music stand. Stay outta my face until 3:30 recall.

Back at the unit I usually do some writing. We're locked up at 4:00 for count. This lasts fifteen or twenty minutes. Mail call comes right after count. I read my mail and continue jamming on the acoustic I stole from Rec. I can have the acoustic except for Wednesday and Friday nights when Will gives his class. No problem there.

Then we wait for chow to be called. It is called over the intercom that blares away at us all day.

"Unit 2B release for chow, Unit 2B, chow."

Out the door and off to chow hall to wolf down the garbage they call grub.

Make some small talk during dinner.

"Hey, what's up?"

"Yeah, whacha doing?"

"I'll be down in the music room till 8:30."

"Yeah, all right. Later."

Zing. Back to the unit to get my stuff. Todd gave me my own guitar cord because they don't have enough down there to cut it. I grab the strap I stole from Spartanville, my cord and my music. I trot over to Rec. I get an amp, a guitar and a music stand. I then step into my world until 8:30. They actually lock everyone in Rec at night. They call it passive rec. At 6:30 and 7:30 when they call the move, everyone goes out to smoke. I go too, unless I'm locked in a groove.

At 8:30 it's time to pack things up and go back to the unit. Maybe make a call to Diane or Mom. After this, I usually head over to A.C.'s house in cell 222 and play the blues until the 10:00 PM count.

We're locked in at 11:30. That's when I pick up the pen and begin to write. It goes like this pretty much day in and day out. I figure I get a minimum of eight to ten hours of guitar practice a day. I would get more, but I've got to smoke, have a coffee and take a piss every once and a while.

October 9, 1994

Iactually made it to breakfast yesterday. I had to steal some sugar for coffee. I made it out with a pound or two.

Last night my blues band had a practice. It went extremely well. A.C. is an excellent teacher and I strive to play what he taught me so well. Its working out pretty well and I receive a lot of compliments. I'm really pushing myself on this guitar thing. It keeps me out of trouble. I haven't played a single game of cards since I got here. I play only one football ticket a week. I play for one pack. I don't think this is too bad.

Sometimes violence crosses our path. Usually, I just hear about it. A guy in 2A, the unit next door, got beat up pretty badly. They tore half his face off. They used a piece of metal like brass knuckles. He was sent to the emergency room.

Tonight my bass player pointed a guy out to me.

"See that guy?" he said. "He's crazy. Cut a guy up into little pieces and was carrying him around in suitcases. A goddamned nut."

The leaves are changing and geese fly over all the time in their "V" formation. They are fat and flying free for the warm weather.

I can't say I blame them.

October 11, 1994

The last two days have been shitty but I don't know why. I've been tired and downtrodden.

I'm still practicing my music, still learning, still working at it. But I think I'm maybe burning myself out on the music. There's just too much to learn. I was listening to Peter Frampton's "Do You Feel." It has some pretty nasty guitar work on it. I think it's his best.

I haven't been able to get hold of Mom for awhile. I think her phone is messed up.

I got a letter from Diane. She's such a gem. I miss her touch. I talk to her almost every day. I don't know what I'd do without her. She seems so genuinely interested in me, talking to me every day since I've been in. She started sending me mail again. She got a post office box.

So why do I feel like just another notch in her lipstick case? She's been with the same guy for ten years and probably will be with him for life. I can't figure out where I fit in. You know what I mean? Why is she so goddamn aggressive in her interest? Why does she care so damn much? Why am I sweating it? I'm burning bridges like Saddam Hussein torching his oil fields.

Something inside me is vacant. Something is eating away at me. I just don't know what the hell it is.

October 19, 1994

A month has slipped by since I arrived here at the penitentiary. I'm settled into cell 209 with a good cellie and playing guitar all day and a good part of the night.

I took pictures last Saturday. The weather was awesome. Some of the prettiest sunsets I have ever seen have been over the wide open skies of Pennsylvania. If sunsets only occurred once or twice a year it would be an amazing thing. It would be in all the newspapers and all over the networks. People would gather and watch them. But because it happens on such a regular basis, everyone takes it for granted.

The same thing with the moon and stars. Viewed from inside these walls they seem so symbolic. Last night there was a full moon. I argued with Diane on the phone whether or not it was completely full until 12:00 or so. I can see the moon very clearly these past few fall nights and watched it go from a sliver to full and shining.

But I have not seen one star yet and this is most unsettling. Once, during a cigarette break from the music room, I thought I saw one. It turned out to be an airplane or a high flying helicopter. There were mutterings that it was some "government aircraft snooping around."

Someone stole a metal bar from one of the guitar stands in the music room. They came down and took pictures of an existing stand and photographed the bar and how long it was. A sticker is being made.

As I told Todd, someone has fear in them.

October 20, 1994

The search for the metal bar has escalated.

I went into work today at 12:30. Although I am not officially on the roster, I was told by the Head of the Rec. Department that I would be placed on the roster within a next week or so. I tune and polish the four electric guitars, the two basses and the acoustic and classical guitars. I replace strings and set the intonation properly.

Everyone in there looked at me like I was the thief who stole the metal guitar stand bar. The black guy who works in the equipment room asked me about it.

"It was missing when I came and took all the guitars out to work on them," I told him. "I didn't take it and I don't give a damn because it's none of my business."

October 25, 1994

Someone is going to get their head peeled back. My cellie told me that somebody went into a cell and stole a pair of sneakers and some other stuff. There is nothing more detested in prison than a jail house thief. Except maybe a snitch.

I put up a couple gallons yesterday. Some mega oranges and grapefruit. If I don't get popped it should come out some killer brew. Halloween is coming up and it should be ready just in time. I'm going to sell half of it. At least half, and give Eddie from Boston a quart, Johnny and his cellie a quart and my buddy Cameron a quart.

I just hope my luck holds up. My poor mama would be going crazy. But things are tough all over and a guys gotta do what he's gotta do to get by you know. Maybe I can stay out of the hole until next year.

November 1, 1994

Today I met the biggest moron in the world. There was no escaping it as I was assigned to work for the Safety Department. He is to be my boss. I think I was screwed because I intentionally skipped A&O (Admission and Orientation), which is nothing but three hours of boring speakers and a video. At least that's what I heard.

Mr. Wilson is fat, balding and possesses the beady, shiny eyes of a ferret. His taste in suits is severely lacking. But it is his attitude that really sucks.

Looking at the daily rosters, called "Call Outs," I see I am to report to Safety at 7:30 AM. Must be a mistake I figure. No problem, I'll straighten it out. I put on my headphones, my sunglasses and my ragged hi-tops. Pull on my hobo gloves and grab a full cup of coffee.

Then I stroll into the Safety Department with Metallica jamming on my headphones. I see Mr. Wilson and another C.O. His lips are moving. He looks pissed.

I shut off the headphones.

"You Legacy?" he demands.

"Yeah. Listen man, this is like a total mistake. I work in Rec, Dude."

Mr. Wilson pushes his fat face close to mine.

"I am not a dude," he says. "Further, you do not work in Rec. I have your paperwork right here. You belong to me."

He snarls with a funny look on his face.

"You're mine!" he says.

"Bogus," I'm thinking. This guy is really an asshole. I better keep my mouth shut or I'll get myself in trouble. I've learned to keep quiet in these situations.

"First, Mr. Legacy," he says, "you will return to your unit and retrieve your safety shoes and report back here immediately."

I curse all the way back to the unit. I put on the heavy black steel-toed shoes and report back. I was told by Mr. Wilson that I could not wear headphones. I had a pair of earphones that I fit in each ear and run the wire down the back of my shirt. My long hair conceals them perfectly.

"Come with me," says Wilson. It is not a request.

I hate his guts.

We walk past the chow hall. Past CMS and UNICOR and up the long, long hallway all the way to the hospital. At the hospital he stops and turns around.

"Do you see this hallway, Legacy?"

"Yeah," I answer fearing the worst. All of a sudden the hall looks to be about a quarter of a mile long. In actuality it is really about one hundred yards long.

"This is your hallway, Legacy," Wilson says. "You report to me each morning, then you report to the hospital. You will mop this hall three times daily and make sure that the glass and heating registers are clean."

My fears are confirmed. It appears he hates me as much as I hate him. The entire right side of the hallway is glass which is about six feet high. I console myself with the fact that the people in Rec will straighten this out. It will only be a day or two and this asshole will be off my back.

It's been one of those days.

November 11, 1994

Eagleview is in a deadlock and the whole prison is locked down. Yesterday a cop was beat up and there were two stabbings.

They were separate incidents. They locked us in at 9:21 last night and are interviewing everybody. They want to know if there were any rumors circulating previous to the stabbings.

"No," I tell them.

"If you did know, would you tell us?"

"No."

After the interview, it's back to the cell. The stabbings were to be expected. Everybody knew this place was going to heat up soon. Once it does, it's going to get hot.

This increasingly hot situation is largely the result of the nation's prison laws. On November 1, 1987, the United States amended the Federal Guidelines and abolished all good time, parole and furloughs. A mandatory 54 days a year was to be given to all sentenced inmates after November 1, 1987. Prior to November 1, inmates received good time in quantity. There was good time for going to school, for completing programs, for good behavior.

Under the old law, the convict was given something extremely important to the smooth running of a prison system. He was given incentive. Under old law, if you could fly straight you'd average one third of your actual sentence. In effect, my four year sentence equals an 11 or 12 year sentence given prior to November 1, 1987.

There are many repercussions from this loss of incentive. Eagleview is full of convicts with a high security level. Many here are doing big numbers like thirty, forty, fifty years, life and double life. Under the new law, all sentenced offenders will do 90% of their time. Period.

It's been a few years and everybody has waited to see if things are going to change. With still no change after the Comprehensive Crime Bill, things are beginning to heat up. Convicts are starting to realize they are screwed. They will be old men when they get out. With incentives gone, depression, anxiety and bitter apathy settle into the system. When a convict becomes apathetic, he becomes dangerous to everyone.

There are two current philosophies about prisoners. One is to forget them and let them rot. Don't give anything. Make them pay. The other is to let them live a with little comfort. Give them this and that. Keep them content because we don't want them coming out of prison too hardened.

Within the next two or three years, I think something is going to happen with these philosophies and it will sway one way or the other. The convict has already lost the incentive of good time. If they try to crack down harder by removing creature comforts such as commissary or recreational facilities, the convicts will break. Riots will sweep the nation. Guards will die. On the other hand, if it sways the other way and incentives are given back, who pays then? The United States government, that's who.

The Federal prison system is designed to suck money out of the convict one way or another. The factories in federal prisons generate millions of dollars annually. But they pay the convicts pennies. The factory here makes lots of expensive furniture. The convicts do the plumbing, electrical and the carpentry. It saves them thousands of dollars. They mark up everything in the commissary. Things from the outside, like guitars, have tremendous mark ups on them.

So, the government gets the short end of things if the prisoner gets out early without doing his full time.

November 21, 1994

Today is manic Monday.

I still haven't gotten my Rec job and am still mopping that friggin' hallway at 7:30 in the morning. It's tough to dodge the work because you are supposed to be there all day. But I'm becoming adept at avoiding work. I hide out down in passive Rec a lot. I try to stay lost in my music but its tough because of all the politics involved.

I'm supposed to get my band slot this week. There is a concert this Thursday, a Thanksgiving thing. My band, Bad Shoes, will be playing a few numbers. I'm also in the rhythm and blues band, Unique, and we'll do a few songs and back up some singers on other ones.

This will be my second Thanksgiving and winter inside. It seems like so long ago. I hate the holidays like everybody else.

I drank some wine recently. But mostly I like to smoke pot. Everybody raves about heroin and how good it is. I broke down and tried some yesterday. I didn't like it too much and probably won't mess with it again. I had to try it though. Christ, if my mom knew she'd have a stroke. I'm just going to stick with reefer. I was pissed twice at Spartanville and came up clean on both of them. They haven't pissed me yet since I've been here.

I've been breathalyzed three or four times though. The last time is worth writing about. I was about to smoke some weed with this guy when another dude stuck his head in the door and said he had some wine. When it's around you've got to jump on it and I jumped.

I had my little pipe made from a toilet paper tube and a pencil eraser. I was smoking and drinking. These guys had about three gallons and I'd drunk about a quart of wine when there was some commotion in the cell.

"Oh shit, here comes the cop!" one of the hawks said. The guys were all Hispanics.

"What's he doing? What's he doing man?" another asked.

"He's going to cell 209."

Through my haze there was something that sounded familiar. It was my cell! There was some action.

"What's going on?" I mumbled.

"Man, the lady is giving out breathalyzers down there," said one of the Hispanics.

I know I'm on the hot list and that cop is looking to give me a breathalyzer. I'm sure about this.

"Here comes the cop man," one of them yells.

Two guys run out the door and a big one dives under the bed. They leave me sitting there with wine everywhere. I put my back to the door and look out the window.

"Man you gotta go," the dude under the bed says.

"Screw that," I say. "I'm too gone."

The cop opens the door.

"Legacy," he says.

It's Shorty and I pointedly ignore him.

"Legacy," he repeats.

"What man?" I growl.

"Somebody wants to see you."

"Yeah? Who's that?" I ask.

"The little lady at the desk."

I head for the door and casually reach in my pocket to pull the bowl off the pipe. The bowl has the resin on it. As I get to the door I throw it in the toilet and flush the toilet. Shorty doesn't say anything. I'm gone. I know I'm gone. My cellie is out on the rail as I walk by.

"See ya," I mutter to him as I walk by.

Later, he told me I smelled like a walking brewery.

This very cute Hispanic girl with a fine set of breasts, braces and a big ass is smiling at me. I am not smiling back because I'm trying to look as menacing as possible. She gives me the tube and I attach it. She holds the breathalyzer and shows me the zeros on it.

"Blow," she says.

She is grinning at me.

I put my lips to the tube and inhale loudly.

She laughs.

"No, no, no," she says, "you gotta blow."

She holds her hand up to feel the air at the end of the tube.

"Ah screw it," I say as I blow straight booze through the tube and into her face.

She looked at me and shut it off before the numbers even came up. She wasn't going to even test me.

"OK," she said. "You're all set."

I beat the proverbial hasty retreat right back to my wine.

What a night.

I was a hero and all because she just didn't want to do the paper work.

Thanksgiving 1994

I think I always try to write on holidays. At least the major ones. Its a real bitch for everybody I guess. Both those inside and those outside. The memories, of course, suffer. You count how many Thanksgivings and Christmases it's been and how many more to go. The end of the year is important because it's always a major increment of time.

The weather is another mark of time. It snowed yesterday for the first time this year. The snow marks another winter. It snowed so hard you couldn't see across the yard. The radio said flurries. I long for the snow because I fell at the tail end of the winter in '93. It seems like so long ago.

They are already playing Christmas songs on the radio.

"Please come home for Christmas," the radio sings.

Today we had a show in the gym and a lot of guys came. My band went on first and did three numbers: "Another Thing Coming" by Judas Priest, "Fire" by Hendrix and the Guns & Roses version of "Knocking On Heaven's Door." I think we did an excellent job. Those Carvin amps really sounded good cranked up. I received several compliments. Old man Gus, who plays in the oldies band Main Street People, came up to me afterwards.

"You know what Rick told me?" he said.

"What?" I asked.

"That you are ten thousand times a better guitar player than me."

I laughed.

"Ten thousand times," he muttered.

I don't know about that but I do know we sounded pretty good. My bass player sang great. We only had one practice to prepare for the show and we did alright.

I called home and talked to mom. I also talked to cousin Sarah who is marrying my old friend Jerry Baker. Sarah is a super girl with a great personality. She writes to me occasionally. She is a very intelligent girl and the first grandchild to get married. The first girl grandchild that is. My brother Tony was the first. I should have called Grandma and Grandpa, but I guess that can wait for Christmas which is coming right up.

They really put on a good feed in the chow hall. The show was supposed to start at 12:30 but they didn't even release us for chow until 12:30, so I kind of rushed through the meal. They gave us two pieces of turkey as big as a damn pay phone. I pecked a little bit at one and smuggled the other piece out to make turkey soup because everybody's got the flu. I also got away with some celery and carrots and bummed an onion off of the Spanish guys. Two cups of soup, some salt and pepper, and a dash of Tobasco. It came out all right. I cooked it in the microwave. Last night we had steaks smuggled out of the kitchen. Tommy says he's going to make a cook out of me ever since I burned the microwave popcorn. The bags were really smoking.

On top of the good feed and the show, I entered the pool tournament and did pretty good until I lost to a bum. I played in the Spades Tournament and was soundly thrashed in the first round.

All in all it was an OK Thanksgiving.

The Cubans burned out some dude on my tier. Another Cuban, I think. They evacuated the block. It was pretty smoky. I went over to the barbershop and got my beard trimmed up. It looks pretty good. I have a new cellie named Kenny. He's a good dude, wrapping up a smoker with only ten months left. The only bad thing is that he snores loudly. Like now.

It's pretty late and I've gotta get up at 7:30. When I do I'll have another Thanksgiving behind me.

Tick, tock.

December 2, 1994

Yesterday they took away Dodger, my next door neighbor in 2A. He is a member of the Dirty White Boy gang. The circumstances leading up to him being taken away almost caused a full riot. It makes me realize how close this place is to really going off.

I came back from work a little early and saw a bunch of guys looking towards the front of my unit. The units are like "Vs" with the doors being at the apex of the "V". When I got closer I saw Dodger up against the wall on his side of the unit. There were maybe half a dozen cops around him.

I went walking down the sidewalk that splits the two sides of the units.

"What's up, Dog?" I asked him.

He was drunk.

"Man, these mothers pissed me four times in the past three weeks," he angrily said. "I told 'em the next time they come they'd better bring a crew. There's stinkin' rats in my unit. Man they brought down a breathalyzer. Someone ratted me out. My units full of rats."

He turned to the nearest cop.

"Get away from me, pig! You better call some more guys down here."

At this point, a number of guys started to gather. More cops showed up. Dodger slipped out to the middle of the field and started walking around. He led the cops in circles.

"Who's gonna be first, huh? You, punk bitch?" he taunted.

The Captain appeared and tried to talk to him. At this point, for some reason, they did the stupidest thing imaginable.

"Recall, recall, recall," came the words over the public address system. "All inmates return to their quarters. Recall."

About four hundred inmates hit the yard. On the outskirts of the yard there were maybe twenty police telling guys to move along. Yeah, right. The Captain was close to Dodger and Dodger was shaking his head. He was going hard no matter what. When the Captain reached out and grabbed his arm, Dodger swung his arm wide and shook loose of the Captain's grip.

Tensions continued to mount.

A number of cops began to stalk Dodger by pacing around him. One of the cops reached behind and grabbed his cuffs.

"Come on Sean, let's get on this," Cam said.

I wasn't going to let him get the shit kicked out of him and we headed out on to the field. They jumped on Dodger. There were four hundred yells of protest and everyone converged on the field. Old Bullet was out on the field waving his cane and yelling, "Get off him, let him go!"

Bullet was a legend around the place. He got his name from being shot fifteen times by the Marshals in a courtroom when his wife handed him a pistol while he was in a black box. He had also been stabbed thirteen times at the Hut.

Everyone was hot. Dodger was flattened and cuffed. One swing by anybody would have instantaneously started a riot. It was so close but no one did anything. Would I have become involved? Damn right I would have. All for one and one for all. The ultimate of us against them.

I had gotten to know Dodger when he worked with me as a safety orderly. He sold me some wine and we hung out together. His first urine was dirty. So was his second, third and fourth.

"Screw the man!" he told me one morning. "I'm gettin' high and stayin' high. Hell, I'm high right now."

It was 7:45 AM.

Dodger just had that way about him. He had a personal code. Screw it, man. He just wanted to get high. He was doing a smoker anyway. He had nothing coming. The kid had no incentive whatsoever. So, he went hard.

Today, I ran into Country. He's an older guy who, yes, plays country music. We were talking about how this place is ready to go any time.

Country brought up an interesting point. Most of the old school convicts, he said, have gone home. The ones now here are in for such a long time, nothing really matters to them.

December 3, 1994

I'm sitting in my cell sipping on half a gallon of holiday cheer. I'm listening to tunes and just relaxing.

It's Saturday and the weather is nice and warm. This is odd for a Pennsylvania winter.

Even though it's warm, I'm wearing my gloves. They issue you army green wool gloves. I believe they're really liners to good gloves. I cut the fingers off of them and wear them everywhere whether it's cold or hot. They're my "hobo" gloves, my own kind of trademark that separates me from others. They also double as good workout gloves.

I'm in a weird kind of mood. Lately, the stress of this place has been getting to me. I feel the tension a lot. A drink now and then helps a lot. Prison really makes you bitter. You develop a hatred for the cops, the government, the blacks, the Cubans, the Spanish, the whites, everybody. A general lousy attitude permeates your environment. Nobody in here gives a damn about anybody else one way or the other. Talk is plentiful.

I see my self destruction building and the layers of dignity, civility and literacy that separate me from the common human animal, are beginning to fall away. A few years ago I was fairly literate. Although on paper I still try and retain my disciplined English, my language and dialect today is altogether different. What comes out of my mouth is pure prison slang. It is an extremely foul, guttural English with a smattering of bad Spanish.

The Spanish guys on my block are pretty cool. They make incense out of cinnamon. You put some Polo or Obsession on the sticks and it burns nicely. It covers up the wine smell. My cellie, Kenny, is always bitching about the smell of the wine. The incense takes care of it. Kenny works the early 4:00 AM morning kitchen shift.

But there is tension in the air and the incense can't get rid of its ominous smell. I was talking to Heavy next door and told him how this place is getting to me.

"The tension is pretty tough," I told Heavy.

"Yeah," Heavy said, "you could cut it with a knife."

At least I'm not alone in my feelings.

December 15, 1994

I was called to the Lieutenant's office twice today for the same bullshit. My boss is an asshole.

Kenny moved out leaving me with a single cell, at least for the weekend. I'm listening to the Door's "Love Me Two Times." I've only got one more day in Safety, mopping that friggin' hall. Only one more day of putting up with all the crap from my boss. He's gunning for me pretty tough. Maybe I'll pull an idle tomorrow, if I can get up on my time.

I'm exhausted now. One more day and then back to passive recreation and the old evening shift. One more day and then I can sleep each day until 11:00 AM. I can't wait. I've gotta get some rest. More tomorrow.

December 18, 1994

They screwed me over again and didn't put me on the change sheet to go to Recreation. They hired two guys in front of me.

I'm really pissed.

The San Diego Chargers beat the Jets. The Patriots beat Buffalo at home. Bledsoe is a great quarterback and I think the Patriots will actually make it the Superbowl. Maybe they'll even win it.

I drank a little wine last night.

I hate December.

It's almost over, though. My second Christmas in prison. Only one more full year to go and then another eight months.

I'm thinking of getting some more tattoo work done. It's a cover up job on my arm to cover the tattoo I got when I was twelve. The same year I had my ear pierced. It's hard to believe it was fifteen years ago.

I'll be twenty seven next March. It will be my second birthday inside. My counselor says he can transfer me to an F.C.I. in California to be closer to my family.

To get the transfer I've got to stay out of trouble. This is somewhat easier said than done. I'm by no means an angel. I drink, smoke pot and steal stuff from the kitchen. Steaks, and sugar to make wine. I also block for other guys so they can steal. I keep watch for guards while guys are doing stuff like tattooing and cutting up heroin. I gamble, but very sparingly. Maybe a pack a week. Two packs at the most. I make wine to sell. I steal and sell speakers from wherever I can get them. I arrange cigarettes for guys in the hole. Occasionally I sell reefer. I steal guitar strings to give to the guys that do the tattooing. I stole a whole guitar and had it for a couple of months before I was caught. I hide stuff in my cell for other guys. I hid ink for one guy and steel for another. I connect guys with other guys to get the stuff they need. You want a wine connection? You need ink to do some slinging? Want some steaks for the holidays? A blade because you're scared? There's a cut in everything and if I'm not making the money, someone else sure the hell is. It's called survival.

My two biggest concessions are drinking and smoking reefer. I find myself smoking more and drinking less. But if there's nothing to smoke, I'll have a drink. A man could go crazy in here in no time flat trying to keep his head above water every day. Pressure is constantly building up inside and if you can't relieve the pressure, you'll explode like an over-inflated tire. I'm not going to let this happen and plan on leaving this place with my head on straight. I don't plan on coming out as some screwed up psychotic kid. I'm leaving like I came in.

December 24, 1994

Christmas is upon us.

The Jolly One is now undertaking his historic task and streaking through the skies to deliver treasures to the good little boys and girls.

And the bad boys?

They're hanging tough at Eagleview and the other prisons across the country. I wish I had a dime for every convict I've heard say, "Christmas is just another day. It don't mean a thing to me."

Everybody puts up their own little decorations and their own little signs. I have plastic snowflakes and Christmas bulbs that stick to the glass. A Hispanic kid named Billy down the hall has a sign on his door that says, "Caution: Do Not Enter Without knocking." On the sign there is a picture of an Uzi submachine gun spitting out bullets and coughing out shells. I asked him who drew the Uzi.

"I drew it," he told me. "I got thirty years for one, so I guess I can't forget what it looks like."

He's not even twenty yet. Under the new law he has no parole for good time. Billy's a good kid.

Today I called my brother Tony. His wife is back and I talked to her for a minute. My little nieces and nephew are probably nestled all snug in their beds with proverbial sugar plums dancing through their heads. Waiting for the Jolly One to come.

I cut paper snowflakes out of folded paper and hung them on my door. I am listening to Christmas songs on the radio. I borrowed A.C.'s guitar for the night. I will probably still be writing when Christmas rolls right by. I stopped to pick up a song off the radio called "Soul Shine." It's a great new song by the Allman Brothers.

I should have called everybody today. It will be impossible to get through on the phones tomorrow.

We had band practice tonight and it was one of the best yet. The dynamics were good and we really tightened it up. I sang "Born To Be Wild" by Steppenwolf and "Jealous Again" by the Black Crowes. I do the back ups on "Knockin' On Heaven's Door," "Another Thing Coming," "Fire," "Ain't Talkin' Bout Love," "Living After Midnight" and a few others. My singing is coming along slowly. Very slowly.

I received six Christmas cards in time for Christmas. Tom and Dori sent me a cool one with a biker on the front. My brother Tony and his family sent one and, of course, Mom sent one. Aunt Peggy and Mr. & Mrs. O'Sullivan sent one and Debbie and Doug sent one. I got a letter from way-cool Susie from Greenfield. She got an O.U.I. and was on probation. They gave her nine months. Damn, that's her second bit since I've been down. I think she did three months or something.

The other night I got busted for drinking. They said they heard me on the phone talking to my brother. All I said was, "Yeah, they busted the bass player tonight and locked him up." They came down and grabbed me ten minutes later. They gave me a breathalyzer and I failed it. I got the shot the next day. Tommy and I got locked in our cells because there's no room in the hole. A few others also got locked in their cells. I was the only one to get a shot. Tonight some more dudes got busted and sent to their cells. I better not be the only one getting a shot. I'll tell you that. I hope I just get extra duty or something not too important.

After band practice tonight, I helped Todd move the amps and equipment over to the gym. I then came back and cooked the steaks. I cooked eight of them. I bet I've cooked a hundred steaks in the past couple months. It's cheaper to buy them in bulk and spread them around. Everyone gets a crack at buying them. Tommy just bought twenty for a carton of cigarettes. I am designated the chef, probably because it was my idea to steal the salt and pepper from the chow hall and put it on the meat. Tommy, Mac and I are on Viking status. Viking is slang for living comfortably.

Well, I'm sure that it's gotta be Christmas by now. I'm going to eat some of this steak and read myself to sleep. Merry Christmas everybody. I still remember what a pine tree smells like. Or even a blue spruce. Brenda Lee's singing "Rockin' Around The Christmas Tree."

I'm signing off.

Captain's log Stardate December 25th, 1994.

December 25, 1994

The guard woke me up at 6:00 AM and said the Lieutenant wanted to see me at 6:30 or as soon as they opened the doors to mainline. I figured that they were going to breathalyzer or piss me.

I went down to see the Lieutenant. It was still dark outside. The lights were off in the Lieutenant's office. This seemed weird. He asked me to sit down. He then asked if I had any problems on the compound. I told him I didn't have any problems. He asked me if I owed anybody money. I told him that I didn't owe anybody money.

I asked him what this was all about.

He said that someone had dropped a note on me.

"Get Sean Legacy off this compound," the note read. "We are going to kill him."

He asked me if I was scared. I told him that I wasn't. Assholes write notes to staff all the time. Usually they take it pretty seriously and lock you up. He asked if I had a problem going back to the compound, into population. I said no. They usually have you sign a waiver, but they didn't ask me to sign one.

I figured that it was someone in the music program who wanted me out of the way. Or someone who wanted my single cell. Whoever did it was on this block. I have narrowed down my suspicions, but you never really know. Shorty, the cop, asked me tonight who I thought it was. I told him I didn't know. He said they were keeping an eye on me. When I go to the yard, towers 7 and 8, the only two towers overlooking the yard, will be constantly watching me.

I've pretty much written it off as a petty threat. But there's always that little thing in the back of my mind. Maybe someone really wants to kill me. I really doubt it, though. It's not likely.

So, I woke up Christmas morning with a death threat on my head. Merry Christmas.

We put on our Christmas concert. The drummer murdered us. He played way too fast and increased the tempos too much. Maybe the threat was from him and he was fulfilling it with his playing? He really did kill us.

After the concert I came back and fell asleep. I didn't wake up until 6:00 PM and missed dinner. They gave us Cornish game hens with stuffing at lunch and I filled up on that and cheesecake. It was pretty good.

Christmas is over.

I didn't call anybody like I was supposed to.

But screw it.

I've a right to be depressed, don't I?

December 31, 1994

It's the last day of the year and I've made no resolutions. I am not quitting smoking. I am not cutting down on salt or sugar or going on a diet. I am not going to be nicer to people, nor am I going to try to be a better person in any way. I'm the Grinch of New Year's Eve and I'm not looking at the miserable year of incarceration that has past, but rather the next cursed 365 days to come.

I am the pessimist of 1995.

Beware.

It is 11:35 PM. Almost that time.

I played in a concert again today. The sound was terrible but overall it was all right.

My wisdom teeth are going to be worked on next Thursday. They are going to cut out the gums around the teeth to allow them to grow up. I can hardly wait. The dentist and the dentist's assistant are both sweethearts, especially the dentist's assistant. She's very cute.

My glands are all swollen and I haven't been able to eat for a few days. My teeth are killing me. I'm on 1,000 milligrams of penicillin a day and I've got a medical slip to get real salt out of the kitchen to rinse my teeth and infected gums.

Samantha went back to Jim. There is now talk of marriage. This sentence probably doesn't mean a thing to almost everybody. It's funny how much it means to me. I didn't talk to Samantha on Christmas or New Year's, but I did call her in between to see where her head was at. She sounded miserable again. It is none of my business anyway. I only wish she could be happy. I miss that mean old bitch. I miss my daughter and cannot wait to see her again.

My mom may come to see me in April of this year. Maybe I can get Diane to come with her. I need somebody to come and see me pretty damn soon, I'll tell you that. I'm going batty.

Walking down the hall a couple days ago, I had a sudden realization that I had slipped further into an apathetic state of depression. Everything sucked. My head just hasn't been right. I'm sleeping all the time. I don't like anybody. Everybody sucks. Everybody seems to be a liar, a thief, a piece of shit. I'm stuck in this slime pit. My music is going to hell. My hair is falling out. On top of everything, I got another shot for drinking, even though it was my first one here. The shot will prevent my transfer to California.

With this realization, I felt something funny inside and heard this strange voice say my spirit was dying. I know this sounds corny but I know it to be true. There's a big thing about being weak in prison and the general consensus is that if you are weak, then pretty soon someone is going to be screwing you.

The reality is that everyone has fear. I don't give a damn who you are. When someone has stashed away a knife or weapon, the first thing I think is that this person is afraid. I don't necessarily think this person is one to be feared. Everybody is just trying to get through this shit the best they can. This means without getting killed and with the least possible wear and tear to the human psyche. In the penitentiary the tension wears on the psyche twenty-four hours a day.

It kills your spirit.

Looking back on this year, not one good thing happened except the visit from my mother back in May. I went from a sweet county jail to an

F.C.I and finally to a friggin' pen. I can't manage my money for shit. That may be the thing I'll change next year. I'm not going to borrow nothing any more. I can barely get by on the $150 a month I get from home. Once I get this F.R.P. up off me, I should be able to make an extra $30 or $40 a month at work. Maybe I should go to industry or CMS where the pay is higher, but I just can't make it up that early any more. Not for the amount of money, anyway.

I received about eight shots last year. That's pretty bad for me. To some guys, it's nothing. But for me its pretty screwed up. Five of them were for drinking. My rebellious attitude has not changed. I don't feel that I've gotten anything out of my incarceration in the last year. The system is not designed to rehabilitate you. Its designed to make you not want to come back.

It's designed to kill your spirit.

It's also designed to make money.

Maybe this year I won't get into as much trouble.

Today I finished reading a book. It was your basic good versus evil story based on a post-war setting, in which the hero went out to destroy the villain, who was out to destroy the world. One of the points in the book was that good will always triumph over evil. There will always be more good than evil in the world. Evil is greedy and makes a move to destroy something. It tries to make its power stronger by squashing inferior forces. But the forces of good will unite and eventually conquer evil.

But what happens when there is more evil than good in the world? The Devil is doing one hell of a job now and what happens when he gets control? Is this day coming? It seems like everybody is already self centered. My country has over a million people incarcerated. From personal experience I can say that maybe half of them belong here. But definitely not three quarters of them.

They are playing "Dream On" by Aerosmith on the radio. It is one of my favorite songs.

Lately my dreams have been very vivid, detailed and easily remembered. They border on the macabre. I am a firm believer in dreams and the meanings within them. Sometimes I have flashes and remember pieces of dreams I had years ago. Sometimes I have visions of dreams

I've had before but didn't remember. The visions come to me in brief bursts of clarity. It is startling to say the least and unsettling at times.

There was a period of time in my life when I had vicious nightmares. The nightmares were accompanied by pains in my chest and troubled breathing.

Maybe I'm finally living out the nightmares I once dreamed about.

1995

January 6, 1995

The new year is rolling right along.

I'm still in my single cell and it is late at night. I am tired but can't sleep. I feel the urge to write.

I had minor surgery on my teeth today. It ended up being a catastrophe with me blacking out under the knife. I totally freaked the dentist out. They had to move me from the chair to a stretcher, and then into the Emergency Room. I told them they needed to knock me out, but all they had to offer was general anesthesia. I always freak out whenever I'm getting worked on by a doctor. I just black out. It was quite an experience. I go back for a follow-up tomorrow.

I am on a liquid diet and they give me a big can of juice at every meal. I am going to save up and try to get a batch of wine going. It will help me to pay my bills, if nothing else. They gave me commissary restriction for a month, but I don't know whether or not it will stick. It's already been two weeks, anyway.

Time is ticking away. There is nothing I would like more than for this year to just fly by. Winter has just started, but I'm already looking forward to Spring. There have been sub-zero temperatures the last couple days. The sun shines, but the cold bites right through your clothes at your ears. It's the kind of cold that makes it hard to draw a breath when you first walk out into it.

I'm holding my job in the music room. We blew up all the equipment so there's not much to work with. I'm happy with the acoustic I stole from Recreation to play in my cell. It helps me to have it here to learn how to play new songs. I've recently figured out the new Green Day tune "When I Come Around" and the new Allman Brothers tune "Soul Shine." Both are excellent tunes. I want to start working more on my acoustic stuff and classical technique, in particular. Playing those fast rifts gets boring after a while. I'm at a point where I need a break from electric guitar anyway.

I've been working on this journal for close to two years and wonder if I'm actually trying to accomplish anything, or if I'm just writing to write. Do I want anybody to actually read this? Sometimes, like now, I just babble and don't really say anything. Good writers think about what they are going to say. Their words have meaning. My words wander. I don't really sit down at a certain time with anything on my mind. It seems that I just scribble every now and then.

The holidays are over and the next big event is my 27th birthday, on March the 3rd. I hope I can get a buzz on. It's hard enough just trying to make it through the week. The only thing that's really different each day is that one more day is behind you and you're one step closer to the door. I have five hundred and eighty-five steps to go. I'll break five hundred days sometime in April. That's seventy one weeks. There are all kinds of ways to look at it. Am I obsessed? You bet your ass I'm obsessed. Someone once said that "Freedom oppressed then regained bites deeper than freedom never threatened." It's true.

I think a lot of things going on in the outside world. The free world. Drunks being thrown out of bars. Girls having their hearts broken. A guy stranded at the airport. The beach on a Saturday afternoon. Tiajuana, Mexico on a Friday night. A family driving through McDonald's in a station wagon and ordering a ton of junk food. A little league baseball game in a small town. The hitchhiker on the side of the highway in the middle of the country. The young couple sitting on the rocks watching the sun set. The hard rock band dreaming of making it to the top. The single mother wondering if she'll have enough to feed her kids this month. The girl that used to sit in front of me in history class. The little kid catching his first fish. The old man breathing his last breath.

I think about these things a lot.

I can't forget.

I will not forget.

January 13, 1995

Sometimes you just want to scream, go berserk and smash up some shit. I gave up punching steel, bricks and glass a long time ago. But being locked up night after night, day after day, month after month, does something to you.

At times you can appreciate life so much. Other times, you feel like dying. The isolation from familiar people is the worst. Last time I saw Diane was January of last year. God, was it just a year ago? It seems so long ago. Last time I saw my mom was nine months ago.

They pissed me last Sunday. What a waste of time.

The pressure to get high is staggering. There's a guy who wants me to help him bring some drugs in. He says he'll hook me up with this girl he knows. I badly need the money but told him I'd think about it. I'm going to tell him no.

I'm still making my wine. I made four gallons of wine last Wednesday and sold it all in forty-five minutes.

I hope this year goes quicker than the last one. Ninety four seemed five years long. I have to take things day by day. One step at a time like they tell you in AA.

January 14, 1995

I gotta get out of this place.

I went next door to collect some money from the guy in IIA. I smelled burning plastic when I walked in. The dude was making a knife.

He had broken a piece of plastic off a chair and was sharpening it with sand paper. He said he had to go collect some money. I told him I had a much better knife and he could use it if he liked. He said "That's OK, mine is finished."

I go back to my cell and soon this little asshole comes in and tells me he wants to screw me.

"You're out of your mind!" I yell at him.

"Please," he begs. "I'll pay you."

I got up to smack him and he stepped outside the door.

"I'm comin' back," he said, "and when I do you'll do what I want."

He split and I figured he was going to get a knife so I quickly got my knife out of its hiding place. In a few minutes, he was back at my door with two big dudes. This is it, I thought, as I pulled out my knife.

But when they saw my knife, the two big dudes dissolved and the fag was left standing there by himself. His eyes bugged out as I jumped towards him. He ran and I chased him down the tier all the way to the ice room where he jumped the rail and went right to the cop.

I couldn't believe it. These are the tough killer fags? They were only pussies. I suddenly felt very confident.

I dropped the knife on the floor and kicked it under the door of my dog's cell who stashed it away for me. After chasing the guy all the way across the unit with a knife, I felt I sure I would get busted. Everybody saw me and this place is full of rats.

But nothing happened.

I still can't believe it.

The fag checked in with the cops and asked to be put into protective custody.

January 26, 1995

I'm back in the hole for possession of a weapon. The idiots ratted me out and they found the knife I chased the fag with in my jacket pocket during a "surprise" shakedown. I knew it was too much to believe that no one would say something about the chase incident.

I've been in the hole for eight days. By some strange twist of fate my old dog Cameron is my cellie. Cameron was in the hole with me at Spartanville.

I am still in administrative detention pending an investigation of the incident and have not been found guilty yet. I might wait weeks to see the disciplinary hearing officer. I might see him tomorrow.

I had the little amount of property allowed down here delivered a week ago. Most of my property was ripped off by inmates before the guard on duty could pack it up for me. My clothes, cosmetics, pictures and personal items are all gone.

I'll probably get sixty days in Disciplinary Seg. I'm also waiting for a urine test to come back. I'm pretty sure it will be dirty. If it is then that will land me another thirty days.

The knife will get me a transfer out of this shit hole. It's the only good thing that could possibly happen out of this whole mess.

If prison is a different world, the hole is like a moon circling this different world. It is an altogether separate existence from prison. Your universe is eight feet wide by twelve feet long by ten feet high. Showers are built into the cells. This is one luxury that you do not take for granted. At Spartanville it was three showers a week which was pretty disgusting. Two steel bunks, one bed on top of the other, take up a quarter of the room. The shower takes up another quarter. The sink combo toilet and the small steel desk with swing out seat leave little room to pace or exercise.

Both Cameron and I have spent a considerable amount of time in the hole.

There is only one thing to do.

Make wine.

Making wine in prison is a tradition that has lived on as long as prisons have existed. There are hundreds of recipes and different techniques, all producing something a little different. Long periods of hole time means you live from batch to batch. If nothing else, it kills time. Some wine gets knocked off. Some turns to vinegar if you don't know what you are doing.

The basic ingredients are simple. Fruit, water and sugar. Fruit and sugar comes in through that wonderful little slot in the door. Water comes from the sink. It took Cameron and me no time to whip up our first batch which is brewing at this very moment.

One of the important factors in brewing wine is temperature. Cold air kills the brewing process or slows it down tremendously. At Spartanville the sinks were big enough to heat the wine in. But here the basin only holds a gallon. The showers can't be controlled like they could at Spartanville. You push a button and water comes out for however long it feels like coming out. This is somewhere between ten and fifteen minutes. At Spartanville the showers had variable control handles.

The first step is getting a bag to brew the wine in. The orderly took care of this for us. For the first few days of hole time, Cameron and I deposited vast quantities of trash outside our door. The orderly brought us a trash bag to put all of the trash in but we simply put our trash on the empty food trays.

The cell is cold and this means a problem with the temperature needed for the brewing process. I solved this problem with a bit of ingenuity. The sink and toilet are one piece of stainless steel. The water is so cold that when you flush you do not want to have your ass on the steel seat. Sitting on socks on the toilet seat alleviates most of the problem. The cold water makes the bottom trap of the bowl sweat cold water. We run water in the basin until it is as hot as we can get it. Then we fill our cups with the hot water and flush the toilet.

Our particular toilet is a real power flusher. It can suck down socks on the blink of an eye. It also goes for about thirty seconds and is pretty noisy. After we flush and the cycle is nearing the end, before the water level rises, we dump the hot water from our cups into the toilet. Our cups are big and hold two quarts of water. We do this over and over. The water level rises. The toilet gets warm. We have to take turns sitting on the cold steel and warming it up with our asses.

After a while the bowl is full of warm water. The stainless steel retains the heat excellently. We then place the bag in the warm water bowl and cover it with a pillowcase to further retain the heat. The brew in the bag heats up and begins to "cook." It bubbles and froths processing sugar into oxygen and alcohol. The cooking process slows down when all the sugar is cooked off. You have to catch your wine before all the sugar cooks off. If you don't then it all turns to vinegar. This is a real drag, especially after all the work.

Dodging the Man during the brewing process is another thing altogether. Shakedowns occur once a week but they have to handcuff you before they take you out of the cell. Last time they came around we simply told them to write us shots. They said OK and moved on. We never got the shots so we caught a lucky break last time.

I may be in the hole six months this time. If it comes to that and I am thirteen months short, I hope they send me to some decent place. I will be going crazy and bouncing off the walls anyway at the prospect of leaving. Can you blame me after four years of insanity, violence, death and apathy?

Time is a fickle master that bends only to fate. The closer I draw to my release date the more tense I become. Please God, don't let anything screw up my walking out of this place. By this time next year, I'll only have seven months left. I hope they don't take away any of my good time for this. This would push the release date back even further.

My schedule in here is already nonconformist. I stay awake until three AM and try to sleep for twelve hours. I skip breakfast but get up for lunch only to try to go back to sleep for a couple more hours. It doesn't do any good most of the time.

I've got a pretty solid work out schedule. I do a lot of work on my legs because I know I'll be in the hole for a while. The schedule involves a lot of stretching, toe raises, toe touches and deep-knee bends. It's important to keep the legs in shape because you do a horrific amount of lying around in here. I think my hair grows faster in the hole than anywhere else. Being in the hole probably preserves you pretty well but I would prefer to have been deep frozen two years ago.

Cameron is also pretty hard into working out. He might only get 15 days of seg time, but they are "dropping notes" on him left and right back in his unit. With any big white boy like Cameron, they cry racism and then drop a note threatening his life if he gets out. It usually ends up in a transfer.

I do a lot of reading in here. So far I've read Cussler's *Dragon*, Clancy's *Patriot Games*, Segal's *Love Story* and *The Donner Party*. I have *Sophie's Choice*, *Plato*, *The Thornbirds* and a couple of trash novels. It would not surprise me to know that by the time I get out, I will probably have read hundreds of books. Somewhere in my readings I came across an interesting quote that somehow relates to this situation. It is from Giacomo Leopardis Pensieri and reads: "Men do not so much hate an evildoer, or evil itself, as they hate the man who calls evil by its real name."

I am only allowed one phone call a month even on A.D. and that is a real drag. I miss the telephone most of all. I miss talking to Diane, my friends and my mother, my family. Diane might come with my mother to see me in April. That would be extremely nice since I have not seen either in a year or so.

I'm afraid Diane has stolen my heart. She is truly one in a million. I miss her a lot.

February 2, 1995

I'm on a reverse schedule now. The Hole Zone. Like one of my favorite rock singers says, "I'm on the Night Train." I just finished my workout and shower and decided to knock off a few pages.

Today is day seven, day seven of captivity as Rush Limbaugh says. I saw the DHO on Friday and he gave me sixty days in D.S. and suspended twenty of them for 180 days. He also gave me a Disciplinary Transfer which was suspended for 180 days. It's suspended until I get into trouble again. I've never been able to go six months without getting into trouble since I've been in the federal system. Cameron is babbling away at this moment, talking about skiing and doing his best to distract me. He only got 15 days.

I received a pleasant surprise today. A few weeks ago I entered a short story contest. A few days ago I requested the results. At dinnertime the screw came and handed me a bunch of papers and a brand new dictionary. I won second place in the contest. It was a bright spot of the day.

February 5, 1995

I don't know what time it is. It's dark outside and two or three inches of snow is on the ground. I didn't get to bed until 6:00 AM yesterday. I was up at noon and stayed up until dinner. Then I fell back to sleep and slept until sometime after midnight.

Cameron got his haircut today. I couldn't get mine cut because we couldn't both leave the cell at the same time. We have too much stuff we'd lose in a shakedown. Cigarettes, pillows, clothes, towels, razors, stacks of books. The guards would undoubtedly take all of this during a shakedown if we were both gone. But if one of us stays in the cell at all times then they won't come in and we won't lose our stuff.

I slept after dinner as if I was drugged and wonder if I actually was drugged. Dinner was gross. Roast beef as tough as leather with a sprinkling of dried up rice. I ate the rice with contraband hot sauce, which made it almost taste like food.

I spoke to Mom a few days ago. She's mad and wants me to sign a release so when she calls she can find out whether I've been bad or good. Like Santa Claus or something. There is no way I'm going to sign a release. It will only give her something else to upset her and she doesn't need this. And I also don't want to feel like she's watching every move I make. Sorry Momma, but we've made it this far. We're both just coasting now.

I received pictures in the mail of cousin Sarah's wedding. It was very nice and everybody was there. There was a good letter from Mom.

Diane sent a card and wrote about a thousand little words on it. It's been so long since I got mail from her I forgot what her writing looked like. She didn't send pictures. She says she looks yukky. All girls say this though. She drives me nuts. I wrote her several letters.

I wrote to Danny, Tommy and Suzie. I even wrote Susan a letter although I don't have her address. I'm waiting for Mom to send the address to me. I'll probably write my little brother Jimmy a letter tonight. Mom says he might come with her in April to see me. I look forward to this because I know it will be my once a year visit.

I keep trying to get out to Lompoc so I'll be close to home. It feels like I'm deep underground and light years from any place. The only contact I have with the real world comes through a 4 inch by 13 inch slot in the door.

The DHO said they'll release me to the A.D. for transfer on March 7th. Four days after my twenty seventh birthday. I feel like I'm at least forty years old. Exercise is helping me to stay in shape though. I'm especially working my legs which are constantly sore.

February 10, 1995

Cameron has gone to A.D. to wait for his transfer. I was moved to the Dungeon side of Disciplinary Segregation. It was one long wall of steel doors so you couldn't see anybody.

Some familiar faces have arrived in the hole. My whole band is now down here. My bass player, George, is in the cell with me for a dirty urine. Kevin is in for fighting.

I got a letter from cousin Sarah who is now happily married and residing in Ocean Beach. It's an excellent place to live.

Ocean Beach brings back lots of memories and memories are the only thing I have now days. It was the first place I went when I came to California for the first time. My mother was living in Ocean Beach. I was fifteen and had hitch-hiked across the country. I had a dollar bill in my pocket and a bag of pot. I lost the dollar.

The night I arrived the Padres won the game that put them in the World Series. They closed the streets and had big bonfires in them. Everybody was smoking pot and getting drunk.

I liked Ocean Beach a lot and returned there many times during the next eight years. Once I had a job at SeaWorld that actually lasted a couple of months. It was a pretty cool job even though I was just a temporary hired slave. They treated me good and I took full advantage of them. After they fired me they sent a very polite letter saying I should never apply at any Sea World for employment again. I kept the cool jacket they gave me, though.

I remember all the times I used to party in Ocean Beach by the pier. Once, I arrived on the pier shortly after a murder had happened near it. A guy was stabbed to death and the white outline remained in the street for a few days. Homicide cops came by the house the next day asking me questions because they knew I was always hanging out at the pier.

February 12, 1995

I'm in my 17th day of D.S. It's really not so bad.

But it would be good to get back to the compound. George is pretty confident they will let us out after half our time is served because they need the room in the hole.

I am not too sure though, because I have to beat this petty shot they gave me for refusing to cuff up. They are supposed to deliver a copy of the shot to you within twenty-four hours, but I still have not received my copy. They did try to deliver my copy, but it came at mail call and was eight hours late. I told the cop delivering to initial it and put the down the time. He got real confused and left and we never got the copies.

My counselor wanted to pull us out to U.D.C. us. This is where he reads the shot and makes a recommendation. In this case, he recommended 15 days. After he reads us the shot we are supposed to get a blue copy of the shot, with the recommendation. We still haven't gotten this copy. I never received the blue copy of the U.D.C. for my knife shot either. It's a bunch of paperwork bullshit.

A lot of rumors circulate about you when you're doing hole time. A guy I knew from Spartanville left the hole in the middle of the night on a writ. He was only gone a few hours when rumors began to circulate about him. How he was a rat, a SIS, a member of the WPP. All kinds of crap. A lot of the low lifes in here start the rumors because it makes them feel more secure about themselves.

The rumors are circulating on the compound about me. As soon as I came to the hole, people started saying I had checked myself in. When I get out I'll put things straight with the assholes that started the rumors.

I got my bangs cut today and it looks OK. I still haven't had a full haircut for two years but it doesn't seem to be growing too fast. That's not surprising. Nothing seems to grow much in prison.

I've put up another batch of wine. It's my fourth attempt. I came up with the novel idea of hanging the bag in front of the heating duct. It heats the wine quite nicely and I can hear the sugar cooking off at night.

February 14, 1995

Valentine's Day. Across the nation, lovers express their feelings for each other with flowers and candy.

Here in the hole it is different. I'm trapped in a cell with another dude smelling his gross smells.

Happy Valentine's Day.

"I gotta crap man, put the shit sheet up."

"Awww . . . man, hand me my powder."

The commissary sells baby powder which we squirt into the air to lessen the smell.

"I'm not sure whether I gotta shit or not. I might just have to fart."

There is the sound of the toilet flushing a minute later.

Clouds of powder fill the air.

I am lying on my bunk reading Conroy's *Prince of Tides.*

"God, Dude, that reeks, get some powder on that!"

"You got powder up there?"

"Yeah, but why do I have to use all my powder on your shits?"

"Well, I gotta use all mine on yours!"

Life has been reduced to pitiful levels. Cigarettes are hard to come by. Some days we might smoke two if we're lucky. Some days we don't smoke any. It is difficult to be stripped of everything and allowed nothing. Somebody must have once proclaimed, "Yeah, put showers in the cells. We'll just throw food at 'em." I get tired of reading, tired of writing, tired of doing absolutely nothing.

By having nothing, when anything comes along, like a cigarette or a letter, it is an event that is savored. Our lives have become reduced to nothing. But give us a smoke and we are for the moment content. This is a state which I call Point Zero Bliss. It is for these moments a prisoner survives, for without them the strain of living would be too much to bear.

Every prisoner experiences Point Zero Bliss in some way, shape or form, whether it is a cigarette in the hole, a money order for a few dollars that allows us to go to the commissary, or a letter from somebody we haven't heard from in a while. Nothing is really good enough for everybody. If everybody had to live with nothing for a little while, there would be a whole lot more understanding going on. Every situation that presents a reward is relevant to the rewardee. What may be nothing to somebody may mean everything in the world to another.

That is the imbalance of life and it has been that way forever. It is like that in life. It is like that in love.

It is like that in prison.

It is cold as hell out today. I received a Valentine's Day card from Momma. She sent me some books from home but they won't let me have them. I've just finished Clancy's *Sum of all Fears*. It's an excellent thousand page book by a brilliant writer.

I applied for the orderly's job since he is leaving. At least I will be out in the hall for a couple hours a day. I probably won't get the job though. I'm not too well liked by the police, it seems.

Cameron is over in A.D. I got a letter from his deceased brother's wife. She is my link with Cam. He is getting a transfer because he single-handedly almost started a racial riot in the TV room of Two A.

February 18, 1995

I got up bright and early this morning. It's hard to sleep because things are so cold in here. The heat went off yesterday at about noon and only just came back on. The natives were restless with no ventilation last night.

I bought two packs of cigarettes and paid twenty dollars for them. I have a gallon of wine brewing but the cold does not help at all. This batch is much too big to hang from the vent. I may have added too much water to it, so I'm not sure how it will come out.

George thought he was getting out yesterday. He was a little irate at not being released with over half his time served. But it is his second dirty urine so they are keeping him longer. I hope to get out on my half time date which is March 1st. My birthday is on the third and I let the Lieutenant know this. He said maybe we could work something out.

I received my once a month phone call last night. I actually got hold of Mom. She is still expecting to come and see me in April.

I asked for and received information on correspondence courses.

The University of Ohio has a degree program and I decided to pursue my Associate of Arts degree. I'll try and talk to my father about paying for it. I haven't called him in six months. I'm not sure at this point what he will say. I want to take a full load of several courses and spend my time studying and playing guitar.

Today marks one month down here in the hole. Twenty three of those days are D.S. days. After the smoke cleared I ended up with 67 days. As I've said, they generally release you after serving half your time. Day to day is how you do hole time. I'm glad I only have this little amount of time to do.

Mom sends me letters and books. Diane actually sent me two cards back to back. I haven't heard from Suzie and I fear she screwed up her furlough and ended up in the joint to finish up her nine months. Maybe I'll get a card from her this week. We'll see.

February 20, 1995

Mama said there would be days like this.

But she never said there would be so many of them.

I'm still in the hole and hoping to get out within the next 10 days or so. I'm reading books like a mad dog.

I have a gallon of wine hanging from the heater. I guess it's going to be my birthday party tonight. It appears as though this will be a particularly strong batch. We are going to wait until after the 10:00 PM count, if we can. They are due for a shakedown on Wednesday.

George was certain he would be leaving tomorrow but he has now downgraded his optimism to "reasonably certain" he will leave tomorrow. Time will tell. It always does.

I can't wait to get back to the compound. It's funny, but getting back to the compound seems like getting out of prison in some strange way. I think I'll change my evil ways for a while and try to behave as best I can.

I really look forward to having access to the phone again. Getting back to a normal sleep pattern will also be good. This on again off again, a few hours of sleep here and a few hours of sleep there, is not good. It deprives one's system of deeply needed REM sleep. Last night I actually got about six hours in. I hope to stay up until lunch and sleep the rest of the day until dinner.

After dinner I have a pack of cigarettes that are owed me. I need them when I drink or it won't be a pleasant experience. At $10 a pack, one expects delivery on time.

February 21, 1995

I can't sleep and am haunted by thoughts of freedom. It's far too early to entertain these notions but I can't avoid them. Like the bear by the honey tree who shakes his head to clear the bees only to have them furiously return.

I've been at Eagleview for six months. I hope to finish the year here and receive a transfer to Lompoc where I'll serve my remaining six months. This assumes I don't lose any of my good time. It might be assuming too much though. The DHO made it crystal clear he can't stand me. Pointing out my bad attitude, he declared the next time he saw me, for anything, he would strip me of my good time. Nice guy.

The police in all their wisdom decided to conduct a shakedown today and, of course, we had to flush the wine down the toilet. It seems I'm destined not to drink. Of the five batches I've made, I've only been able to drink one of them.

I wrote to Diane and kind of let her go. It was tough but I'm surprised she lasted as long as she did. They say hindsight is 20/20 and I have a lot of time for hindsight. Diane has now been with Mike for a number of years but she has not been able to commit herself totally to the man she loves.

I wonder why she has been unable to do this. Is it fear of rejection? I think she needed the "what if he does this" option and this option was me. Maybe my stepping aside will give her the extra shove she needs to grab that extra security in her life. Maybe she will find the option in another man. I only want to see that girl happy and content.

I woke up this morning with a powerful thought about alcohol and drugs. It was a very clear and lasting thought. I always ask myself why I drink. I can live without everything else except alcohol. Cocaine reduces me and any man who has used it for any period of time. Heroin simply neutralizes me. Marijuana makes me content. But alcohol enhances me, brings out my emotions and stirs my imagination. With women it strengthens my endurance. When I'm drunk I can be ten different things. I'm capable of just about anything.

But alcohol is also the cross I bear. It tends to strip me of focus and pull me towards irresponsibility. It causes emotions to surface that sometimes might have been better buried. It causes irreparable damage.

The things I'm becoming aware of are the things I've always known. But it's the act of becoming aware, the acceptance of knowledge, that brings wisdom. The application of wisdom is another matter entirely. Sometimes I think wisdom has more to do with not doing something than with doing something.

February 26, 1995

While the nation sleeps the prisoner writes. Serving his hole time for possession of a knife. He's been in this little cement box for over a month now. One month, one week, two days, three hours and forty two minutes. Doing hole time can be extremely easy or extremely difficult. Some days are better than others. The closer you come to getting out the longer the days drag.

I'm in a cell now with Shorty who was also at Spartanville. He is one of the multitude who gets heavy medication to help him sleep. I took just two of the little pills he gets daily and I slept for 24 hours. Last night I took four of his pills and my muscles got all knotted up. It was like doing acid with strychnine in it. I slept for a good sixteen hours and missed all three meals today. Shorty, however, was considerate enough to save me a sandwich.

In the last few days I haven't eaten much because of all the sleep. The long periods of sleep were good though and much needed. It helped smooth out all the irregular sleep I've gotten in the hole.

I look forward to getting out on Wednesday the 1st. It will be my half way point and since it's my first time in the hole here they should let me out. I need to get back to the guitar. George told me that there is a real keyboard player that showed up in the compound. I hope he nailed down our band slot.

I've got plenty of cigarettes thanks to Cam. He came over to D.S. for a week and went back to the other side of A.D. to await his transfer. He sent me a whole pack of smokes.

My new cellie likes his coffee and heats it up in a milk carton late at night. He showed me how to make a Bunsen burner out of a roll of toilet paper. He keeps his tobacco in a bag tied to a string, which is tied to his drawers, in case the man decides to come in. He calls the cops "boss" as in "Yes, sir boss" and I have to admit his subservience allows him concessions.

The orderlies are pretty worthless to us and it has been the man that has been delivering our smokes. Although it is not exactly scraping, I still can't find it in me to give in even a little bit. I refuse to grovel. Only when I am in deep shit do I revert to "Sir." Otherwise, it is a simple "yes," or "no" or silence. The prisoners that grovel to the cops don't realize that they're laughing at us every day. They go home every night and drink beer and screw while we are locked in a cell, smelling another man's bad odors, wondering if we will live through the next day.

The next time I write I will hopefully be on the compound. Shorty and I have started a half gallon. I showed him my method of tying the bag to the vent. I think he likes it very much. I learned my lesson on the last batch and will drink it when it is ready. Mom sent me some more AA books and books on recovery. I think she understands I do what I have to do to get by. If I need to have a drink every now and then, well it's better than having a heroin habit, I guess.

Prison is not the place to do anything to excess unless you are "retired," and that means doing life. I guess I've learned to control my drinking. But that's easy to say when you don't have easy access to alcohol. I can clearly see in my mind what alcohol does to me. It's the reason I am lying here on this bunk surrounded by cement bricks, razor wire and guard towers. And if that's not enough to open your eyes and make you aware, then come with me, walk in my shoes, share with my despair. Taste the bile that is incarceration and heed it well.

It's mid afternoon. I look into the piece of metal bolted to the wall that's my mirror. Haunted eyes with deep dark circles stare back. I've been awake for over twenty hours now. In this time I've done a thousand push ups. I'm dead tired. The cement box is my world now. My universe. In here there is no clock and no time. Light shows through the thickly barred window. Then it is dark again. Food trays come through the slot in the door. Then later, the slot is opened so that the tray can be passed back through. The meager rations of tobacco are slid under the door. If not for friends, even this would cease to exist. One book is allowed, although others may be obtained. All magazines are forbidden.

There are two kinds of recreation. Outside and inside. Outside recreation means they take you from your little cell and put you in the Kennel, a fenced in area possibly twice as big as the cell. As many as three inmates per kennel. There is a chin up bar bolted to the brick wall. There are fences on all sides and overhead. Sometimes there is a ball.

Inside recreation means you go from your small cell to another small cell with as many as three inmates. The cell you go to is hardly any bigger than your cell and has a chin up bar on the wall. I've never seen a ball in the inside rec cells, but then again, I've only gone to inside rec once.

Letters are spun from gold. I write them endlessly it seems. Last Monday I received three letters in one day. One from my mother and two letters from girls who continued to exist long after the others have faded away. Both of the girls' letters had perfume on them. I put one under my pillow so I could smell her while I dreamed and fall asleep with her perfumed scent in the stale air. I put the other letter under my pillow the next night. I never put both letters under the pillow at once.

The letters are read and reread. Then they are carefully put away with the others, almost like they were bottles of fine wine. Over long mailess stretches this "stash" is broken into and certain letters are read again. Some are simply picked at random and read.

I exist in a peculiar time zone. Tomorrow only exists on a calendar. It is not important. The beginning, the middle, the end of a month, of a year. These things are important. You might know somebody for a few weeks or even for a month. If he is suddenly gone and his name comes up, people say, "Yeah, he was here for a minute."

Yesterday is not important. Every past day in prison is only a savage reminder you've failed. You learn to take it in stride. Going from event to event helps. Valentine's Day just passed and my birthday is coming up on the 3rd of March. Spring is the 21st of March. The end of March marks a quarter of the year. It'll be here in a minute.

I look into the metal mirror on the wall and a strange face stares back at me. I have asked myself all the questions a hundred thousand times. It's even possible I've answered them all at one time or another. As the *I Ching* says, "One thing moves, all things change."

I have said it before and I stick by it. Life is like a kaleidoscope. Sometimes it is green and yellow. Sometimes it is blue and red. And sometimes, if you get it just right, you get the perfect rainbow.

But it's been a few minutes since I've seen one of these.

March 4, 1995

I finally got out of the hole on the first of March and moved over to unit 2A. There are more white guys over here. This includes George, my bass player.

The day before my birthday I got extremely intoxicated on tomato wine that was very potent. The day before that I smoked a little weed. The wine was a birthday present to myself. I was put in a cell with a guy named Mark who has since gone out on a writ. The night before my birthday I talked him into splitting a gallon with me. He wanted to be sure it was good. It was friggin' rocket fuel is what it was.

I also had band practice that night. It was good to be out of the hole and be able to get drunk and play guitar. I hung out with Mike, my Viking friend. He's over six feet tall, blond and heavily tattooed. He's a good dude and just came back from a writ from an outside court case.

"I carved Viking runes in my arm before I went to court," Mike tells me. "It brings me luck."

George was drinking with Mark and me and I split some of the wine with Mike. I was really messed up. During band practice I had to take my shirt off. I was lying on the ground playing Judas Priest and having a great time. Back in the unit we drank some more wine and at one point I went over to Mike's cell. I reached for the handle on his door and missed it by about a foot. I stumbled backwards and almost fell off the top tier. I ended up on the floor instead.

I had fun and boy did I need it. The next day I was pretty badly hung over along with George and Mark. I ended up doing some exercise out of boredom. There was nothing else better to do. Although I've had the opportunity, I've stayed clean today and probably will stay clean for at least a week.

Mike does tattoos. I'm going to get some work done on me. I've got a really cool pattern of tribal art for him to do.

For some reason I'm really amped out tonight. Its after lock-up and pushing midnight and I've got nothing better to do but read.

I tell you it's nice having a single cell again.

March 6, 1995

Today I found out they put me on the morning schedule. I hate mornings with a passion. I'm not a nice person in the mornings. In addition to this little piece of unpleasant news, I just found out they locked up my bass player George. He was the reason I moved over here.

The more time I spend here the more I dislike it. You're around people all the time with devious, slimy characteristics. I don't have to deal with them all the time, but they sure seem to come across my path a lot. What makes it harder is that people aren't always what they seem to be when you first meet them. A convict will go out of his way to make a good first impression. You quickly learn to be selective.

Sometimes I wonder about everybody and don't want to associate with anybody. But prison means living daily with a lot of people you don't like. I wish I could set my own schedule and do as I please but that's impossible. It seems that things are always messed up. Either another prisoner is in my business or the man is messing with me. Something always seems to be going wrong.

I could run off and get high or drunk every time things got too tough, but I think I'm beyond this. When I came to prison I made a conscious decision to stop running and face reality. Drugs and booze are methods of running from reality. Facing reality is supposed to make you a stronger person. But I sure had fun when I was running from it.

I've always had feelings of rage but there was something that overrode them. I know my weaknesses. I also know my strengths. Fear is my worst weakness. My mind is my best strength. Thoughts are painted with so many colors. I've always sought inner peace, but for years was unable to find it inside. I searched myself and I really didn't like what I saw.

Sometimes the truth is ugly and hurts. Becoming aware of truth often causes pain and confusion. All of these things, emotions like confusion, love, hate, passion, apathy and despair, lie in that cosmic maze of the mind. It's all in your head. If you want to know what makes you tick, you can find out. If you don't want to know, you never will. It's as simple as that.

The rage I'm dealing with right now is a bitch. My daily life seems to compound this rage without me noticing. It's like watching a puppy grow. If you see it every day, the growth is hardly noticeable. Then one day you are surprised because the puppy has turned into a dog.

I see myself as much harder than I ever thought I could be. In a way, it seems I have no choice but to become hard.

In this environment you can't help becoming conditioned to this hardness. Before you know it you find yourself thinking you'd like to kill or stab someone. Maybe just hit them with a pipe or kick their teeth out. When you feel this way, you know the monster of rage has taken over your spirit like a great dark force. It is a structured, calculated and out of control force. It's the real monster that the prison system creates. That's the terrible price of committing a crime and going to prison. You are now preyed upon by this great dark evil force.

There is little effort made to face this force. The official prison system makes very little effort. There is no rehabilitation to be found here. Prison will twist your psyche and kill your spirit. It will change you in ways you never thought would be possible.

It is only in awareness of the great dark force of rage that the seeds of its destruction might be planted. Memory is crucial. It is one of the few things you have. You need to remember who you are. Remember where you come from. Remember that this nightmare all comes to an end someday. There is light at the end of the tunnel, although the light might be a mere pinprick in the darkness, like a dull star from a faraway galaxy. There might not be shelter from the storm, but the sun is damned sure going to shine again. You've gotta keep that little mantra ticking in the back of your head.

It has passed.

It is passing.

It will pass.

And it does.

March 13, 1995

When the confusion ends, and the last of your fears are defeated, when you've finally attained what you sought for so long, the circle is complete. There is no more denial and no more running. You have faced things and it has brought you strength. Perhaps the search has been an emotional one, but emotion cannot be that which has controlled the search.

Questions and not answers always lie in emotions because they are constantly changing entities. One day I feel a certain way about a person, and another day, I feel totally different. Emotions make us unpredictable. How I handle a situation one day might be handled differently on another day. Unpredictability can be good. It breathes life into otherwise predictable times. In the long term, though, a life subservient just to emotions is a life without direction, a boat without a rudder.

Controlling emotions brings self discipline. Although I hate too much discipline, the lack of it has had a good deal to do with landing me in prison. Then again, all the self discipline in the world will not help to get me out of here. It may help me, though, once I get out.

I now find myself writing more when I am bored. I write long letters to girls I haven't seen in years. I hand out advice freely. They write back and tell me how smart I am. I can't tell I'm smart by looking at my surroundings.

Every day seems such a waste. No more than dead time. The only thing I really accomplish are these pages. They stack up in tribute to these lost days. But is it really an accomplishment? What will ever become of these long ramblings of a man locked in a cell? Will I look back years from now and laugh? Or Cry? Will there be a long sigh followed by another cigarette and glass of whiskey? I think I write these words to remember.

Recently I got a tattoo on the inside of my left forearm. It is very thin skin there and it is a large tattoo. It took two and a half days to complete. First they did the outline and then the shading. There was lots of shading. All done with a single needle. The work on my arm kept getting interrupted. By the roving cop. By the count. By the lock up. It seemed like it was taking forever. And when they pause during tattoo work, the skin becomes very tender and when they go back to work, it hurts twice as much. It was finally finished. .

Now I have something besides these pages to remind me of my time in here. I have other tattoos from prison, but this one is large and came out well. And the other ones are on my back. Every time I look at this tattoo I will remember being in U.S.P. Eagleview. I will remember the staggering hopelessness, the stagnant environment, the tension so thick you could cut it with a knife. I will remember the eyes through which I watched ink being put into my skin forever. I will remember the feel of the needle like a red hot poker. The blood and ink running off my arm.

Maybe, just maybe, this memory will help keep me out of here. I'm probably going to have its twin put on my other arm in the same spot.

Sometimes I wonder about myself.

Unpredictable.

March 15, 1995

It is around 2:00 AM in the morning. I spoke with Diane last evening. She told me she might be getting married this year. The misery continues. There goes the best damned woman in the world, right through my fingers.

Locked in this cell I look out at the steel, the rock, the wire. They shoot you if they catch you on the wire. But I feel like I've already been shot. I laughed, though, of course, when she told me. I wished her congratulations and told her all I wanted was for her to be happy. This is true. The worse thing right now is that I have absolutely nobody to talk to. Time to buck up once again.

March 24, 1995

"Writing does not cause misery. It is born of misery." Montaigne.

As a boy I lost myself in the make believe world of books. Around third grade I began looking at *Reader's Digest* and a number of other books. Some of the books were factual but they still forced me to conjure up my own images. The story might mention a dog barking in the distance and immediately I would see a beautiful German Shepherd, black with brown markings, faithfully patrolling his master's yard. Perhaps he was barking at a multi-colored calico cat frolicking in the garbage and trying to dig up the remains of his master's trout dinner.

The images from books caused a lot of day-dreaming and lack of attention in school.

My teacher at the Christian Academy in Tulsa, Oklahoma was one of the first to recognize this lack of attention.

"While I find your reading abilities outstanding," she would say to me, "I simply cannot tolerate your lack of attention."

I would then be sent to the closet for a beating. When I was young I believe it was the final few years when legal beatings were allowed in the school system. A comical sign from those days comes to mind.

"The beatings will continue until morale improves," the sign said.

When I returned to Massachusetts a few years later I discovered they don't beat the kids in New England like they do in the Midwest.

I was often beaten as a child. I think it was all the rage in the Midwest. I would get beaten at school. When I got home I got beaten for the beating I took in school. I never heard the words "This hurts me more than it hurts you." There is something bizarre about getting beaten by a nice, middle-aged, Christian woman. They seem so meek, timid and caring. I see how parents could hand over their children with little resistance. But you put that cutting board in their hands and watch them beat you until they sweat. It was a side of them only us kids saw.

I was once beaten with a Bible for stealing a yo-yo. I'm not even sure I really stole it. I think I just borrowed it. But one thing I am sure of was that big, black, hardback-Bible. I had to bend over a chair while the teacher gripped the big Bible with both hands and gave me a very substantial "whomp" on my ass.

To this day I believe that this teacher was trying to beat evil out of me or good into me. Maybe it was a little of both. Regardless. All it really did was piss me off and taught me to despise all authority figures. As a matter of fact, it may have contributed to the fact that I am sitting here in a U.S.P. right now, writing these words.

But books allowed me to pack up the bruises from these beatings and disappear into story land. I find it amusing that once upon a time I found solace in reading words and never imagined that one day I would be writing them. And, escaping the same way as I did then. Only these pages are not fiction, but fact. This makes it all the more interesting.

March 30, 1995

As I sit and write once again I contemplate the past as I find myself often doing. For me, the present is constantly turning into the past because nothing really changes. The words I wrote mere seconds ago are now in the past and it is in this strange period of incarceration that I have found myself changing from a boy into a man.

It has been said that "The person who has had only passions knows but one side of life; he who has had only reason is no better off; and he who upsets the natural order of the two periods has been nothing but a fool from the start." (Baron Philippe Regis de Trobriand, written in the last seconds of 1867 while sitting at a crude desk in hostile territory. *Custer and the Battle of Little Bighorn*, Evan S. Connell). And so it is, possibly through my forced abstinence, that I pass from my age of passion to my age of reason. Also contributing to this mental growth period is the staggering amount of time that I have with which to do nothing but contemplate both past and future.

A few days ago the Hispanic guy in the next door cell hung himself. In some bizarre way I had something to do with saving his life. The cop was at the gate of iron bars at the end of the tier. He was waiting for another cop to finish up on the other side. I called him over to give him a couple packs of cigarettes for my friend George who is on the slam side of D.S. After he took the cigarettes from me through the bean hole, he saw the Hispanic guy hanging in his cell.

To my dismay he threw the two packs of cigarettes on the floor and went to get the other cops. They were in an envelope and I thought for certain they would get stolen by the orderly.

All the cops came running and I watched them carry his body out of the cell. I don't know how bad off he was but I was told he lived.

I got a good look at the Hispanic kid in the time he was next to me. He appeared to be quite angry at the world and constantly cursed the cops quite vehemently. When he was not cursing them he banged on his door for hours. This, of course, was somewhat annoying to me since he was right next door.

One time he flooded his cell and the flood spilled over to our cell. My cellie and I slept through the flooding. We were enraged when we woke up and found out he had let us sleep through the whole thing. We would have wanted to block the bottom of the door to keep the water from coming in. I screamed at the young Hispanic kid. He was very disturbed at my anger but for some reason, this pleased me.

Later I felt bad when I realized that I may have scared him and in some way contributed to his attempted suicide.

April 2, 1995

I am approaching the fourth day of my hunger strike. I've refused eight meals.

The long, slow, laborious process of starving myself began after breakfast last Friday. It was a pathetic last meal and I wish I had savored it. I refuse to go back to the compound because I am sick of it. Twice they've attempted to throw me back out to the compound. I was given incident reports for refusing to go back to the compound.

So, I am on a hunger strike officially protesting "the gross apathy towards human life and human rights."

I'm told they'll begin the weight and blood pressure tests tomorrow. Even now I am experiencing light headedness and dizzy spells. I can't believe their crassness and audacity. The worst part is that I believe in what I am doing. I am right. They are wrong. I continue, undaunted, to this end. I'll continue until relief is given to my satisfaction. My wish is to refuse all medical treatment in the event I become unconscious.

Maybe my fate is to make my final stand here.

Time will tell.

Tick, tock.

April 3, 1995

They rudely woke us up last night and told my cellie, Perry Delton, to pack his stuff.

He was soon gone.

I am now isolated in my cell pursuing my hunger strike. My stash is two small boxes of cereal, six oranges, three apples, six little containers of maple syrup, and one sandwich (of undetermined origin my cellie saved from lunch), a small piece of cake (that I ate for my daily meal), one-half bottle of Tobasco sauce and a small bag of coffee. This completes my entire cupboard. I am assuming that they will come in to shakedown and that they will take all of this and leave me with nothing.

I am mentally prepared to do battle. Today after my refused lunch, the doctor came and weighed me, took my temperature and blood pressure and a bottle of urine. I weighed in at 186 which is preposterous considering I weighed 205 the last I know. I suspect the scale is rigged. That way they can set it properly in a few days and claim that I am gaining weight. The doctor comes every day and I will make sure it is set correctly. I'm a little weak but still feel pretty normal considering today is the fourth day of the hunger strike.

I am settled into my new single cell and cleaned up with all my trash thrown out. I've thrown out my salt and pepper, condiments and one rotten apple. I am now drinking a hot coffee and deliberating the staggering decimation of my stash. Being not entirely foolish, I've made an agreement with my pal Cameron. He will save various morsels of food for me by placing them in a coffee bag and stomping them flat. This is to accommodate sliding it under the door to the orderly, who will then pass it to me. This way I should be able to hold out longer than they assume.

I am not hungry, although I did eat an orange in addition to the sandwich and piece of cake. This is a preposterous amount of food for a man on a hunger strike. But the coffee tasted good and the proverbial smoke with it assured me I was once again putting one over on the man. To further my state of bliss, I have become hooked on Sinnequan. I depend on three little yellow capsules to sleep my regular 14 hours. The Sinnequan is being purchased from an anonymous donor.

I don't want to fool myself, though. I see rough road ahead.

My ex-cellie, Perry Delton, proved to be both a benefactor and a problem. He greeted me with brotherly aplomb when I came into his cell on the 9th of March. At first he spoke much of God, but less often later on. I can only describe him as a thoroughly miserable cretin of average to low intelligence.

One aspect which reflected this was his continual letter writing and his inability to spell. My dictionary became his friend very quickly. But that soon faded away as I became his automatic, instamatic, living, breathing dictionary. The Seanasauras. In between his frantic scribbling he would pause and ask the spelling of a word. I would patiently spell the word and he would continue his scribbling for a few seconds until he came to another word he couldn't spell and the whole process would repeat itself.

And so it went. He was thoroughly impressed with my ability with letters and sulkily pouted until I first helped him. Soon I was composing entire letters for him. I had my own letters to write but didn't complain. Mr. Perry seemed overfilled with disgust at everything.

The writing fests were broken up due to our mutual enjoyment of cards. First it was gin, but then, inevitably, poker. We opened a little box of Cheerios and used them for chips. Mr. Perry was not a very talented poker player. In poker slang he was a "chaser." He was fairly miserable all the time but definitely at his peak when losing to a youngster like me. I would dance around, raise and fold on him, so that he never knew exactly when to call, or fold, or even bet.

In spite of all of these faults, he was one of the best artists I've ever seen. The man could paint and sketch like God. I have a feeling that he painted only copies of things he saw and could not draw from his mind's eye. Nevertheless, his talent was nothing less than remarkable. I hesitate to say idiot savant.

Mr. Perry was missing most of his teeth but had bridges which he kept in a cup on the sink. They sat there for pretty much the entire month of March. He had tattoos and they seemed random, scattered. A butterfly here, nicely done. The rest were a mess. Little lines here and there. Single letters that were certainly the beginning of something that was never quite finished.

When I discovered he was married, I was confused at first. My confusion soon gave way to constant speculation. I remembered the quote, "Do not let us judge others lest we grow vain; for there will always be others greater and lesser then ourselves." I speculated if someone could love Mr. Perry enough to marry him, then it was easier to believe I could find a wife for myself some day.

April 4, 1995

Day five of my hunger strike.

I am now isolated from food. I foolishly gave away my four oranges and ate my sandwich yesterday. I started to throw out another mushy apple today, but ate the best parts of it, which were a couple of bites. Then I ate my last good apple. Besides this, I've only eaten two slices of bread which Cam flattened out and sent to me.

The Doc came and weighed me again. He told me I had gained weight and I told him I was drinking water. He wants to have a daily urine sample. I drink a lot of water before he comes and piss pure white. I get dizzy if I move too fast but am not overly concerned. I still have my coffee and trade an occasional cigarette for some sugar which has to be done on the sly. I figure if I make it for two weeks, I'll be OK, I'll go the distance.

They also came to U.D.C. me today, telling me nothing new except they must notify the district I live in upon my release. They said it's part of the new crime bill. I think its a crock of shit. They tell me my release date is August 16th but I know it is August 30th. Rejects and bums these damned cops are. I'm sure if you look in my file you'll find "Asshole" written across the top of it in big red letters.

I am at a loss for now. I don't know who to write or what to do. So, I won't eat. Screw it. I've got a feeling it means nothing to any of the staff here except perhaps the P.A.

I read Chaucer's *Canterbury Tales* and have a distinct memory of listening to Steely Dan and reading this literary masterpiece.

I received a letter from dear, sweet Momma today. Now that Diane has fluttered into the past like dust on a windy day, her memory burns forever in the hollow place that lies in my heart. I sent her a poem and a letter consisting of just three words. "*Amour Vincit Omnia*" or "Love Conquers All." I stole it from Chaucer, but he undoubtedly stole it from someone else. I am supposed to be writing something meaningful and worthy, but what? I know that prison sucks and I have resigned myself to the fact that I will lose 108 days, or half my good time.

It sucks to be me.

But you know what?

Tick, tock.

April 5, 1995

The memory of my childhood in Oklahoma comes drifting back to me. And with these memories the memory of the giant cow pasture behind our house. The cow pasture with the fishing pond where I encountered the water moccasin snake.

The great cow pasture was vast and flat. It seemed symbolic of Oklahoma. I've already recounted some of the adventures that occurred in that pasture. Some are etched in my mind forever. Some long forgotten.

The corner of the big cow pasture was half a mile from our property. It had oil pumps in its corner. They were mysterious devices which looked like rocking horses with their perpetual rocking motion. I once heard about a boy getting ripped to pieces playing with these oil rigs.

In the corner of the field were dry creek beds which filled with the spring rains. The creek beds were bare in the dry heat of the summer. In them you could find a wealth of fossils. There were more fossils in the creek beds than I have ever seen in one place.

It was all pretty much uncharted territory. When I struck out that day it was drizzling. An Oklahoma sky is big and when it is gray it is really gray. I found myself with nothing better to do than investigate the mysterious region we had been warned countless times to stay away from. I was alone. It was only a pasture. Closer inspection of the oil rig's monotonously pumping revealed nothing. But as I turned to look out into the field, I saw a little girl about my age. She was in my domain. In the middle of nowhere. I stared at her and she stared back.

She was on my turf.

Or maybe I was on her turf.

"Haven't seen you around here before," I said, like I went there every day.

She was shy. I immediately liked her.

Although she was a girl on my turf, she was also a fellow adventurer. I liked her.

I took her home. We were both soaked. Mom was appalled, but I was delighted. I had a new friend. I remember sitting on my bed with her while mom dried our clothes.

That's all I remember.

I wonder what became of that girl.

So many times in our life we meet people for only a short period of time. Certainly that little girl has forgotten about me. Then again, maybe she remembers me, remembers that chance meeting under the gray, drizzling sky of Oklahoma.

I received a letter yesterday from a very courageous young lady friend of mine. She is going through a very positive transitional phase in her life. She, very wisely, and unlike millions of today's poor sheep, has decided to conquer her demons. She chose to dredge what tormented her and not run from it, or deny it, but to face it. For this, I give her great credit and immediately sat down and wrote her a full ten page letter covering both sides of a legal pad. In a time when I was having immense difficulties, and even wrote her a short and rude letter, she wrote to tell me of this great accomplishment.

This woman is a very important person in my life. She is one of "Them" that believes in me. And, though it may be a small group, it is the best group in the world to me. The Koran says, "Without hope, man is but an animal." This is true. It is difficult to believe in one's self if you first do not have others who believe in you. I gave this woman a thousand reasons not to believe in me, but she chose to believe in me. Once, during my many travels, she picked me up at an airport. She told me that day she thought one of my problems was that people did not believe in me. It stuck with me. I will never forget it.

Her husband is a also good friend. If you asked him if he was a good friend he would probably deny it, but if you pressed him he might admit to a partial acquaintance. It's kind of like when I read Howard Stern's book and started in the middle and read it to the end, and then started in the beginning and read it to the middle point where I started. That way I could deny reading the book all the way through.

There are those who like to get involved in something controversial but can't make any forthright decision or stand behind either side of an issue. And there are others who will choose which side of the controversy they support and stand behind it. There are still others who try to avoid controversy altogether. I admit my friendship was somewhat thrust upon my friend and that we had our differences. But we went through a lot. While rock climbing one day, I watched him plunge over 100 feet off a cliff. Miraculously, he lived. Whether or not I had something to do with saving his life is irrelevant. God's will or something like that.

Anyway, it was very nice to hear from this lady and it is always good to hear about an almost superhuman achievement. In this day and age, as I wrote to her, most people would simply fall over, curl up in a fetal position, and suck their thumbs. And probably whimper. Three cheers for her. A true woman.

Well, my hunger strike fizzled out yesterday evening. I talked to the Lieutenant who told me I should write to the warden, which I did. I took a cellie because they needed the room. My new cellie smoked all my cigarettes then went to the D.S. this morning.

So, I find myself with a single cell. Bottom bunk, peace and quiet, privacy.

April 9, 1995

It is so nice to have my regular white paper back. For over a week I had to suffer with just legal pad paper.

Many things are going on in the outside world. My grandmother is very ill. And my Diane is getting married this year, she claims. I have not heard from her in a long time. I made my once a month call and could only get hold of my brother. He was depressed so I ripped off a sermon-on-the-mount type of letter to him with the hope that he gets things back in perspective. I sent out nine Easter cards. Most important, I wrote a medium sized length letter to my father.

I am enjoying a hot cup of Joe. I never could figure out why coffee got the nickname Joe. I've drunk myself batty with coffee this weekend.

All the orderlies got fired leaving me with no direct link with Mike. This shut off my drug supply from my dog, so I'm back on strange hours. One orderly is a young kid that couldn't be more than 19. I asked him his name and he replied, "They call me Diane." Such a waste of a man. Not only is he young, homosexual and in prison, he's also devout.

It takes all kinds I guess. Diane was a good orderly, though. He'd bring hot water for coffee and pass things from cell to cell unerringly. To get hot water in the cell, a piece of paper, or preferably an empty Taster's Choice bag, is slid through the crack in the door frame. The hot water is then poured through. Otherwise its the old Bunsen burner on the toilet seat trick. Empty milk cartons and all that.

I wrote a couple of decent poems. I wrote several short letters to send off in my Easter cards. Must get the full 32 cents worth, don't you know.

I am currently stimulating my mind with *Tim*, an excellent piece of literary genius written by Colleen McCullough, author of *The Thorn-birds*. A very good book. As I am all by myself in this cell, conversation is fairly limited. Today I surprised myself by laughing out loud. It was a deep chuckling kind of laugh. I had almost forgotten what true laughter sounded like. Yes, I definitely recommend *Tim* to any reader.

I expect to see the DHO this week and shuffle on over to Disciplinary Seg. To prepare myself for this I have hidden a little over four packs of cigarettes in a clean, but otherwise empty, conditioner bottle. I also placed the larger portion of an 8 oz. bag of coffee into my mouthwash bottle. Whether or not these items will make it remains to be seen. I also have cigarettes hidden in my paperwork.

Forget going without over there. I did 34 days of that last time. This time I'm prepared. They can't give me more than 14 days, of which I will serve 7. Hopefully. I have not received a blue copy of my U.D.C. hearing telling me what they will recommend yet. Cowards.

Most importantly, I am becoming increasingly anxious as each day to the door draws closer. I have spoken to both the psychologist and the psychiatrist about putting me on something so I can get some sleep. Two years to go and I am already bouncing off the walls. I shudder to think of my pulse rate when I can begin to count the days. I take my time now in monthly increments. Only when I get to two or three months will I actually begin to count the days.

Kerabe? (Do you have peace?)

Kera Dorong. (Peace only)

Fend Kilivg dorong leh warrata ka otch tee. (Behold, the only thing greater than yourself)

Mandinka.

April 11, 1995

The following are excerpts from a letter to a woman friend.

I have the capability to be brutish. All females are fairly delicate. It is a female attribute that has been carefully cultivated and indeed encouraged throughout history. Maybe because it makes us men feel that much stronger. I have always felt that I was emotionally strong, stronger than most without question. One of the countless curses in life is that I can be unfeeling, uncaring, even apathetic towards someone's weaknesses. This stems from my seemingly apparent self-centeredness which is actually a result of my long years of independence. This coupled with my "I am an island," added to my deep philosophical searching, then mixed a little with my metaphysical talents. This makes me a very confusing individual indeed. Even though I am familiar with most aspects of my mind, there is an unpredictability about me which is always compounded when I drink.

I once figured out it is much better to listen in a conversation if you want to learn something. Because anything you say, you already know.

But to distinguish what we need to learn from what we already have learned, we must ask questions about what we don't know.

I don't know about my Christ-self. That's a little much. (She said she experienced my Christ-self when making love to me). I don't compare mortals in any sense to Christ, except that they are born of His breath, and pass with His tears. I do know that I have some Prince Charming attributes, and I am aware of my animal-like sexual nature. I daresay, I may even have an ability to captivate one. I hate to sound a little vain, so that is where the credit to myself ends. My bad qualities always seem to far outweigh my good ones. But that is not reflected with a cursory acquaintance, nor even with an intimate relationship. For my demons are both within and without. My battles to balance my spirit (which when balanced correctly gives me the ultimate inner peace) lie not merely in a conscious and subconscious level, but my wars rage on several different planes. This is what makes me both conflicting, confusing, and outside the realm of common understanding.

This is the most I have spoken to you of such matters. I hope it helps you to understand a little why some things about me are so complex and others are so simple. I struggle to conquer what appears to others to be small things, but the true relevance of such things are actually vastly important to me.

Sigh.

Probably sounds like so much babble to you. Life truly interests me, possibly to a further extent and on a much deeper level than others. (Did prison do this to me?) For example, it fascinates me when people compare themselves to others. It is entirely a mute point, as there will always be others greater and lesser than one's self.

April 17, 1995

I made it into Disciplinary Seg with my cigarettes. I actually got away with six and a half packs. But the coffee never made it.

That was six days ago. I saw the DHO and he graciously gave me ten days, but then ungraciously took five days of my good time. Easter came and hopped away again yesterday. They brought us hard boiled eggs for Easter breakfast. I saved mine and then soaked them in the grape Kool-Aid they brought for lunch. I therefore made my own Easter Eggs. They came out pretty good with a purple color and somehow a light blue pattern of cracks spread all over them.

"Only Sean could do something like that," the orderly said.

I have a pretty good cellie now. Like most people you meet in the federal system, he's been in jail forever.

"Prison has changed a lot," he tells me.

I questioned him further and he explained it like this.

"There used to be honor," he said. "Mostly nobody told, now everyone's a rat. It used to be when things were done, they were done right. The white guys looked out for the white guys, the black guys looked out for the black guys and the Hispanics looked out for the Hispanics. It seems like now everybody just screws every one else and the only question is who's first."

This only served to strengthen my belief that the criminal element has gone to hell. The other day on the radio they said, "Nearby Eagleview Penitentiary houses 800 of the most violent criminals in the nation." I laughed out loud when I heard that. What they should have said was "Eagleview Penitentiary houses 800 of the biggest junkies in the nation." I've never seen so many people in one place hooked on heroin. The Captain walks around here like this place is so tough, when in actuality, everybody is laughing at him and thumbing their noses because the compound is flooded with drugs. It's a joke.

There are lessons to be learned and some of them are hard and at other's expense. The first and most primary lesson is "Don't trust anybody." One example would be a guy asking you to give him a crime so he can confess. If he confesses to an unsolved crime, he can go to a county jail and has a better chance of escaping. It's been done. More likely though, the guy would rat you out to get a reduced sentence. You've got to be more than cautious. More times than not, it'll be the last guy in the world that you thought would turn you in. Another lesson is to never get involved with anything that isn't your business. If it sounds too good to be true, it probably is.

These two lessons were shown to me in a story I heard from a guy in here named Billy.

Billy was in Clayton for years and was finally ready to leave and go to Raybrook. Things were going real good for him. Before he left he was approached by an Italian guy who told him to look up a friend named Jimmy at Raybrook. The Italian guy told him that Jimmy would take good care of him.

When Billy arrived at Raybrook he was put in the same unit as Jimmy and before long Jimmy approached him and asked for a favor. He said that Steve, his cellmate, owed him $150,000 but was balking on paying it. He said Steve was terrified of guys from Clayton and asked Billy to scare Steve into making him pay the money.

Billy didn't want to get involved but Jimmy told him that he would give him $20,000 if he scared Steve into paying him. He told him he would send it to Billy's teenage son.

Billy didn't want to get his son caught up in the whole thing but $20,000 was too much money to decline. So he told Jimmy he would scare Steve. When Billy got Steve in his cell all alone he put an ice pick against his head.

"If that money ain't there by Friday your dead," Billy told him.

Jimmy told Billy that he did a good job and that Steve was scared. But Billy was worried that Steve would rat on him. Jimmy assured him that Steve would not rat.

At lunch one day the guards called Billy's name. Billy knew they didn't know what he looked like and started to edge out of the lunch area. But they spotted him and took him away and put him in the hole. Jimmy was put in the cell next to him with Steve.

Jimmy told Billy that he had everything under control. From his room Billy could see the interrogation room and men in dark suits in the room. They soon came and took him into the room.

The men were F.B.I. agents and they asked Billy what he knew about extortion and bad checks. Billy told them he didn't know anything. They put him back in his cell and took Jimmy in for questioning. He was in there about twenty minutes. When he came out they took Steve in for questioning. Steve was in there about an hour.

When they were finished with Steve they split all three of them up and didn't let them near the phones. Billy was praying the money wasn't hot. He was locked up in solitary confinement for a month. After he came out he went to the law library and looked up extortion and found that the sentence for it starts at thirty years. He felt he was really screwed.

The F.B.I. agents came back to see him again but he didn't tell them anything.

"We got you now Billy-Boy," one fed kept telling him. "And when we nail you, we're putting you away for a long time."

Billy didn't doubt it one bit.

After a few months he got a phone call from his ex-wife, the mother of his teenage son. She was yelling and angrier than hell. She told him that her son had received a Federal Express package with a certified check in it for $150,000. Her son was not there to accept it and she had signed for it. She freaked out when she opened the package and saw the check. There was a letter from an attorney with the check and she called the attorney and he told her some things and mentioned Billy's name.

His wife tore-up the check and mailed it back to the attorney by certified mail. This saved Billy. When she told Billy about the incident she was yelling at him over the telephone. Billy told her he loved her but she hung up on him.

"This saved me," Billy told me. "She didn't know it but she saved me."

The next time Billy saw the feds, he knew they didn't have anything on him.

"Everyone got shipped to different joints and that was the end of it. But if that check ever got cashed I'd be doing some serious time, probably life."

April 20, 1995

April is ticking by and this is my last night in Disciplinary Seg. Tomorrow I'll go to Administrative Detention to wait for my transfer. It's going to be a long wait. Possibly all summer. I don't mind, though. It's only time.

I find myself writing less these spring days. As I am locked away from the compound, I really have no insight as to what's going on out there. I only pick up little pieces here and there. The compound is flooded with heroin which is nothing new. Some crack, that's new. I'm really glad I never got wrapped up in the drug scene. Guys are chasing that bag all the time.

I spoke to the psychologist on a couple of occasions. The last time I spoke with him, I found myself intrigued. I spoke in generalities about my alcohol problem. Mostly, I've been experiencing sleep disorders because my time table is completely reversed. I wake up at 4:00 PM and I'm up until about 5:00 AM.

What the psychologist said that interested me most was that he thought that I drank because I had a mental block. This made sense to me. Alcohol changed me into a different person. It had its drawbacks, but the good points outweighed the bad ones. Booze gave me courage, confidence and sparked new ideas. I've never been a great speaker, but with juice, I could speak smoothly and easily.

It's all about being aware and what I'm aware of now is that I have the capacity to do these things, and be this way, without the use of alcohol. I used booze as a tool to break this mental block and lower my inhibitions. It was a great relationship, but now I know that I no longer need whiskey to be the man I want to be. That doesn't mean that I'll never drink again. But I can realize the reason I drank and know I can succeed without it. I can adjust my actions accordingly. It's really so simple. I can't imagine how I never saw it before.

So, I learn something every once in a while.

I've recently been writing a lot of letters. If you write enough, you will eventually get some back. Sometimes I'll get a totally unexpected letter out of the blue. Any mail is good mail though. There's a feeling in here that if you don't get any mail one day it means "No one loves me." If neither you nor your cellie get mail, the feeling is modified accordingly to "No one loves us." It is with this feeling that I pace the floor after the 4:00 PM feeding.

"Does any one love us today?" I ask my cellie.

"Naw," he says.

This horrifies me and I frantically write letter after letter in the hopes that when the mail does come, I will find that indeed, somebody still loves me.

The Stinking Man prowls the confines of his captivity chamber. He strolls nonchalantly the few paces searching for a victim. Across the captivity chamber, he spots his prey.

He pauses.

"Why you lookin' at me like that, Sean?"

The Stinking Man casually strolls towards the end of the captivity chamber, where the victim lies unknowing, reading a book. He pauses near the victim only to turn on his heel and walk away. He is building the confidence of the victim.

He turns again, circulating the captivity chamber. The moment is near. He reaches the victim and casually turns and detonates. PPPPFFFFFF!!! The Stinking Man flees.

"You bastard, you goddamned bastard!"

The Stinking Man, able to annihilate entire galaxies with the lift of a cheek if he so chooses, has struck again. Tune in for further adventures of the Fabulous Farter, the Sultan of Stink, the God of Gas, the Father of Flatulence. The Stinking Man!!!

April 28, 1995

T he world sleeps and the prisoner reflects.

I am now in a cell on Administrative Detention. I find myself celled up with my old pal Cameron, who I've known him since my F.C.I. days. We've done almost a year and a half of time together.

Pop music now drones on the radio. Cameron has always liked country music, and I have acquired a taste for it. It is good we listen to a variety of music because we can only pull in a few stations. Clayton and other prisons are nearby and the radio keeps us updated on incidents that occur in them. It seems like the news flashes only come early in the morning during our "wake" time.

I hear over the radio news that shots were recently fired at Clayton over a knife fight in the yard. Here in Eagleview a man was stabbed "a lot of times" in the neck. They were trying to kill him but failed. The news reports incidents when shots are fired because this violates local laws and must be reported to the police. The news also reports incidents which send prisoners to outside hospitals when they're too messed up (or too dead) to be taken care of inside.

I've read in the newspaper about casualty reports of surrounding penitentiaries. The reports are incredibly understated and you can't believe what they say. I do believe the convict who told me he knew of twenty people killed at Clayton in the three and a half years he was there. Along with the killings, he also told me that there had been a couple hundred stabbings. That's why they call Clayton the Graveyard. It's a serious place.

I try not to think about all this. I keep trying to see the forest without getting lost in all the trees. I try to focus on the real world, the world that matters. Inside these walls lurks evil in its purest form.

Human life stripped of all pride and all amenities. The real world is only memories.

Here apathy flourishes. Contempt spawns a bleakness that people in the real world, the world that matters, could never comprehend. Perhaps people on the outside see a small glimpse of it in the homeless woman begging for change. Maybe they brush the outer edges of the world in here when they see the wino with the thousand yard stare, shuffling along with no particular direction or purpose.

It is so easy for people in the real world to simply avert their eyes, and turn away, and subconsciously deny the image access to their memory banks. In these walls there is hopelessness, there is life with no parole, there is AIDS, there is rape, there is heroin addiction, there is death. And there is madness.

I believe that any exposure to this environment results in some degree of madness. How the real world defines madness is different, altogether, from how it is perceived in here. Here the word "valuable" becomes confusing. Value is an ever changing thing. A pack of cigarettes on a Tuesday is not as valuable as a pack of cigarettes on Sunday night. A carton of cigarettes is certainly worth stabbing somebody over.

Your mind becomes the most valuable thing in your entire existence. It is your mind that keeps you from being killed. Your mind screams "Survive!" and you must comply. A chance look at the wrong person, on the wrong day, after he's had the wrong phone call, could spell doom.

It goes on and on and on. Day after day. Every single day. Week after week. Every single week. Month after month. Year after year. Footprints of misery following a path that only leads to insanity or death.

I try not to think about all of this.

Instead, I try to remember.

I try to remember what it was like to leave work on Friday afternoon with the whole weekend to myself. I try to remember the fun times at the beach with my friends, drinking beer. I struggle to recollect the holidays with my family. I try to remember what it was like to touch a woman, to be held, to kiss. What if I forget how to kiss? I try to remember the laughter, the joys of just being free.

I remember hugging my little girl at Christmas of 1992. I remember her little girl scent. I try to focus on what it was to have responsibility.

To drive a car. I try to remember what it was like to help other people. Helping them move furniture when they changed their residence. Giving an unfortunate person a couple of dollars at the beach. I remember playing my guitar in the sand at the beach with the waves crashing. I try to remember what it was like to feel pride in a job well done. To feel tired after a long day. I try to remember encouragement, people that believed in me. I try to remember that warm feeling of contentment that comes from sitting around the wood stove, or the fireplace, with good company. I try to remember her sweat, mixed with mine, and the way our bodies fit together like we were created for no other purpose. I try to remember looking into her brown eyes, looking into her as deeply as she was looking into me, and feeling that closeness, that oneness that bonds two people together. I remember looking up at the stars and the moon and feeling so small and the private talks that I'd have with God when I sought solace and consolation.

That world is so far removed from me now. I grip my memories with all the fervor of a seaman clinging to a lifesaver adrift in the ocean. Sometimes I become desperate, like the time I started to forget the names of friends and had to write them on a piece of paper to keep from forgetting them. That was bad.

I love life. I want mine back.

For now, though, I just fight becoming institutionalized. To me, the meaning of the word "institutionalized" means you accept that you have to do an amount of time, and you bow and grovel to the cops, and comply with everything, for fear of reprimand. I will not comply because I do not accept the ideals of incarceration. Period. Incarceration is a mind trip. Unless you have a ridiculously short amount of time, you will be permanently altered.

The system is designed to either entirely break the will of the convict or turn him into a monster. Maybe it's designed to do both. And also make money for the system. But I don't even want to get started on this vein. The only thing you can really do to fight the system is to try to beat the mind-trip, to reduce the amount of alteration of your mind to a minimum. You must stay focused. Some of the ways I've changed are for the better. I take note and make myself aware. No changes are abrupt. Most are slow and gradual.

Sometimes a guy will just snap and try to hang himself or cut himself. Like this fellow I know called Zarf who was unstable to begin with. Zarf had tattoos on his head and when he came to the hole he snapped and started hacking away at his leg. He'd stab it with pencils and shove human feces into the wounds. He refused all medical treatment. When he went to see the barber, who was my cellie at the time, Zarf showed him his leg which had putrefied.

"I want to win, I want to win," my barber friend told me Zarf kept telling him.

Zarf was shot out. Do you think they did a good job trying to rehabilitate him? Do you think he had hope in the future that someday he would be free and happy? There was no hope for Zarf. His sentence was too long and he simply gave up. For him there was only one way to be free, to win, to beat the system. To "win" Zarf wanted to kill himself, piece by piece.

You see, the Bureau of Prisons does not want you to die, believe it or not. They want you to stay alive to do that next thirty, forty, fifty years. And, they maintain that their power is absolute. You lose because you are a loser. There is only one way to "win," only one way to beat the Bureau out of the complete control of your life. And that way is to die.

It seems harsh and almost unreal doesn't it? You say that you don't believe it? There is a lot in common between convicts in penitentiaries and people who have served in the military during war. Maybe the vets would castrate me, but I think its true. The B.O.P. is a government branch, and they mostly have military or ex-military personnel in it. Death is a very real threat that could strike at any moment of any day.

There is an audible tension sensed by the entire body. Radios crackle all day. When an actual incident occurs, they "hit the deuces" and a hundred police run stampeding to the area the altercation is in. Like the military there is rank among police. C.O.s are "Correctional Officers" instead of "Commanding Officers." There are scores of Lieutenants. A Captain heads up this or that. Every cop with a title has its initials capitalized like the military. For example, the S.O.E., Superintendent (or something) of Education. The A.W.s are Assistant Wardens. Everything is structured.

Convicts know what I'm talking about. I think the major difference is that a soldier is a noble character and one who has chosen to fight or serve, whether from patriotism or self-satisfaction. A soldier goes into combat willingly, with courage in his blood and glory in his eyes. Yes, there is courage here, but the convict is thrust into a world of chaos, insanity and apathy, not by choice, but by punishment. Some, like soldiers, adapt better than others.

But the biggest difference between soldiers and convicts is honor. A convict has no sense of the word. And if they do, it is an extremely twisted interpretation of honor. The head cheeses are that way because they push dope, and whoever has the most dope gets the most respect and the most money. If one were to adhere to the true and traditional aspects of honor like honesty, integrity, and courage, and the tenacity to pursue these traits, he would be quickly killed. There are probably veterans who are convicts who remember honor. But, like I said, the definition of honor in prison is far different than the definition of honor in the military.

The sun is now up. I've been writing for two hours and I'm exhausted. The prisoner goes to sleep while the rest of the world begins to wake up.

May 11, 1995

Thunderdome exists.

It is here in the penitentiaries.

Those movie scenes where the man tapes two knives to his hands and goes into battle is very real. The federal prison system is smaller than people think. Subsequently, when a gladiator makes a stand, or a "Thunderdome" situation occurs, it gets around.

One "Thunderdome" situation existed out in California at Lompoc and the story was related to me by an Orange County Hammerskin. The Hammerskins are an elite racist group who accept few into their ranks.

"The kid had heart a mile wide, he liked to get icy (do coke, slam coke) a little too much. But he taped up when they came for the cash and it was Thunderdome dude. Knives, pipes, everything went. And in the middle of it all stood this kid. A knife taped to each hand screaming, 'Come on, you mothers, come on!' and dude he made it out."

The kid was only about twenty-two. Not long after the "Thunderdome" he was violently killed. Different messages are conveyed according to the way you are killed. Generally, if you are killed in your own cell, the message is that you were killed by one of your own race. In this case, the kid was stabbed at least a hundred times and his eyes were punctured. He didn't pay his bills. He was a kid. He had nothing. He just liked to get high and try to forget about the disgustingly long sentence the government gave him. He went hard.

I am now awaiting my disciplinary transfer. I've been sitting in Administrative Detention since March 9th and only five more days until the month is half gone.

It's been raining and the little patch of grass that was dead and brown outside my window has turned thick and green. I've been going out to the dog kennels with my cellie on nice days and getting some sun. The latest news on the Oklahoma bombing is that they will seek the death penalty against McVeigh. He's in a federal holdover place that is visited by practically every federal prisoner who gets the opportunity to travel.

Mail comes less and less these days. The trickle of mail that does come under the door is mostly stuff I have sent away for: music catalogs, magazines, letters from the Region. Recently I sent away for my sentence computation form. When I received it, I discovered that there were horrendous mistakes and that by my estimates they owed me at least 50 days. Who knows when I will hear about that.

I totally shaved my beard off. I do this when it gets to the point of being annoying. I've grown a few in the past couple of years and have begun to grow another one. This may be the last one. I might have one or two more in me.

There are fifteen and a half months left now. Sometimes, in perspective, it seems like such a short amount of time. But sometimes it seems like an absolute eternity. Sometimes I wish I could just close my eyes and dream sweet dreams for a year. As I often find myself doing, I wonder where I will be next year at this time.

May 17, 1995

By my own estimate, I have been in the hole for about one hundred and seventeen days this year. My mind is like a washing machine with thoughts loaded inside like so much laundry. People push buttons and my musings are then sloshed around. Sometimes I just spin.

Even my reverse schedule has been upset. Now I get up at 9:30 PM and stay up until whenever. It makes me angry that I am not on a 12/12 cycle. I like to sleep for 12 hours a day thereby robbing the Bureau of Prisons of half of my sentence. It makes me feel smug.

I've been in the dungeon since Friday, the same day I received a nice letter from home. I haven't received any mail since Friday.

The Bureau of Prisons answered all my letters and politely told me to bug off. I made requests about my sentence computation. I felt they were robbing me of about 40 days. I appealed to the inmate systems board. I also appealed the good time they took from me. I also filed on my lost property and am waiting to hear more on my tort claim. I wrote letters requesting my transfer of supervision to California. I am the proverbial bug in the ear, the thorn in their paw, the squeaky wheel screeching for grease.

In this case the squeaky wheel may just get nothing.

May 18, 1995

Drunk, drunk, drunk.

The squeaky wheel got hammered up yesterday.

My old cellie Tom went to A.D. and my new cellie moved over and brought two gallons of rocket fuel with him. After months of stress and bullshit, it was good to just get juiced and hang out and rap with Tony.

The cell looked like a scene out of *Apocalypse Now* and I once woke up to catch Tony pissing on the wall. We both had vicious hangovers. Tony, in a superhuman feat, drank a quart this morning that was left over in my cup. I passed out on the floor smoking a cigarette and cranking my radio with my homemade speakers. The screw came back and said the Assistant Warden was coming by and asked me to at least try to stand up. That was the last I remember, besides Tony pissing on the wall. I don't believe I was standing when the A.W. came by.

After Tony passed out, I wrote a stupid poem to Diane in a moment of weakness and mailed it. I put a stamp on it and tried to get the hack to take it, but he eyed me suspiciously as I stood there swaying with cup in hand.

"Go lay down with your drunk ass," he said.

I attempted to cuss him out but could only manage an unintelligible grunt. I was having fun.

I've taken a shower and eaten a little breakfast. I took a vitamin along with multiple cups of coffee. I'm unsure if I can eat lunch as I'm still recovering. Tony is already planning our next mission. We are waiting for them to come in and shake down so we can go up with our next batch.

It feels good to once again get one over on the system. Yesterday I laughed deeply and sincerely for the first time in months.

It was a long laugh.

May 24, 1995

There are clouds out my window but it is still a hot day with temperatures reaching into the 80s. Today there is no outside rec.

I am still in disciplinary segregation but will be going back to Administrative Detention. I have filed for a Hardship Transfer stating that I have only had one visit in the past sixteen months. The counselor just came to the door with my 8 1/2 Administrative Remedy Procedure Form.

Their response was that I was transferred to this institution for disciplinary reasons. I'll retort that I was already too far from my people at the institution to which I was designated. I'll also tell them that the disciplinary measures consisted of transferring me from a medium to a maximum security institution. Must I be further punished by not being allowed to do my sentence within a reasonable distance from my family?

I'm so sick of the Bureau of Prisons and all it entails. Instead of some fine oiled mechanism spewing forth justice, dealing in remedies, assuring the convict is pacified to an acceptably humane level, individual characteristics play more into the scheme of things. Personal differences, racism, and discrimination rule with reckless abandon. Some screws give prison snitches preferred treatment. Other screws cater to the convict. The former are beneath contempt. The latter will give respect if it is given to them.

I despise my unit team, my counselors and those who are responsible for my paperwork. I have always held contempt for those who actually control other people's lives. To do so with dedication and the belief you are doing right is one thing. But to be in a position of power and do your job poorly, or in a discriminatory manner, is totally disgusting. In my case, it's blatantly obvious that I've been flagged as a hard case. To this, I bare my posterior and flatulate.

I am beyond rage, beyond anger, beyond denial, beyond disgust. I am at the epicenter of apathy. All this shit that happens to me inside these walls is exactly that, a bunch of shit. I've learned my lesson about a couple of years ago. I don't imagine I'll be turning back to crime. I find it repugnant and contradictory that the system jams itself down one's throat to the point where it breeds disgust and almost demands some type of reprisal.

You've got to look beyond all this to where freedom lies and this daily control is just a thing of the past. You've gotta look beyond the bullshit to the day you can laugh the deep, hearty laugh that only freedom and happiness brings. When you can look over their heads and tolerate the day-to-day grind and wear on your mind, can tolerate it because you can see beyond it, this makes you a winner and this puts you on top.

All I can do is try to get a little up on them every chance I can. I smuggled my radio down here to disciplinary seg by an ingenious little harness which puts it behind my scrotum. I've got plenty of cigarettes and even drink a little wine once every couple of months. Actually, I've only drunk twice this year. One time was on my birthday and the other time was the other day, with my old cellie who just left. I guess I've gone soft. I just scribble my little words down and write my letters.

The hell with letting all the despair and oppression take over. These characteristics come in waves. Some waves are bigger than other waves. But, as with all things, they wash out into tiny bubbles and sink into the sand to be washed over again with a myriad of other thoughts.

June 2, 1995

We are experiencing what the weatherman in Pennsylvania calls "torrential downpours." Before the rains started we had a few days of outside rec and these were nice. Last Thursday I went out and played handball and beat poor Tom 3-1. The cages were particularly animated with the life breathing exhilaration and fervor that fresh air and sunshine bring.

But there was a solemn note also. On Wednesday a man died upstairs here in the hole from a heart attack. His cellie repeatedly pushed the "panic button," but the cops, characteristically, did not show up for a while. In this case, it was too long.

Once again death rears its head in the prison system. Only this time, it quietly took an old man in the night, without all the violence and blood that usually proceeds death in the penitentiary.

Too long in this goddamned cell. I guess, not really, when I look at it in perspective. But the dull grudge of repetitiveness tends to grate on you after a while. June is here though. It is another important month. When it is over, half the year has evaporated into that fine gray mist of dead prison time.

I begin to look more towards my freedom and my future. I speculate about wasting hours in the sun at the beach. Maybe forming a band. I keep trying to visualize a girl. I know that there is someone special out there for me somewhere. Or, am I destined to a life of bachelorhood? Too many unanswered questions. Too much uncertainty.

The shrink tells me I'm pretty together in the marble department. But he also tells me I'll be very paranoid when I get out. I imagine he means paranoid about coming back in. I believe his warning is true and must now take preventive measures to deal with this. Who wants to walk around a paranoid nervous wreck? The solution is simple. I will utilize an amount of all this time I have and think. I'll anticipate and develop scenarios and solutions to situations. I'll start with the obvious ones, and when those get boring, I'll dwell on the inane. It's a psychological preventive, self assurance technique developed by ancient Indians. It sounds good anyway.

I wrote about twenty letters in the last few weeks. This week I only got one back. It wasn't even from any of the people I wrote.

I got weak and finally wrote Diane after three months of no contact. Much to my dismay and consternation, she seems to have disappeared off the face of the earth. But the loss of a loved one, or someone we deeply care about, are things the prisoner learns to deal with. I have always considered myself an altruist and it is strange to have to learn how to detach myself. Even in prison I have a soft spot for the guys who don't have anything, or the ones who are really messed up and having a bad time. Is this altruism a curse or a blessing?

But nonetheless, I've grown accustomed to my isolation. All experiences produce lessons. The lessons are there if we wish to grasp them. I find myself asking what this test of loneliness is meant to produce. From the system's point of view, I guess I am supposed to be "learning a lesson." But I piss on their perspective. It is what I can draw from this experience to use to my advantage that concerns me.

The human psyche is very flexible and adaptable. I've learned patience. I've learned to converse with myself on these pages with these words. I've learned acceptance in the sense that when life deals you a shitty hand and forces you to play it, then play the damned thing. But that doesn't mean you've got to bet the hand. Ride out the rough waves and surf the good ones. Throw out a life preserver once in a while if you have to.

And always remember those magical words of the Good Book: This too shall pass.

June 5, 1995

I suppose there is no denying any longer that I've been on a serious drinking bender for the past couple of weeks. Alcohol has come back to me with open arms, offering her shoulder and patting me on the head saying, "There, there now, it's OK, Sean, everything's gonna be all right." I sniffle and gratefully accept the two-faced bitch's comfort.

I wonder why I do this. Is it my interminable lack of self-discipline? Is it such a weakness to break down and get drunk after such a lengthy period of solitary? Does it really matter? It's not like the letters are flooding in under my door from all the people who care about me.

Before I try to justify my actions with excuses, let me first answer my own question. Of course it matters. Where does self-discipline begin? And what about "Be true to thine own self" and all of that? The answer to this dilemma, I believe, lies in a balancing of the scales. I agonize over what I feel is the injustice of sweating out time boxed into confinement. It seems a ridiculous punishment to crime ratio. I agonize over my sobriety. I drink and agonize over my non-sobriety. I suppose it involves a selection of the lesser of two evils. Who are you to judge? What could possibly happen to me getting smashed, locked in a 12 x 8 cell?

Isn't this why I'm here? Society does not trust me to drink among the innocents. So they put me in a little box, inside a bigger box, that's surrounded by triple fences and guard towers with guns. With the key snug in their pocket, they tell the innocents, "You are safe, there is no way he can possibly attain the same levels of consciousness in that little box we've got him in as he did out there."

As far as my current situation, I am in the Twilight Zone. I'm neither here nor there and extremely uncertain about my future. I am the steel ball spinning around the roulette table. Black or red? Even or odd? Worse than this, I wonder if the table is rigged.

Jimmy Page is whaling his solo to "Livin, Lovin, She's Just A Woman" and right now, life is groovy. I've grown my beard back and even got a haircut. It takes me years to grow any length of hair and I've lost a good four inches. My head feels lighter and the heat of the approaching summer is not so bad.

The weather here is weird. Torrential downpours one day are followed by sunshine and heat the next day. The sun was out today and it was fairly hot. I played handball outside against Tom. The final score was even with each of us winning two games. I've seen some good sunsets here in Pennsylvania, but I sure as hell would not want to live here.

June 14, 1995

I am celled up with my Nazi friend, John. He is a true Nordic Aryan and the walls are covered with Aryan/Klan/Skinhead sayings. A poster of Hitler now glares down at me from the wall above the desk where I write.

Tomorrow marks the halfway point of the month. It will be much better at the end of June when half the year is gone. Overall, time seems to be picking up the pace a little. Some days and hours are slower than others. Weeks seem to click by with astounding rapidity. I often find myself scratching my head and asking, "It's Thursday already?" or "The weekend's over?" Sometimes minutes just drag by. I have to admit that my little drinking binge helped kill some time. I'm trying to hit the good doctor up for a sleeping medication called Vistoril.

I'm currently reading *Spycatcher* by Peter Wright. It is the "book that Britain banned" and is about a ring of five spies: Philby, Burgess, MacLean, Blunt. Who could the fifth spy possibly be? Wright points his finger at Hollis. I think it was Peter Wright.

I'm finally getting weekly phone calls after six months of one call a month. I'm trying to get a hold of Diane, but she's no where to be found. What can I do? I received two letters yesterday from the two Suzies.

June 21, 1995

Today is the first day of summer. The marker for another increment of time. I have 61 weeks and a day left before I go home. Next week, on the 29th of June, I will have 60 weeks. Thirty weeks from then, I'll have thirty weeks left. Pish-posh you say? Far from it, my friend. For these careful calculations are the sum of my life's incarceration. Nothing to be pishing or poshing about.

I find myself writing less and less upon these pages. Perhaps I am already trying to avoid memoirs of these long and lonely days. I have never really accomplished what I wished this book to convey. When I started it I lacked the vision of what it should encompass. Certainly, I have not said all there is to be said or described all there is to describe. At times I have smoothed over the true somberness of prison life and have written nonsense on page after page. It is possible that I had wished to consider myself some sage, locked away in a prison cell, spewing forth wise philosophies with great depth.

The hardest thing to battle in prison is yourself and your conflicting emotions. On one hand, you reject adapting and acceptance. On the other, you accept rejection and try to adapt to it.

Cut off from ready access to liquor, money and drugs, your mind clears and you begin to grow again. It attains a clarity you never sensed you possessed. All things buried come to the surface and must be dealt with accordingly. There is no warning. There is no running, no denying, and absolutely no help anywhere. It is time to pay the piper for all your shameless deeds.

So, prepare yourself for a very tough war. You might fight and win small battles in prison. But you must win the big war within yourself to survive.

June 22, 1995

The weather is rather pleasant today. It is warm and breezy, although gray and overcast. I judge the warmth by the radio D.J.s proclamation and the breeziness by the dance of the fiddle heads outside of my window.

I phoned home like E.T. last night and spoke to Mom. My brother is going through an extremely difficult time, so I sat down and scratched out a letter and tried to fill it with constructive and uplifting words. For all the bullshit that my older brother and I went through, I believe we've both come too far to give up on each other. I have a strong belief in family unity. It was my Aunt Betty who instilled this characteristic inside me. Even though she has a large family of her own, she never turned me away from her when I needed a place to stay.

July 14, 1995

It has been some time since I last wrote. One of the reasons is the time my new job takes up. I have been "given" the orderly job at Eagleview in SHU or segregation. After four months of laying on my back in the hole and only a couple of weeks on the orderly job, my feet took the worst end of it. They are healing up nicely though.

There are over 100 people to feed on my orderly job. I am also in direct contact with the two A.D. ranges which hold about 75 convicts. The 200 range upstairs in the range designated to me and houses only 31. The nuts are all up there.

This range either makes or breaks the orderly and is given to the fresh grunt. The feeding involves loading and unloading over 100 trays. There is also the constant clean up downstairs which has to be cleaned and mopped. On Mondays, sheets, towels, drawers, t-shirts and socks have to be handed out. Everybody wants "good shit." Hot water is passed out every night. Tuesday nights we clean up for inspection on Wednesday. Wednesday night is clothes night again. On Thursdays we clean up for the Liars Parade when counselors, assistant wardens and case managers come through after lunch on Friday. Friday is also the commissary day.

In addition to all of this, the orderly is also responsible for running kites (letters), magazines, cigarettes, wine, newspapers and all kinds of shit from convict to convict. This in itself is very demanding. I've also got a responsibility to the guys on the Disciplinary Seg to run kites for them to A.D. and to get them coffee and cigarettes.

All of this is highly illegal and grounds for instant dismissal. It must be done under the nose of the "man" who is ever watchful. The "man" also uses cameras to help him be watchful. There is a camera mounted to observe the gates of each tier of D.S. range. The office is about 15 feet from these gates and fully glassed in for full scale observation. The towers might observe something at any time and call down here to identify you. When this happens you're shit-canned.

Things get done anyway. I've gotten busted once but that was shortly after they started double shifting me. Now I am head orderly and work from 11:00 AM to around midnight. I am pretty much exhausted, but it feels good to work again and burn up calories.

My disciplinary transfer was denied, so I am still in limbo. My tort claim was also denied. I gave them receipts to the Region as proof and provided much evidence to back me up. They still denied my measly $54 claim for clothes they lost. My counselor made me sign some bullshit paper. I didn't want to sign it at first. But I asked them if it went into my file and they told me it did. So I scribbled "You are crooks" in big letters at the bottom and signed it.

I sent a ghastly letter to the warden. I should probably write him back and apologize for calling him an incompetent fool. But I don't know.

If I keep up this pace and don't screw up, time will fly right by. It already is. Over half the year is gone and now over half of July is almost over.

I received a letter from Diane. It made me very, very happy. I know she really misses me. She is also confused. I let her know exactly how I feel and told her when I said I'd love her forever that forever was what I meant. Whether or not we will ever be together remains in destiny's hands.

I'm so damned tired I can't scribble another word. One last thing. Governor Weld decided to abolish music and art in all Massachusetts State prisons which really pissed me off.

Tick, tock.

July 21, 1995

There was never really any specific time that I actually spent some time thinking about my feelings. Maybe this means something. Most of the time I tried to think about bettering myself by concentrating on being "aware." Also, studying thought processes and thinking patterns. What I forgot, but remembered recently, was that old formula: when I felt like *this*, I did *that*, because it made me feel like (fill in the blank).

My feelings. Personal animals. I realize I spend a lot of time thinking about how other people feel. Possibly, I'm insecure because I want to be liked and want to be accepted by others. It is becoming more and more apparent that society as a whole would consider my childhood a tragedy. I felt unwanted. I felt unloved, and I was sad because I was often spending my time alternating between being punished and being ignored. The victories of my youth were small. When I ran away at the age of twelve it is possible that I felt empty inside, and I was curious to what existed in the rest of the world. When I was twelve and lived in the runaway house in Boston, I learned loneliness and pain were everywhere. When I went to court after my mother found me, she gave me to the custody of the state. Said she couldn't handle me. My fears were fulfilled. I was abandoned. This seriously fertilized my insecurity garden.

One result of this was that I became independent at a young age. I attempted to grasp the concept of life's fluidness. I wanted to know it all and learn as much as I could to protect myself from being hurt. Whenever I got too close to a girl, I would push her away or just drop the relationship. There began to develop a repetitious pattern in my life, a pattern not just in girlfriend type of relationships, but with anybody who cared about me.

I strove to learn through my life about all types of things like music, poetry, literature, plumbing, psychology, weapons, explosives, computers, crime, charity, love, hate, sex, cars, surfing, skiing, chemistry, astrology, history, geology and politics. I wanted to know about everything. I falsely placed myself on this pedestal, like I was some great sage or something.

I had a counselor in a halfway house who utilized a writing exercise for our group. I wrote what I thought was a good paper. Everyone in the group thought it was excellent. But the counselor told me I used my intelligence as a shield to hide behind. At the time I dismissed his opinion because I felt he was incorrect. But it bothered me. Could he have been right?

I'd like to think that I'm more in touch with myself these days. I can't look back and say at this point I was confused. But I can look back and say at this point I was sad, or lonely, or scared. Maybe this is a big step. When you have so much time to utilize positively, you find out there are more questions than answers. I feel like my personal growth is a day to day process. I accept it as such.

Still, I am having a problem. Although I feel it is good I'm doing all this work, I am unable to apply what I learn to "real life" free-world conditions. I can only assuage my doubts by accepting the fact that the work is getting done, that there is progress as I come closer to understanding myself.

This is a good feeling.

And, right now, I feel pretty good.

August 4, 1995

Last night I had the most astounding dream. It was one of the most beautiful things I've ever dreamt.

I was on the beach and the weather was fairly good. I was hanging out with a few people. Suddenly, a rolling, boiling cloud appeared from the left traveling over the ocean. It looked like a speeded up video tape of cloud movement. The turbulent cloud reached a point directly in front of me on the beach and a being somersaulted out of it. Someone shouted, "It's an angel!" and my breath was taken away.

The angel performed a dazzling array of aerobatics.

It was maybe forty feet tall and was made of this cloud like substance. After performing the beautiful aerobatic configurations, it paused. Then, with wings fully spread, it dove straight into the ground and disappeared.

It was the most captivating dream I've ever had.

I told my cellie Todd about it.

"Sean," he told me, "that was God talking to you."

I told Todd I thought he was right. I believe it was a message to me that out of my turmoil, I will eventually find peace.

Life is so amazing.

August 9, 1995

We are now in the thick of summer and the days are hot and muggy.

I am just barely holding on to my orderly job. Lieutenant Splitfoot works days now and they say no orderly has ever survived three weeks under his rigorous, structured, iron hand. I desperately need to survive three more weeks until Lieutenant Angel comes back.

We worked until 11:00 PM tonight to prepare for inspection tomorrow. My case manager was down here today and I spoke to him about getting back to an F.C.I. Specifically, we talked about Sheridan, Oregon and getting myself phased out of this marvelous system.

I've been writing and sending bits and pieces to publishers. One poem I submitted will be published in 1996 in "Treasured Poems of America." I sent a couple songs out to some music companies. They sent me these weak ass recording contracts and I turned them down. I should be hearing from more publishers soon.

I finished my poem "Tale of the Bottled Eye: The Legend of Iron Hand." It is seventy-six verses long. I wanted to submit it to a poetry contest, but my cellie told me it was too valuable and I'd just get ripped off. Right now he's writing his mom and telling her to try to find some big name talent agencies or something. Who knows?

Anyway, I'm happy just to have the one piece published and content with the way my writing is going. I guess it's virtually impossible for a poet to make any money until after he has croaked. So, I guess my legacy lies in the words of this book that might be published someday.

Prison life pushes onward like a bumbling giant. The steps may be heavy, but the movement is at least forward. Todd got busted for passing a razor blade to Disciplinary Seg tonight. Sprout got all sucked up, but Fishman was cool about it. Because Fishman is a Senior Officer Specialist, that's all that matters.

Todd was really bummed out and thought he might lose his job. I'm sure there will be repercussions. It's the asshole's fault who gave him the package. It was supposed to be coffee, smokes and dip, and the guy wanted to get it to his boyfriend on Disciplinary Seg. But he didn't tell Todd it was a "hot one" and to be cautious about passing it. Idiots like him put us right in a cross.

There is always a chance the man's going to catch you. But a good orderly gets things where they are supposed to go. Todd and I had this fairly large, dangerous dude try to extort us. It was mostly me he tried to extort until I let him know what time it was. In the words of some great sage: "I ain't the one."

People that deal in negativity have negativity come back to them. I've seen it before, but it becomes more apparent in this closed environment. I think I've done much better since I've begun thinking positively. One of the real important things I've learned is to spend more time developing your strengths and positive traits rather than dwelling on your troubles and sorrows. It opens up a whole different spectrum and you begin to feel better about yourself as a person.

I do feel better about myself than I did six months ago. I've talked to Mom, Tony, Diane and Tom on the telephone. They all said I sound real good. It make me feel good I'm accomplishing something along the lines of straightening myself out. I also know it makes my friends and family happy. This is really what full circle is about.

There is a cop named Sprout that works weekdays. Being an inmate, and especially an orderly, you get to see these cops day in and day out. You get to know them. A convict will always be a convict and a cop will always be a cop and never the two shall meet. They give us respect and we respect them. Us convicts keep our convict code, and the cops keep their cop code. No matter how good a rapport there is with a cop, there is still a barrier that is not crossed.

Sprout is in his late twenties to early thirties. He is the spitting image of a Boston Gentleman's Quarterly yuppie. He has close cut hair, a beveled watch by Omega and round wire rim glasses. I have caught him babbling enthusiastically about the price of golf clubs, and he has told me that he "surfs the net" whatever the hell this means.

Being from Massachusetts, I get along pretty well with Sprout. But I hound him mercilessly about his Boston accent which is hilariously apparent when he orders us to get the food "caught" or the clothes "caught." His vain attempts at properly enunciating his r's have caused me and my co-workers great pleasure when we mimic his accent.

Sprout is both intelligent and professional. Although I can't help but admire his panache, I can't accept his line of work. In the free world, Sprout is a character I would have seen at parties: a computer geek with a firm grip on reality and an eye for the future. Some people are born with success minded spirits. Some have it inbred. I believe Sprout is a combination of both of these.

Tonight Sprout was pissed off at the razor being passed by Todd. His anger stemmed from fear. I can't say I blame him, but he's kind of naive about stuff like that. No one wants to be on the receiving end of a razor cut, but practically everybody has one for dozens of reasons other than cutting somebody. Sprout will get over it. It's just another example of one of the things that separates "us" from "them." Sprout's smart. He'll figure it out.

August 15, 1995

Todd left on Monday morning and I was sad to see him go. It was maybe the second time I allowed myself to get attached to anybody. But Todd was not anybody. You get to know a guy when you are locked in a cell with him for 17 hours a day and work with him for another 8 hours. Our conversations ranged from personal tragedy to global politics. Now that he's gone, I feel as if I am experiencing the loss of one of my brothers all over again. I'll miss his companionship.

Only sixteen days to go until I can begin the countdown for my final year. Since Todd left, I'm hanging tough with being the only tier orderly for 95 guys doing time forever. I'm sure that half of them are probably lifers. All of them are pissed off at being in the hole.

And all of them know me by my first name.

"Sean!"

"Yo, Sean."

"Sean, I need to see you quick man!"

"Yo, Sean."

"Hey, Sean! 108 man, 108!"

"118, Sean, 118."

"Orderly."

"Yo, Sean."

The tier I live on is A.D. 100 and it holds 50 inmates. The second tier only holds 45. Frosty works in the laundry and was recently promoted to the 200 range. He has what's termed "sepratees" on my range, so he can't come down here. The 200 range used to be my area. All the nuts are up there.

It's hard to get all the assigned work done plus pass newspapers, magazines, cigarettes, batteries, extra clothes and towels, wine and whatever else fits under the damn door.

When the door first breaks, I have to get the counts of where everybody is. Besides A.D. 100 and 200 range, I also set up food carts for Disciplinary Seg. I feed Disciplinary Seg first. Nineteen down and ten up. There are less people up stairs because the food carts have to be hand carried up the stairs. Nineteen regular? No. Seventeen hot, seventeen cold, one common fare and one bag. Juice, bread, plastic gloves. When I'm finished, I roll the carts to Disciplinary Seg. Then I set up A.D. 100 and 200. Let me see: 50 guys minus 2 bag lunches minus two common fares minus me. 46 is the count because Larry gets a bag lunch and a food tray. I set up just the cold trays for A.D. 200.

Then run to fill up a mop bucket and get a broom, dust pan and push broom for D.S. 100. They take turns with the supplies. I time all of this. Then I clean up the mess the day orderlies left, clean the supply closet and ice the milks. When this is done, D.S. is almost fed. Again, by timing, I begin to stack the hot trays on A.D. 100 anticipating the E.T.A. Sure enough, they're done. I spend more time cleaning up the mess the day orderlies left.

Frosty needs help in the laundry with four laundry carts piled high with clothes. Sort, fold, sort, fold, sort, fold. Then feed A.D. 200. Is the mail sorted yet? Sort, fold, sort, fold, sort, fold. When D.S. is finished eating, load the hot boxes with empty trays. Wipe down the food carts. Take out the trash. Sort, fold, sort, fold. Peek at a letter.

If there's time, run up and do the last minute favors that you forgot last night. I try to stay off the ranges until feeding is over, because once you hit the range for the first time in the evening, you're trapped in perpetual obligation to the convicts. All it takes is the first dude to yell your name once, and the cat's out of the bag. Just when you think you've made it safely off the range and are about to hit the gate, they catch you and begin demanding things.

"Sean!" one yells.

"Yo, Sean!" someone else joins in.

In a few seconds there is a chorus, all singing my name and demanding things.

As Head Orderly, I'm not only responsible for feeding the ranges and making sure everything gets from A.D. 100 range to A.D. 200, range but also for getting stuff from the A.D. ranges to D.S. without the man knowing.

When 124 trays are loaded and the carts wiped down clean, they are put away. I then set aside 6 trays for us orderlies, if it's any good. The man eats too. I roll them out over by the door. Here the hall carts perfectly block the view of the D.S. 100 gate from the central pod. This is when I make my first move to pass stuff to the D.S. orderly. Transfer of cleaning supplies from D.S. 100 to 200 range.

Monday, Wednesday and Friday nights are clothes nights. Frosty and me set up D.S. 1 and 2 and A.D. 1 and 2. Frosty passes out A.D. 2 and I pass out A.D. 1. After the clothes are exchanged there are clothes all over the range: 95 underwear, towels and t-shirts and over 190 socks. Sheets are handed out on Mondays. Everyone gets two sheets. There are 190 of them lying on just the 200 and 100 ranges. Clean them up. Tie them up in sheets. Load up the now empty laundry carts. Laundry on D.S. also.

Go on a pass run that ends up being forty-five minutes. Seven thirty. Got to start D.S. hot water. Run up to give the nuts cigarettes out of my stash to keep them complacent. Diaz owes me a pack anyway. Stop, pick it up. Uh, oh. Caught on the range. Pass out almost the entire pack of cigarettes and flee. Shit, eight o'clock and gotta start D.S. hot water. D.S. hot water gets started at 8:15. The floor has to be mopped and swept. So does my range. Shit.

Frosty covers 200 range and I do 100 range. Streak down the tier proclaiming loudly, "Back in a minute, back in a minute!" because I have to get the mop. After filing the mop bucket, I stop to get the hot water jugs to put them in the microwave for the A.D. This has to be timed with a large plastic container set for 15 minutes. Two plastic jugs at ten minutes and one jug at five. I hit 15 minute timer on the microwave and pray that Frosty sets the other one at 10 minutes. I run to my mop. Pick up kites, coffee, cigarettes while I'm mopping and pass them out. When the range is clean, I finish heating water and set up the 100 A.D. cart to pass out the hot water. And then start passing shit everywhere.

When the hot water is out, I stop to deliver stuff I picked up, and then start Frosty's hot water for him. That dog carries his weight. No question about that. By now I owe roughly a thousand promises and demands like "Check 108 for cigarettes" or "214's got my newspapers" or "111's got some wine for me."

And so on, and so on.

Around 10:30 in the evening, things start winding down. The D.S. orderlies get locked down at the 10:00 PM count and the calls are less frequent. Tonight I've earned the *USA Today* newspaper, the *Boston Globe* and various magazines, one quart of wine, a little mota and two packs of cigarettes (of which I already gave 18 away). I gather up my laundry and speak briefly to the man about global politics only. I get my ice and walk that last thirty feet to my cell 106.

My doggies are barking and my cellie is sleeping. I pour off a cup and fire up the mota.

And I begin to write.

Life in the hole. U.S.P. Eagleview SHU.

Stardate August 16, 1995.

August 17, 1995

I'm feeling sad, lonely and tired.

The guy they put in my cell turned out to be psychotic. While I was working, he went through my address book and copied down all my addresses. He then held it over my head, in effect threatening my friends and family. The cops pulled him up when he tried to mail a letter out using my full name and registration number as a return address. They know my writing, because they see it every day. Needless to say, he left my cell before I came back from work.

I'm working hard at my job which is both physically and mentally demanding. I continue to write and concentrate on the positive aspects of my life. Every once in a while a guy comes along like the one they put in my cell last night, and all of the treachery and scandal and violence that I try to avoid, is thrust upon me. The epitome of a convict is a hard thing to look at.

Doing life with no hope of ever seeing the outside does certain things to the mind. It fosters an altogether different mentality than that of a man doing even a long sentence. There is no hope at all. And when there is no hope, nothing matters. And when nothing matters, a man can become very dangerous. It is sad and tragic to have a conversation with a man imprisoned until death.

I'm listening to the news. As usual, there is no good news.

I'm tired.

I'm weary.

Once again, I find myself utterly alone.

After all these years.

August 31, 1995

I have been totally irresponsible in the sense that I have disregarded the importance of my writings in the past few months. I have refused compound twice, because I am separated from my people and have filed against the Bureau of Prisons regarding their incompetence in keeping me from my people.

I am disgusted with their incompetence. But they make the rules as much as I hate to admit it. I continue to "do the right thing" by keeping my job and striving to get to an F.C.I. There is so much I need to write about, but I have absolutely no time to dedicate to my writing. Hopefully, I will soon be able to delve into the months I've spent here at U.S.P. Eagleview.

But now, I simply don't have the time to express all of this in writing.

September 4, 1995

Today is Labor Day. I woke up earlier than usual and have found time to write.

I have been in the hole for six months straight. This year I've spent a total of seven months and twenty-one days in lock up. Next Wednesday I am due for my Team where they evaluate your progress and then screw you accordingly. My case manager, Klingor, seemed to be doing fine until he stopped by last Wednesday and told me that he was going to ship me to U.S.P. Florence. That's a new prison in Colorado.

"We need to get you closer to home" he said to me.

But what's the difference between 3,000 miles and 1,500 miles? I don't want to go to the North Pole. I want to go to California or Sheridan, Oregon. Inevitably though, I'll probably end up at the North Pole.

My job is going well enough. They've begun a different system now. They have three black evening orderlies on D.S. 200, A.D. 100 and A.D. 200. The morning orderly is also black. Of the other two evening orderlies, one is Indian and the other Hispanic. I am the token white boy in the group.

My new cellie, Marty, is a veritable treasure chest of prison knowledge. He has served sixteen years and is serving twenty more right now. His time encompasses prison experience from all over the country, from the southwest to the eastern seaboard. He has been in Sing Sing, Danamora and Leavenworth. He has been thrown out of Terre Haute for allegedly possessing escape paraphernalia and planning escape.

Marty is getting ready to ship to Atlanta where he's been trying to go for a while. He is tall and thin with bleached blond hair and has a gift with the English language. He uses hand and body language to accentuate his tales. Marty is extremely intelligent and quick to laugh. He is totally hip and able to converse about almost anything.

But there is also a very deadly side of Marty. Make no mistake about it.

I knew Marty on the compound. Although we never hung together, we were on friendly "associate" terms. I saw Marty in the hole about a month and a half ago. He was there for some bullshit investigation. The next time I saw him, he had 28 stitches in his back and 13 on his right forearm. His arm was cut completely in half requiring 10 stitches inside his arm as well.

Unlike most stabbings, cuttings or assaults, Marty's assailant was never found. Marty simply refused to tell them anything, which really pissed the cops off.

But Marty's like that.

I was responsible for getting Marty into my cell.

"What's up with Marty?" I asked Fishman the other day.

"He's on single cell, he ain't talking," said Fishman.

"Get this nut case out of my cell," I told Fishman, "and put Marty down with me. Me and Marty are all right. Obviously, you've got him on separate status from everybody on the compound. Stick him in with me and you open yourself up a bed."

Fishman couldn't refute my logic.

After my talk with Fishman, I paid Marty a visit.

"Hey, dog, come on down to my house man," I told him. "I'll give you the bottom bunk until that shit heals up."

"Yeah?" said Marty. "Want me to pack up now?"

I thought about it for a second.

"Yeah, man, go ahead and pack up."

I was pretty sure the move could be made.

It was.

September 17, 1995

I spoke with my mother today and found out that her husband is seriously ill with emphysema. The news came hard. Jay has always been a good man to me and my mother. In fact, I have never seen my mother as happy as she is with my stepfather. She told me that he has been ill for some time now. She didn't want to tell me about it because she did not want me to worry. In the time I grew to know Jay I realized I genuinely liked the man. In fact, I came to refer to him as "Poppa Jay."

Another one of life's unfair turns. It's wrong. It's just so very wrong.

One of the cruelest aspects of being in prison is the inability to offer any type of assistance or help to somebody close to us. When you are sent to prison you are yanked out of your circle of friends and family. Where there was once a walking, talking, breathing, lean-on-me person, there is now just a vacant space.

It sucks to not be able to be there.

Sure, I can write and call and do everything within my limited powers of communication. But nothing in the world can replace human interaction.

I went to Walter, the barber, yesterday. My hair had grown almost halfway down my back. Walter has been a prison barber for years. I've known him for about a year and he gave me a moniker "Hippie" or "Hairy Hippie." Walter's getting ready to transfer and it is his last day in the barber shop. In my two and a half years of incarceration, I've had a total of three haircuts. The first one I gave to myself with a razor blade because, at the time, I was down. The second two haircuts are equally not worth mentioning.

Originally, I told Walter to cut the front and sides short but to save the length. We discussed the usual prison barber chair gossip.

"I guess Jamie and Larry broke up, huh?"

"Yeah, said he's through with 'em. Goddamned homos are the strangest breed."

"Ayuh."

"They got you on the next chain outta here, huh?"

"Yeah. I'm hoping they send me to Atlanta."

"Hey Walt, hey go ahead and cut all that shit off there."

Walter stops.

"Hippie man, you sure about that?"

"Yeah," I said. "Come on with it. I been having long hair for 15 years now. I think it's time I made a couple of adjustments anyway."

"All right, Hippie. You're gettin' short so I guess I can see that."

Snip, snip, snip.

He did a damned fine job if I do say so myself.

My cellie Marty has to have the largest collection of bad jokes I've ever heard. But he's got his moments. Tonight we had chicken, but Marty didn't want his chicken and politely asked if I wanted his.

"Nah, save it," I said.

"Save the chicken?" he asked.

I nodded.

Marty held his piece of chicken aloft and began to rant.

"In the name of the Loooord . . . repent your sins so that you may be saaaaaved! Bend down on your, uh, wing and cluck for forgiveness . . . "

Yeah, Marty's got his moments.

October 3, 1995

Fall has fallen with a resounding crash with the realization that this will be my last autumn in prison. I've been writing less upon these pages without any apparent reasons. I'm still working the tier.

The quarter has changed and brought in new staff. There's a new sheriff in town. Got to break him in. The tier was in a fairly large uproar until around 10:30 this evening. Things will calm down pretty soon. One orderly quit after losing his cool and getting locked in.

I know I have to play it cool. A new staff could be stepping in to root out the old and start from scratch. I played it cautious and patient and it paid off tonight.

But every day I wonder if I'm going to get fired. I am entirely expendable. It goes with the job. I've been orderly now for a while. I'm not even sure how long it's been. At least a few months. It's hard to believe it's October already. My hand-designed calendar has the "O" in October made into a pumpkin.

Today I received a letter from my old pal Cameron who is out at Lompoc. It's hard to write between prisons but easier if there is a go-between person. Cameron's mother is this go-between person.

Cameron wrote and said the usual small talk. Then he added, "By the way, I was coming back from the movies and I got into a sword fight. Only I'd left my sword at home." He was stabbed five times. Cameron claims it is not too bad because "it didn't mess up any of my tats." By "tats" he means tattoos. He makes various allusions to now being a made member of a large prison gang.

I wrote back to Cameron and told him he was a putz.

October 7, 1995

The nights are getting colder. A sure sign of the approaching fall and winter.

Marty has left and gone to U.S.P. Atlanta and I have been let go from my orderly job. This came as a relief after almost four months of pure craziness. Now I have more time to write and think, which are my two favorite things, since I don't have access to a guitar. It is a holiday and there is no mail. Holidays on Mondays are a drag because there are three days without any mail.

I've been doing a lot of thinking lately about getting out and what I should do. I will have a long three years of supervised release.

I also wonder about my current situation and where I'll be going for the remainder of my time. My counselor seems bent on sending me to Florence, Colorado U.S.P. which is known as America's newest and most secure prison. But why send me there? I have never even been to prison before. And furthermore, I've done a pretty good job of setting up life on the outside with a job, a residence and drug and alcohol counseling.

Last March I requested non-releasable portions of my file through the Freedom of Information Act. Seven months later I received a psychological profile listing me as a "non-threat" and concluding that my status was "favorable" for a lower-level transfer.

October 11, 1995

I received my mail tonight and in it was a long letter from dear, sweet Momma. She has been real positive and supportive throughout this whole ordeal. I don't know if I could have made it without her.

She sent pictures which are always welcome. Among the pictures was a 4 x 6 black and white photo of my grandparents in 1943. What a treasure! My grandfather is dressed dapper in what appears to be a wool, double-breasted suit. My grandmother is wearing a polka dot dress and has taken off her glasses and is holding them in her hand, apparently to facilitate the smooching of my grandfather. They are standing beneath a big oak tree on the side of a dirt road running along the side of a large field. Looking at the photo I can almost pinpoint the spot as Hatchery Road in Montague, Massachusetts. They both look very happy.

My new cellie, Jimmy, has thoroughly abused me on the pinochle table this evening. Jimmy is from San Francisco and is currently serving fifteen years.

October 14, 1995

Yesterday was Friday the 13th and the annual Liar's Parade came through as usual. My counselor came bearing the news that they've decided to transfer me after seven months of disciplinary segregation and administrative detention. The transfer should take place within the next five weeks.

It would be nice if I could go to an F.C.I. and get phased out of the system and into a lower level institution. But I have a feeling they will send me to Florence, Colorado. I've been hearing horror stories about the place. It's built on a nuclear dump site and the water is no good. There is an actual nuclear reactor right next to it.

They send all the screw-ups to Florence. Obviously, I'm not overjoyed about the prospect of going there. They are sending me to a Gulag. I'll arrive there just in time for winter which will probably make the frozen Russian tundra look like Hawaii.

However, I am not daunted. I have too much going for me right now to let relatively small things like geographical displacement bother me. I am bothered by the fact that the U.S.P. is no place to finish your time because there is a far bigger chance of getting into a "wreck" at a U.S.P. It would be tragic to come this far and then trip over something as stupid as someone else's bad attitude.

If I do go to Florence, I'll have to walk on cat's paws for a little while. The real pisser is that I'll have no idea of where I'm going until they tell me to pack up. And they might not even tell me then. They might not even let me know until I arrive.

So now I reflect on my last year-plus here at Eagleview U.S.P. To sum it up in a few words, this place is a shithole and the Captain's a geek. The last thing I'll do before I step on a bus is to reach deep into my belly and pull up a black one and spit on the ground inside the walls of this place. I won't do this as an act of defiance, or disgust, or disappointment with the institution. It will merely be a parting gift. I hope my spit germinates a seed in a little crack in the cement and then splits the crack open. Fogerty is now blaring on my radio about a tall, cool woman in a black dress. He knows what I'm talking about.

I think one of the things I'll always remember about this place is that this is where I came out of my shell in the literary sense. I've developed a confidence in my writing and found a style of poetry that is me. I enjoy poetry that rhymes. I enjoy poetry with meter. I think some prose sucks and has led to the downfall of poetry as an accepted form of expression.

There are many talented prose style poets out there, but they are drowned out by the prose movement as a whole. Anyone can simply meander along with incomplete sentences and call it poetry. I call it rubbish. Of course, this is only my opinion and I could be guilty of vanity. And too, there are a lot of jail house poets that are pretty damn good but do not, or cannot get credit for their work due to their circumstances. This, to me, is a real tragedy.

Light is breaking across the razor wire outside my window. Such a touching sight. Hopefully, today I can get into my property to retrieve my poems so I can mail a few out. I need to seriously try to get some money together for the future.

October 17, 1995

I had a nice trip to the dentist's office yesterday. They came to get me at about 1:30 in the afternoon. First, they had to put me in a belly chain which goes around the waist. Then my handcuffs are slipped through a special link in the chain in front of me. This isn't really that uncomfortable. It gets uncomfortable when they put the leg manacles on that limit your steps to half-strides.

So, dressed up like a Christmas turkey I went to see the dentist. My appointment at the hospital was actually with the dental hygienist. I have been looking forward to this appointment since last February. At the hospital there are four righteous babes. They are all fairly young and very attractive. Especially the hygienist. Being bound and shackled is pretty demeaning and to further inhibit any kind of manly dignity, there is the suction tube perpetually and nosily sucking up gobs of spit out of your mouth.

The hygienist and the dentist, besides both being attractive, are also intelligent. They did an impeccable job on my teeth. They are extremely good-natured girls. Two of the girls entered the room while I was in the "Chair of Death" and said hello. One of them is really cute. She knows I hate needles, but I let her draw blood for my bi-annual HIV test. I had the last one in January and have them regularly because of my tattoos. She has a very light hand.

I'm now listening to some Pearl Jam on the radio and it's bringing back old memories.

Since I've lost my orderly job, I have written probably fifty to sixty letters and have received one from someone I'd forgotten to write.

At least I get junk mail.

October 20, 1995

Federal Correctional Institution Taladega rioted yesterday evening. It kicked off another riot here. Rumor has it that federal prisons all over the nation are locked down. Taladega and Eagleview are in a deadlock for certain.

The AP network news reports that the riots are in direct retaliation to a bill that was either shot down or passed (I can't remember which) regarding sentencing differences for possession of crack cocaine and powder cocaine. According to the AP, it is a racist issue because black men are more likely to be arrested for crack while whites are more likely to be arrested for powdered cocaine.

Whether or not this is the issue that actually triggered the riot is still too early to tell. Taladega rioted in 1991 during the Cuban uprising. An acquaintance of mine was taken hostage for five or six days. My friend says they shut off the water and the electricity. The Cubans barricaded the doors, but on the fifth day, they blew the doors off with C4 explosives and took back possession of the prison. There were a lot of busted heads over that one. My friend won a lawsuit and was awarded a whopping $1,500. He'll be out in December of this year.

This afternoon I heard on WILQ news confirming the riot across the street at the F.C.I. It was a small riot as far as riots go and only took about an hour to break up. Parts of the cafeteria were damaged and a female guard had an unidentified liquid thrown in her face.

Subsequently we're locked down here. All the inmates in disciplinary segregation were moved to the 200 range of administrative detention. This created approximately 24 beds which will undoubtedly fill with the usurpers. Estimates from WILQ news place the number of participants in the riot at one hundred and fifty.

October 21, 1995

I fell asleep for a little while and when I woke up I listened to the AP network news. More rioting occurred in Tennessee and Illinois. This led to a nationwide federal prison lockdown. From what I understand, these mass lockdowns are not very common. The Senate and House committees rejected a bill that would lower the length of sentences for crack cocaine and make them equal to that for powder cocaine. I figure there are a lot of pissed off coke dealers around.

I'm guessing the lockdown goes at least through the weekend and most likely well into next week. Dinner was three hours late and was the usual deadlock meal: a cheese and bologna sandwich, a pear and two cookies.

This evening I learned that Greenville, Illinois F.C.I. has stolen the thunder of the October 1995 federal prison uprisings. The riots in Greenville, Illinois, Memphis, Tennessee, Taladega, Alabama and Eagleview were all small scale uprisings of the F.C.I. facilities. But of the four, Greenville managed to take possession of an entire unit.

Throughout the night, according to news reports, small groups of prisoners were turning themselves in. The whole event, thus far, has been anti-climatic. However, all federal prisons are locked down. This is much to the chagrin of those who chose not to participate.

No one has the right to complain though. It is a movement of "Us" against "Them." It is a hopeless, useless movement, but a movement nonetheless. There is not a single, solitary situation in which I could honestly say the B.O.P. has been beaten. The feds make all the rules and if you attempt to get around them, they will either change the rules or reinterpret them to their advantage.

The Cuban riots of 1988 was a more successful campaign. The entire penetentiary of Oakdale, Louisiana and the entire penetentiary of Atlanta, Georgia were burnt completely and utterly down to the ground. This resulted in the immediate nationwide lockdown of all Cuban prisoners. It also resulted in the B.O.P. designing "Cuban Units" with added safety features which house only Cubans.

When a full scale riot does occur, the end result is always the same. The federal government amasses their Special Task Force and they storm the prison, busting heads, teargassing and handcuffing bodies and piling them into a compliant heap. The damage is repaired, the rebels are punished and another war story goes down in the history books.

The way this could possibly affect me is that a lot of these F.C.I. rebels are going to be sent to U.S.P.s. This will probably expedite my transfer out of here to make room for the real bad boy rioters. Time will tell this story, though.

October 23, 1995

They came yesterday at about 6:45 in the evening.

"Legacy, Reynolds, pack up both of you," they said. "You're outta here."

I was packed in ten minutes.

After over a year in Eagleview, Pennsylvania, bunghole capitol of America's U.S.P.s, I was finally destined for greener pastures. Any pasture would have been greener. Anybody who has ever done time at Eagleview will tell you what a lousy hole it really is.

Barney came to get us.

"Legacy, lose the smoke," he barked.

I had a cigarette dangling from my lip. Who knows how long it would be before I could smoke again. I also had a cigarette behind my ear. Getting processed out takes a couple of hours.

"Legacy, I said, lose the goddamned smoke now!" Barney barked again.

I had worked for Barney for three months as an orderly. I had known him the seven months I had been in the hole. Barney was unusually gruff and short with all of us. Usually, he was friendly and joking. Now he was plain rude. He had reverted to the role of "I'm an asshole cop." But he had a good reason. I later learned that Barney was in the passenger seat of one of the two transport vans. He was packing a 9 millimeter and it was his job to shoot us if we attempted escape.

We were handcuffed and led to R & D. We carried our property in pillowcases. The handcuffs were taken off in the holding pen.

"How many of us are leaving?" I asked.

"Thirteen," came the reply.

The holding pen filled up in an hour and a half and we were led to a separate room and told to strip down. The drill was familiar.

"Run your hands through your hair, open your mouth, lift your tongue, behind your ears, hold out your hands, turn them over, lift up your nuts, turn around, lift your left foot, your right foot, bend and spread. OK. Clothes size, shoe size. Next."

When the above procedure was completed, another cop wrapped a belly chain around our waist and handcuffed us to it. Then he placed leg manacles on us and marched all of us into another holding pen.

The names were finally called. My name was the third.

"Legacy."

"Here."

"What's your number?"

"27063-038."

"Date of birth?"

"3-3-68."

"Next."

The transportation was new to me. We were put into brand new Dodge vans with souped up engines. It was the epitome of a prison transport vehicle with iron bars across the windows and heavy mesh wire separating the driver from us. Between the driver and the passenger seat was a scanner, a radio, a telephone and some more high-tech stuff. They loaded us into the vans. Six of us into one van and seven into the other.

I spit on the ground right before I stepped into my van.

All loaded up we cleared the gates of sallyport. For the first time in over a year I saw trees and cars. The outside of U.S.P. Eagleview looked as miserable as it did when I first saw it. Fourteen feet of straight double-fenced razor wire, then the wall.

But it was behind me now.

There was high spirited banter in the van.

Everyone was glad to get away.

"Look at the deer!" I said.

Four deer were grazing on the road leading out of Eagleview. I saw a number more before we made it to the highway. After a year in an environment of brick and steel seeing something as beautiful as a deer was a sign of rebirth. It was a peculiar sensation, like a breath of life.

I was amazed at the traffic on the road and the little towns with their quick marts and McDonald's. Good-looking girls walked down the streets. It was like another world. Cotton was sitting next to me and shared my wonderment.

"It ain't never gonna be the same is it, Cotton?" I said.

I spoke in a low voice.

Cotton shook his head.

"Naw, it ain't," he answered.

Eagleview U.S.P. had left its marks. Prison had changed us.

We arrived at F.C.I. Martinsburg at around 10:30 in the evening. R & D dressed us out, photographed us, fingerprinted us, gave us medical questionnaires and took us to segregation. The hole.

The differences were immediately apparent. Instead of Eagleview's plastic mattresses, we now had big, stuffed soft cotton mattresses and cotton sheets. They brought us big feather pillows. Even the toilet paper would have made Mr. Whipple jealous. The food was also a big improvement.

Nobody will tell us how we got so lucky, or how long we are supposed to stay, or what the situation is. We assume we're merely on "holdover" status.

They assigned us units and the unit team counselors came down and told us we are pending reclassification and that we may be released to the compound. At least that's what they told my cellie. He saw his unit team. They gave him a pin number and assigned him to 4A. I've been assigned to unit 2A but haven't seen anyone from my team yet.

October 25, 1995

There is a nationwide lockdown of prisons currently in effect. Martinsburg has been on lockdown status since we arrived. Things are in turmoil. Nobody knows what is happening and it will probably be a while before we know anything.

F.C.I. Spartanville jumped off into a riot as soon as lockdown sanctions were lifted. U.S.P. Clayton rioted last night. Clayton is the first U.S.P. to join the riots.

Everything is really messed up and lunch is over two hours late. We haven't had showers since Sunday and today is Wednesday. We were supposed to have a shower yesterday. There are no phone calls and no stamps. Our detention order is screwed up and no one will tell us what is going on.

As a result, we withheld the food trays. It's the only way to communicate with these people. They treat us like mushrooms, but we are used to this kind of treatment. But it's bullshit when they withhold our showers and we start to smell and be treated like animals. I secured our door so that it can't be opened from the outside. We are currently waiting for the assault team to come in and beat us down and four point us. Or, give us a shower.

We persevered and the whole tier got showers. Word around here is that the compound opened back up and the lockdown is over. The Lieutenant told us that they are redesignating us and that most likely none of us will stay here. This is too bad because the food is great.

October 26, 1995

The view out my window is spectacular. The foliage might be past its prime, but it's stunning nevertheless.

F.C.I. Martinsburg sits on top of a huge mountain. All around us are mountains and the colors are splashed red, yellow and gold. The sun rises directly over the mountains outside my window. The dawns are reds, pinks and purples of varying hues. Dark purple hugs the skyline, giving way to a light grayish blue. When the sun peeks over the hills it lights up everything. They are the best damned sunrises I'll probably ever see. I haven't missed one yet.

While I was out at recreation today, the guard told me they lost F.C.I. Spartanville. It was gone, obliterated. They needed SERT (Special Emergency Response Teams) teams from U.S.P. Eagleview and U.S.P. Clayton. The guard said the state police escorted the SERT teams from Eagleview to Clayton at 90 miles per hour down the highway.

Evidently, it was not fast enough. They tore Spartanville apart. I remember playing the 1994 Bike Show at Spartanville, and I remember my friends there and wonder if they are all right.

In Pennsylvania, Clayton has had a minor uprising but nothing has happened yet at Eagleview. Martinsburg is the only other F.C.I. in Pennsylvania. It is identical to Spartanville with the same layout, brick for brick.

October 27, 1995

It has been raining all day.

I've settled for a fairly dull routine of eat, sleep, read, eat and sleep. None of the thirteen of us who came from Eagleview have any property. Tonight we are allowed to use the phone and are patiently waiting our turn. The regulations here do not allow any smoking. The cigarettes come to us. One a day. Two if we are lucky. I break a single cigarette up and roll two out of toilet paper wrapping. We light up with one half a match.

Speculation is all we have regarding our future. A letter from Diane caught up to me last night. She wrote two poems. I really miss that girl and am harboring some powerful feelings for her. It is just like her to come through with a letter when my world has been turned upside down.

It seems every book here has followed us from Eagleview and I can't seem to find one I haven't read.

The phone is taking forever.

The rain is making me drowsy like only a rainy day can.

I'm hangin' out, hangin' in and hangin' on.

October 30, 1995

The rains have passed and the sunrises are back. I try not to miss any. I could watch the sunrises for the next ten months. The sun rising over the mountains may seem like such a small thing, easily taken for granted. But I know I will never look at another sunrise again with uncaring eyes. Like the stars in the sky at night. If it only happened once a year it would be a major event and would receive international media coverage. Everyone would want to see it and take pictures. But it happens everyday and familiarity deadens the beauty. Like a good song overplayed on the radio.

It is difficult to really communicate how I feel but pay close attention. Break the law and they take your sunrises away from you. For someone seeking inner freedom in a place with so little of it, this quote from Derek Van Arman's book *Just Killing Time* comes to mind: "Freedom, not the concept but the courage to find it, the strength to allow it."

I have now been here for a week and nothing has changed except the weather. The lockdowns have been tentatively let up in various degrees for different institutions. We are allowed to shower on Tuesday, Friday and Sunday. Yesterday was a shower day. Today is not. I kind of miss the shower in the cell.

It's hard to describe how I feel here at Martinsburg. Somewhat like being in a hospital recovering from the penitentiary lifestyle. The cell is baby-blue and the beds are softer, with white sheets instead of orange sheets. At Eagleview everything was orange. There is an incredible difference in the food. It's hard to now remember how bad the food at Eagleview was. I refuse to give examples. I'd rather forget.

Yet, everything is relative and as I look around, I realize that if someone was randomly selected from the streets and tossed in this cell, they would probably consider the conditions appalling. There is absolutely no personal property. This means washing my hair with institutional soap for the last week. No cigarettes are allowed in here. We have no idea what's going on and only one phone call is allowed each month.

Martinsburg utilizes its own phone system. You receive an initial 30 minutes where you call collect. After that you must have money sent to your account by postal money order or wait for three weeks until commissary and then purchase ITS (Inmate Telephone System) phone credits and have them transferred to your phone account. You are only allowed thirty phone numbers and there is a two week waiting period for approval of these phone numbers. As I am only here on holdover and could be leaving anytime, it's quite possible I could have money sent into my account only to transfer out a day or two later after the money arrives. C'est la vie.

My cellie, Jeff Owens, is a good old boy from Tennessee and goes by the name of Red Dog. I've had my share of agreeable cellies and Red Dog is undoubtedly one of the easiest dudes to get along with. He's big at 6'3" and 230 pounds. We have a few things in common. Both of us fell at about the same time and we both received about the same amount of time. We are both going home within the next year. Red Dog has got seven months left and I've got ten.

Our conversations are easy and mostly involve Red Dog establishing the finer points of Tennessee girls. If I accept Red Dog's view, there is a whole lot of gorgeous, horny girls in Tennessee. Matter of fact, it seems like all of them are this way. Needless to say I am intrigued to the point where I have promised to come and visit him and see for myself.

As I mentioned before, any average person thrown into these circumstances off the street would probably freak out. But for me, life here is far more cozy than the dungeons of Eagleview.

Besides my view of the mountains and the sunrises, I have a direct view of the sidewalk that runs from the entrance building to the visiting room building. The sidewalk is probably 150 feet from my window and roughly 100 feet long. Along the sidewalk, I see more women in one day than I saw during my whole year at Eagleview. This is no stretch of the truth, but a fact. I'll tell you, I spend a fair amount of time at my window.

October 31, 1995

Halloween. While little ghosts, goblins, witches, comic book heroes, princesses and pirates roam the nation's streets gathering sweets under threat of trickery, I am mooning the Lieutenant through the gate bars of the shower.

"Legacy, that's screwed up," he says.

"It's Halloween," I tell him.

"And . . . ?" says the Lieutenant.

"That was my impersonation of the Warden," I say without batting an eye.

The four screws broke up laughing while the Lieutenant turned red in the face from trying not to laugh. It seems that nobody here at Martinsburg likes the Warden. The Lieutenant did attempt to defend him during a conversation in the yard when I asked him point blank if the warden did indeed resemble the rear of a horse.

I enjoyed mooning the Lieutenant. It was the high point of my entire stay at Martinsburg, so far.

The Special Housing Unit at F.C.I. Martinsburg has approximately 44 cells. There are fifteen cells, each on the 100 and 200 ranges. Each cell was designed for one inmate. But, like all federal prison cells I've encountered so far, each cell is double bunked. The 200 range, where I reside, has forty inmates on a tier designed for fifteen. There are two inmates in the U.D.C. room. It is a cell with no plumbing. Other cells across the hall are tripled up where they throw a mattress on the floor to accommodate a third prisoner. This triples the cell's original planned capacity.

So much for prison resorts. My cellie and I, a sum total of about 450 pounds and portraying the image of good ol' boys, don't want to hear any "noise" about tripling up. Hell, there's hardly enough room for two of us. They leave us alone and we won't mess with them. Except when we took the trays hostage to get a shower. Or when I screamed to get the phone down here.

November 3, 1995

I'm still in the little cell on top of the big mountain. The fog up here really gets thick. You could almost break off a piece of it and keep it as a souvenir.

Twelve days at Martinsburg with nothing but rumors concerning my status. I spend my time from hour to hour, from mail call to mail call, waiting to see if I connect with some one in the real world, waiting to see if they can reach me way up on this ghostly, fog-covered mountain.

Mom has been able to reach me.

So has Diane.

Today was commissary day. Since we couldn't smoke, my cellie and I blew all our money on Zu-Zus and Wham-Whams. I will probably weigh a disgusting 250 pounds by the time I leave here.

I've always talked about how bad the food was at Eagleview but never really elaborated. Tonight I heard an inmate complaining that his carton of grape juice was warm. Obviously this fool had never had Eagleview's ice cold waffles that clunked when you dropped them, shattered like glass when you bit them and tasted like cardboard. Twice a week the morning hot tray would hold the quivering, palpitating, substance that could only be identified by its nickname of Red Death. Lunch was always ice cold except when I was an orderly and heated the trays. Hamburgers were the consistency of hockey pucks and french fries as palatable as anemic nightcrawlers.

During dinner at Eagleview they graced us two or three times a week with the famous "Glub Glub." This is over-cooked rice or noodles with this grayish, brown sauce with alleged vegetables in it and another substance almost like meat. Great big gobs of fat, sometimes with a little piece of meat clinging desperately to it, swam in a roving, search-and-kill pattern through the brownish sauce. This was our sustenance. Eat it or go hungry. I lost some weight at Eagleview.

Needless to say, I'm certain the guy up the tier complaining about his warm grape juice had never experienced the pleasures of "Glub Glub." I don't miss it at all.

But all of this is behind me now and every day clicks me one more step to the gate of freedom. Inside I am experiencing some turmoil, doubts and apprehensions. I can only put them off for so long before they surface like sharks demanding attention.

One of my biggest apprehensions is how I feel other people will look at me. I want to have changed. I want to be better. I'd like all my short-comings to have disappeared and be replaced by wit, charm and intelligence. I would like my alcoholism to have disappeared, my criminal record gone, a stranger tell me I'm rich. I would like to slip back into society like I had never left and have my emotional demons conquered. I would like to have a fresh and invigorating view of life that turns all those around me green with envy.

I would also like the moon to be purple.

Unfortunately, this is not a likely scenario.

However, I do have a few things on my side. I can't view my future with total pessimism. One of the things I have going is that I have changed. When I begin to look at myself and consider how I got into this mess, I see I've really made some progress. A key to this progress is not to place blame on anybody but myself.

Going even further than this, I asked some important questions.

Why did I act as I did?

Where did it go wrong?

What was I thinking about?

Not "who" but "what."

It was her fault. It was his fault.

Whose fault was it really?

It all came back to me.

Myself.

My actions.

My alcoholism.

My demons.

Me.

It wasn't that I didn't have the guidance. I had experience. I'd been around. I was intelligent enough to see I was on the edge. I don't plead innocence. I tended to live in the shadow of myself. I didn't accept that there was a "tomorrow" because I didn't particularly care to see it.

David Reynolds, an American exponent of Japanese Morita psychotherapy, said, "People deny reality. They fight against real feelings caused by real circumstances. They build mental worlds of shoulds, oughts, and might-have-beens. Real changes begin with real appraisal and acceptance of what is. Then realistic action is possible."

Before I came to prison, I spent a lot of time denying reality. I pushed away what I didn't want to accept through alcohol, weed and promiscuity. I ran from myself. But to hold a job and keep an apartment, I had to project things were all right to certain people, like my boss and landlord. They counted on me not to screw up. I found myself juggling aspects of my life. Cubes of reality versus cubes of non-reality. Denial is easy when the delicate balance of non-reality slips too far off the edge, and the pressures of reality become unbearable. This is where I lost my sight. This is where I took that step without thinking.

I found my way back.

I made a little progress.

It took me a long time.

November 5, 1995

I watched the sunrise this morning.

We have been here two weeks and there is still no change and no idea of what the future holds.

I have coffee now. I did my hot water trick and with half a match managed to make two steaming hot cups of coffee for me and my cellie.

Yesterday they served us honey buns for breakfast. Today it was cinnamon buns.

I am steadily gaining weight, but it's OK. In four months I'll begin to physically prepare myself for my release. This will give me six months to slim down, tone out and all that other good stuff. I'm not letting things get out of hand, but I am enjoying the good food. And, not being able to smoke really contributes to the chowdown factor.

I am feeling isolated today. It's a feeling of being alone but not being alone. I am alone in this prison world in the sense that I distance myself from others. It is a common enough trait. Everybody puts up barriers for protection. This is survival. I received a couple of letters in the past few weeks but there is a feeling of separation. I'm not really sure if it's a feeling of loneliness as much as it is this feeling of separation. I miss my people. I have a strong urge to get out and fill the empty niche out there I belong in. I want to take my place in society and do something with my life. Whether it is to write, make music or to be a plumber.

Could it be I feel impatient?

God, not already.

November 8, 1995

The moon, full, white and round, rises right outside my window. Yesterday it was orange. Tonight it is rose white. It seems odd that both the sun and the moon rise over almost the same mountain. I've got a real connection with that moon, a real deep spiritual bond. No matter how many miles I travel, no matter how good or bad a day I've had, Old Man Moon seems to look down and say, "Don't worry, kid. I'm watching you. It's all right."

It snowed today. At first it only spit out a few flakes, but soon it was really coming down. It didn't stick, but it did swirl around like it meant business anyway. Most of the leaves have fallen off the trees and left the mountains the color of rust. They wait patiently for the white blanket of snow that will soon cover everything.

My final winter in prison is beginning. A letter from a friend told me that I could now count my "lasts" like "last" Thanksgiving and "last" Christmas. She's right. It's my "last" winter. I even like the way it looks on paper.

Even though I am only up on this mountain temporarily, on holdover, they've assigned me a unit and a unit team. When I saw my case manager today he told me something totally unbelievable. He told me they might ship me back to the dungeons of Eagleview.

Right now it is snowing outside. I hope it snows ten feet and we get stuck here until Spring. Cigarettes or no cigarettes. Only the Bureau of Prison Gods knows for certain what the future holds. It must be like some giant chess game to them as they decide the fate of over a hundred thousand prisoners. I pull this figure from a few years ago. Who knows how high the figure is now.

I'm really too tired to care anyway. I'm tired of prison, tired of these cold cells and the food that comes in a tray through a slot in the door. I'm tired of struggling to keep my head up. I'm tired of using my imagination and memories to construct a pyramid of sanity in an insane environment. Without mental strength the pyramid would dissolve like smoke on a windy day and there would be the Big Empty in its place. Stephen King might call it "The Wastelands." Some would call it hell. I've seen that place. I know it exists and I'm sure not trying to go there. I've got a destiny.

There are things in my life that I need to accomplish. I feel this deep inside and it gives me purpose. Somehow, in some way, I'm going to make a difference in this world.

Time is the clock of the heart.

Tick, tock.

November 11, 1995

I have been in holdover nearly three weeks now. In all this time I have not seen a newspaper, or a magazine, or heard anything from the radio. I miss the radio and hearing music. Any kind of music.

As a result, I have resorted to singing bad renditions of songs like "Where Am I Gonna Live When I Get Home" by Billy Ray Cyruss and "Friends In Low Places" by Garth Brooks. The latter is one of my favorite country songs. On shower days I change to either Guns-n-Roses or Lynard Skynard, much to the chagrin of the entire tier.

Yesterday was Veterans Day and a holiday. I usually try to write a little on each holiday. I would not want anyone to think Veterans Day is an unimportant day to me. It is important. I've always been taught patriotism and am fascinated with American history. It would be a very easy thing to harbor a grudge against the government because it is the federal government that holds the keys to the locks on these prison doors. But it is my shortcomings, not those of my country, that placed me in here.

My father was a marine. A Vietnam Veteran. It was a war I was too young to remember at the time. But as I got older I made it my business to read and learn as much about it as I could. It took some time for me to accept that my father was a hero. He placed his life in jeopardy for his country and completed two tours. That's a hard image to live up to. Sitting in this cell I'm certain it will be a long road before I can make it up to him. All I can do is try.

Anyway, here's to you vets out there. This American kid says "thank you" for what it's worth.

I fell asleep and had a dream about parole officers and large growling dogs.

November 17, 1995

Winter arrived overnight a few days day ago and has not gone away.

Yesterday at 3:45 in the afternoon, I went out to make a legal call. I happened to be handed to an extreme asshole with a God complex. First of all, this jerk dialed the number for me, spoke to the attorney's secretary and did not even ask me if I wanted to leave a message. I tried to pick up a pen and he got himself in an uproar. With a bad lisp he told me I couldn't have the pen. Then he made his first asinine statement.

"It's bad enough I gafe you thith legal call," he said.

"It's your job," I retorted.

"No, ith not, no ith not," he squeaked. "Juth you wait and thee if I giff you a legal call on Monday. Juth you wait and thee."

At this point, I lost my cool entirely.

"Check this out," I yelled at him. "Screw you, you panty waist bitch! Get away from me you bitch!"

Fifi ran into the office where there were six other cops hanging around, even though I was handcuffed. Only after two burly hacks ran to "escort" me back to my cell did Fifi come out of the office.

"Juth you wait and thee if you ever get a legal call," he said again.

I was furious. I made reference to Mr. Fifi's ovaries and degraded his sexuality all the way back to my cell where I was unceremoniously deposited.

What really made me angry was not that I wasn't able to place a legal call. The call wasn't that important. I don't even have anything going on in the courts. What really pissed me off was this little pipsqueak abusing his authority. I'd waited two weeks for this call. What if it had been important? What if I'd been some poor slob who desperately needed that call? This disgusting excuse of a man has the authority to make important decisions regarding another person's life and he can't even control his own pituitary gland.

There is a guy I know down the hall called Moondance. Fifi torments Moondance on a regular basis by mercilessly heckling, prodding and poking him. Although it would be wrong to personally want to inflict major bodily harm upon Fifi, I wouldn't care less if he got hit by a truck or a safe fell on his head. He is the epitome of all the bad aspects of "Them."

I should only pity the guy.

This weekend makes it a month in this cell. Originally, we were all happy to escape the dungeons of Eagleview. But now it appears we've been cast out of the proverbial frying pan and into the fire. The food is still good, but the lack of cigarettes and our personal property makes it a hard road to hoe. With Christmas only thirty-nine days away, it's time to start thinking about my Christmas card list, but all my addresses are in my property. And I'm only allowed one fifteen minute call between now and then.

I've made a coffee to soothe my battered spirit. And I've begun to challenge the bleakness of the situation by singing as many Christmas songs as I can. Last year I taught myself to play "Noel" and "Silent Night" on the electric guitar. Hendrix style. Was it just last year? In some ways it seems like ten years ago. In other ways it seems like just last week. We're coming up on the end of the year. The most important increment of time. Another calendar down.

I wrote my daughter tonight. Jesus, that's hard. Not that it's difficult to write the letter, but it is difficult to ride the emotions that come with it. The last memory I have of her is Christmas 1992. I was a real mess. Maybe she was too young to notice. Maybe she wasn't. That's something I've got to live with.

That's the damnedest thing about regrets. You struggle so hard to accept them. It's like catching a butterfly. What happens after you catch it? You let it go and it's gone. It's the catching part, the acceptance, that's hardest. Once you can clear that, you've got it knocked.

The Holiday Monster is looming large and stirring up all those thoughts and emotions that can only be evoked in the months of November and December.

In the midst of all of these old memories, I've accomplished a pretty amazing feat that is worth writing about. Three thick steel bars cover my window. By tapping them in various places I am able to approximate a whole music tone scale. To my delight, I dinged out "Jingle Bells" on the bars. My cellie seemed astonished.

November 21, 1995

I'm reading *The Murder of Napoleon*. Napoleon was exiled to Briars in the Isle of St. Helena in July 31, 1815. It is described by Betsy Balcombe, writing as Mrs. Abell, in her *Recollections of Emperor Napoleon* in 1844. Miss Betsy, Napoleon's friend, had this conversation with the great conqueror.

"You see," Napoleon says, "we are both prisoners and you cry. I don't cry."

"You have cried," Betsy retorts.

"Yes, I have," answers Napoleon, "but the prison remains nevertheless, so it is better to be occupied and cheerful."

And so it is with Red Dog and me. We tend to see humor everywhere and have names for everything. Our juice comes in cartons and we refer to the flavors as Grape Ape, Orangeustodeath (we have this a lot), Suicide Lemon (one sip and you're dead) and Iced P which is particularly nasty. There is a female guard who works in R & D we lovingly call Volkswagen because of the size of her ass. Then there's little Miss Buick who's not very little. My little Buttercup works on commissary day. The Catwoman remains a mystery, while Throw Mama makes a fairly regular appearance. Real geekazoid C.O.s we call Barneys. And of course, there is Fifi.

My counselor made it down today and said that a few of us might be released to the compound. I'm hoping like hell I'm one of them. Otherwise, no changes. Commissary is a day early this week because of

Thanksgiving. I'm hoping to get some money in the mail tonight so I can buy a radio.

Yesterday they brought in the SERT team and rolled in on the kid across the hall because he threw piss on one of the hacks. I guess they thumped him up pretty good.

November 23, 1995

Thanksgiving day.

It is not a shower day. Neither was yesterday. There is also no mail today. But there are things to be thankful for. Things like my release date comes to mind.

My cellie, Red Dog, has scored the sacred orderly job which is extremely convenient. All sorts of things like clean long johns, sheets, extra food and occasional cigarettes find their way into the cell now. There are also choice books to read which are real life savers with no radio.

I actually swept and cleaned the sink and toilet using scouring powder and Lysol. I don't know what came over me. We all have our moments of weakness. I swept up a pile of dust as large as an actual rabbit. This revealed to me the origin of the word "dust-bunnies." When I confessed to Red Dog what I had done he actually called me a "gotdamt liar." It took me ten minutes to convince him.

Not much is happening here. Yesterday I went to the law library. The typewriter was broken, but I fixed it enough to type small letters and typed a four page single space poem. Commissary came and my little Buttercup made her usual showing. I typed for a while. There was no typewriter at Eagleview in the law library the entire seven months I was in the hole. No one cared about it, I guess. There was a fair share of apathy around.

I could very possibly get a phone call today. I put $5 on my phone account which will cover my fifteen minute phone call once a month. I'm hoping to get a call today and also one on Christmas Day, if I'm still here. It's all timing and goes back to the clock or the calendar.

It's late and we haven't eaten brunch yet. The food service brings our trays over from the kitchen in big metal containers with wheels. They are all stainless with two doors and look like big freezers. You plug them into the wall. They have some type of heating element in them. Today, while they were rolling these big carts out to us, one of them fell over on a cop. He's probably not too thankful. One cart holds ninety-six trays. We now wait while they recook everything. I'm starving to death.

Yesterday I saw Detroit who came with us from Eagleview. He was coming in from his hour out at rec. He saw me for the first time in over a month even though he is right on the tier below me.

"Jesus Christ, Sean," he said grinning ear to ear. "You've gotten fat as a hog."

Well, as I've said, the food here is good. But I planned on my Thanksgiving meal being my last huge meal. I begin my diet tomorrow.

November 27, 1995

Christmas is only weeks away and I have amassed a veritable treasure: a decent collection of Christmas cards. I look forward to the Christmas card ritual and the reconnection to my family and friends, a reconnection to my past. Memories of Christmas trees, snow-flakes and hunting season. The forceful heat of a wood stove and the smell of a Christmas feast. All of these memories are sacred ones. All are pages in the chapter that is the spirit of Christmas.

Some cons say that Christmas is just another day and that the seasons do not affect their emotions. This is a bunch of BS. No man can disregard the memories and emotions brought by the holidays. Sure, maybe some days were bad and even some Christmases non-existent. But inside every person is the small child who listens in wonder to the tales of Santa, who hangs his stocking and can barely fall asleep, who wakes up to the magic of a Christmas morning with Christmas lights and presents and parents that reluctantly pry themselves from slumber. Soon all are caught in the magic of the moment.

Christmas is a spiritual event in spite of all the commercialism. There is a type of bond with your fellow man, your neighbor, even your neighbor's dog.

I'm not able to participate in Christmas as fully as these old memories. But I am able to make my little contribution. For the past three years, that has entailed the Christmas card ritual.

November 30, 1995

There was a bus out front this morning. I know because I can see the parking lot and entrance to the compound. The whole tier gets quiet once someone yells there's a bus out front. Who gets to leave? Who has arrived? I'm still here.

Since I can see the entrances and the walkway to the visiting room, I sometimes just look out the window to watch the visitors. Especially between 3:30 and 4:00 when they throw a whole parade of the visitors out.

Today, I looked out my window and saw something that hit me with a shock. It was a child of perhaps five or six. The little munchkin was dressed in boots, a coat and mittens and was dancing circles around his mother. I realized it was the first child I had seen since my mother's visit in May of 1994. That really threw me. Little kids have a magic all their own and I could only glimpse a little piece of it. Eighteen months since

I've seen a kid and even now, from no less than two hundred feet away and locked up tight.

There has been talk in the system for the last few months about a new drug called prolyxin. Word has it that one shot of it pretty much lobotomizes you. I met a guy who told me he had a friend he didn't see for a year. When he saw him, his friend didn't even know his name. I keep hearing about prolyxin here and there. It sounds like nasty stuff.

I found out that I might be going to California or Sheridan soon. But it still looks like I'll be here until after the holidays. Holdover status is no big party. I've whined considerably about the no smoking, no newspapers, no magazines, no radio, no property and the showers three times a week. In fact, the only thing I have coming is my once-a-month phone call.

Or so I thought.

The ITS (Inmate Telephone System) that Martinsburg utilizes is mandatory. In other words, if you don't have money in your account, you don't get a phone call. This is a really sleazy move on the B.O.P.'s part. There is no excuse for it but disgusting greed. In order to make some phone calls I transferred money from my general account to my ITS account. I filled out the proper forms over a month ago. The forms stated my numbers would be approved within ten working days. But when I tried to phone home, I found out that my phone numbers had not been approved.

I have a strong suspicion that this is somehow connected to that little spat I had with Fifi the day I attempted to make my legal call. Fifi, by the way, does not stop by my house anymore. He doesn't even come to this end of the tier unless he has to.

A couple days ago all the snow melted. Then, the night before last, it snowed a foot. I woke up and it was deep. Today, the sun is shining and there is not a cloud in the sky. Blue skies over white snow with a little razor wire thrown in. That's my view.

Me and Red Dog are dedicating our lives to the pursuit of the actual possession of a radio.

December 1, 1995

I finally have a radio and I have music. I can't imagine how I survived without it for over a month. A myriad of emotions were brought to the surface. They are even already playing Christmas songs.

I was thinking how I never imagined I'd find myself wishing that years of my life would rush by. Sure, when I was young I wished I was older, wished that these years would rush by. But these were romantic notions and overridden by common sense that tells you things are better off when you are young.

December 4, 1995

I stare through the bars of the small window in my cell. Clouds slide across the full moon and I fall back in time to a world where life was a family, a guitar and a job. Back to a time before that which tormented me, began to drag me down into the depths, into the dark pit with the sides too slick to grasp. Back to a time before there was no way to stop the fall and climb out of the dark pit.

"If only," I silently sigh to myself. "If only."

I shake my head. If onlys are for fools.

Now there is only the future and a rainbow of possibilities that dances before my eyes. I've spent close to three years now unlocking the doors of the prisons in my mind. It's been dirty work but there's been rewards.

The quest is not yet finished. There is more to be done. Perhaps the strongest gates still remained closed. They are big, steel, intimidating gates with skulls and crossbones and the three black triangles on yellow that makes me scratch my head and wonder what they are doing there.

But most importantly, they are within my reach and I can see the downfall of the gate. There is the keyhole. And where there is a keyhole, there is a key. I picture the heavy gates opening. There are treasures on the other side I am desperately seeking.

Peace.

Serenity.

Freedom.

Somewhere in my mind are the keys. I search and search, but the gates remain obstinately closed.

I stare at the moon and remember.

December 7, 1995

The moon is defiantly full now.

I wake up at around 10:00 AM and spend my day in search of the perfect cup of coffee. I ran out of coffee today but a fellow Californian named Pete bought me a bag to last until next week. Roll after roll of toilet paper goes into making the "bomb" that I use to heat coffee. I estimate about forty or fifty sheets rolled around your hand and then made into a small cylinder is just about right.

Red Dog is out working as an orderly so I have the cell to myself. I have had no success in getting to the law library to fool with the typewriter. The cops seem to want to make a little game of it. So I spend the time I'm not getting amped on coffee thinking of collective strings of adjectives to cleverly hurl at the police. This passes the time.

Diane, love of my life, tells me Mike is definitely going to buy her a diamond. I didn't receive one piece of mail this week and I didn't have any bread for commissary. I briefly ran out of coffee and spent the stamps I was going to use for my Christmas cards on cigarettes. My cellie lost his money order, courtesy of the mail room here, and my road dog Jimmy next door, couldn't lend me a book of stamps this week. I have gained at least twenty pounds in the six weeks I've been here. And, to top everything off, today is not a shower day.

But, on the bright side, the moon is full, Christmas is in the air and I now have a full jar of coffee. The clock is ticking and the year is almost over. I'm sending to Diane a real nifty short story I wrote. It's theme is kind of like I'm OK, you're OK, we'll be all right. I've been through it a hundred times already. It's not even worth talking about. Maybe it is, but I'm just burnt out on it.

The radio is a big help. I recently acquired a decent set of headphones and now I get to go away to that place that sets me free for a little while. I really like the Goo-Goo Dolls "Won't Tell 'em Your Name" but the radio is playing it to death. I torture poor Jimmy next door while I practice my singing every day after lunch.

Red Dog comes back to the cell between 3:30 and 4:00 in the afternoon and we usually play a ritualistic game of pinochle. Usually, he brings back something to smoke. Tonight it was Newports. After chow and mail call I'll usually write a letter or read. Red Dog has to go to sleep to get up at 7:00 AM to go to work.

I listen to the radio in the dark and dream about my freedom and my future.

December 10, 1995

Days are bitter cold now. It was seventeen below zero with the wind chill today. The forecast calls for highs in the low twenties tomorrow and Tuesday it is supposed to get up to a scorching

27 degrees. The pleasures of a gulag in December includes the honor of shoveling out my own dog kennel for outside rec. It's been a while since I held a snow shovel.

Red Dog goes out to work at 7:30 AM and I'm locked in the cell alone until about 4:00 PM. It gets pretty boring.

Today I made a Christmas tree. I constructed it out of legal size paper and made little bulbs out of green and red pieces of paper from various sources. One of them was an ice tea container. I made little garlands out of twisted up tissue the toilet paper comes in. I even cut a little angel out of a Christmas card and put it on the top. I made a stand also. All in all, it appears to be a very righteous Christmas shrine I have constructed. There are pictures of presents along the base of the stand. I am very pleased. I also received my first Christmas card of the season from Mr. & Mrs. O'Sullivan.

Last night was the 75th birthday of Charlie Parker. The public radio station did an excellent biography on Mr. Parker with interviews mixed with recordings throughout his career. Dizzy Gillespie compared him to the discovery of Jesus. Everything I heard about the man, including his music, instantly made him a musician hero to me.

The story about Parker I liked best concerns his song "Lady in Red." While doing a solo, a lady in a red dress walked by him and he swung around and riffed "Lady in Red" and then fell right back into his solo without missing a beat. His inventive phrasing was a monumental force in music which musicians gravitated to during the 40s. He had a terrible battle with heroin and with himself.

If only there were musicians around like Parker today. He took 4/4 time and doubled it to 8/8 and then went so far as to double it again, which was completely unheard of. It was a surprise to some when he began to record with Miles Davis, but the mix turned out to be mutually beneficial. Parker favored the upper registers while Miles Davis would usually play the middle or even the lower register. Listening to those early recordings fascinates me.

In the recorded interviews with Charlie Parker, he admits to practicing twelve to fifteen hours a day, every day for three or four years. That's dedication. I am very jealous and also very humbled. I've seen some musicians in live settings that have made me just go home and put my guitar in the closet: Mathias Jabbs, Rudolph Schenker, Alex Skolnick, Eddie Van Halen, Stevie Ray Vaughn, Joe Satriani, Yngwie Malmsteen. Playing an instrument can be quite discouraging in a world so full of talent. But they all started somewhere.

If God came down tonight and told me that I personally could have any gift I wanted, I'd say, "Give me Charlie Parker's musical comprehension."

Charlie Parker was all that.

December 13, 1995

Red Dog is working late this night. His counselor came by yesterday with some papers to sign about his release. His probation officer had already been to his house to ascertain the environment and condition of his home.

Home.

It brought the stark reality of freedom into our little cell and we both read and reread the paper from his probation officer several times, as if disbelieving anybody in authority would even speak of our release.

Alone in the cell during the days, and at times during the nights, my mind reaches out to the future and tentatively speculates upon a thousand scenarios. Will I make it in the music business? Failing that, could I hack it out as a writer? Am I destined to be a plumber until I am old and wrinkly? Most importantly, will something utterly stupid, or someone utterly stupid, cause me to be sent back behind these walls?

My intentions are good. My intentions are great. They are absolutely fantastic. I do not think about anything except being with my family, maybe settling down and getting married, and having about 19 more kids. I long to be a working man once again. I feel as if I am at a stage where I could go in several directions, do almost anything I want to, with a high chance of success.

I mope and despair at the thought of a highly restrictive three years of parole. Three years! Will I even be able to travel back to the East coast to see my little girl?

Questions and more questions, but no one to answer them. I am absolutely powerless over the outside world: requests for addresses, money, people I need found or contacted, or items I need mailed, or even asking someone to stop in and see my daughter to make sure she's all right. The only contact I have with the outside world is my fifteen minutes per month on the telephone. I write hundreds of letters but it's really frustrating to not even receive a response. The longer you're in, the more people fade away.

My road dog, Jimmy, in the cell next to me and my cellie when we left Eagleview, got a sacred orderly job today. There is a hole between his cell and mine, in fact, I think between most cells down the tier. A message is written and the paper folded lengthwise and slid through the hole. Jimmy jams his through so that at times when I am sitting at my desk writing, a message will fly through the air and land on the desk.

I received some mail from Eagleview. Among the mail was a letter from my old friend Cameron who is now at Lompoc. He made certain references to now being made a member of a major prison gang. He is sitting in the hole there, recovering from five stab wounds. He assures me that it is okay since none of his tattoos were messed up. I heartily admonished him in a letter sent to our "go-between" (which is necessary to facilitate writing prison to prison) and I called him a putz.

Cam's a good dude and I hope he makes out all right. It's strange to watch a guy that you came in with go a different route. We were very compatible, but Cam was always more aggressive where I saw things less aggressively. Things were less puzzling to Cam and everything was always cut and dried with him: this is right, that is wrong. There were definitive lines to everything. But I questioned everything.

Granted, we brought out close to the worst in the both of us when we hung out. Especially when we were cellies in the hole at the pen. They would be coming down the tier, shaking down every cell and we might have some wine going.

"I don't feel like giving it up," Cameron would say. "Let's buck."

And I would jump to my feet and pace the cell, weighing the circumstances, probabilities and consequences. Meanwhile, Cameron fu-eled the fires of anarchism. He was good at that.

I suppose I saw him slipping away and I tried to talk to him. But Cameron could easily be led at times, too. Once he left Eagleview for Lompoc I expected trouble for him with the reputation he had. You never want to see or hear about one of your friends being stabbed or killed. You get a little close to them and you say to yourself, "This is a good kid. If I'd known him on the street, I probably would have hung out with him." And you feel like "This kid's better than this, he doesn't deserve this."

And then you see the gangs get an eye on him because he's big and works out and can be influenced. Then you get a letter telling you he's been stabbed five times.

It's sad.

December 20, 1995

It started snowing Monday night and is still snowing now on Wednesday morning. I've heard the song "Frosty the Snowman" about a million times and if I ever see Frosty, I'm going to torch his ass with a flame-thrower. It is far too many times to maintain any type of sanity. I am enjoying the twists on some Christmas songs like "Grandma Got Run Over By A Reindeer (copping dope on Christmas Eve)" and "LeRoy, The Redneck Reindeer." My all time favorite is Chuck Berry's "Run, Run, Rudolph."

My counselor came with a progress report for the relocation of my supervision. Once that is approved, I think I'll push for a halfway house. I hear they are giving away one year and six month halfway houses. If I could get a halfway house for six months, I could be out in two months at the end of February.

On the other hand, my progress report still lists me as high security so I may be sent to Lompoc for the remainder of the sentence. That's not so good. But Red Dog has a worse disciplinary record than me and is getting cut to a halfway house. Another thing that works to my advantage is the overcrowding of federal prisons. It's not that big of an advantage, though.

The S.H.U. unit is very shoddily run. The cops for the most part act like little bitches because everyone is locked in a cell. If there's a beef, a SERT team will take care of the convict and the cop in the hall will never get touched.

They do the damnedest things. My road dog, Jimmy, next door had over $500 on his account when we were shipped from Eagleview. They didn't send him his money when the rest of us received ours. They found out he was on commissary restriction, so someone put in a memo not to send him his bread. Of course, that isn't right because he's entitled to buy stamps and phone credits. He bitched and they sent him an allotment of $50. Jimmy and I were out at rec when the seg Lieutenant walked by.

"You can't just divide up my money and give me however much you see fit," Jimmy said to the Lieutenant.

"Sure we can," said the Lieutenant. "We're the U.S. Government. We can do anything we want."

That's funny, I don't remember voting for this jerk. Pretty heavy claim for a peon seg Lieutenant. I've come to believe Martinsburg seg is where they send the rejects for training. Sure, there's two or three that are almost professional. But out of how many? Thirty? Forty?

My days alone in the cell are taking their toll. There is absolutely nothing to do. How long can one read books, or listen to the radio until you've heard every song? I believe it's called sensory deprivation and it's a real monster. I fight it every day now. I look forward to mail call like a lottery junkie. I have received a grand total of four Christmas cards so far, with only three mail days until Christmas. It doesn't look good this year. Only nine hours until mail call.

December 24, 1995

Christmas eve. Children are nestled snug in their beds while the Jolly one streaks across the night sky.

I begin my third and final countdown to Christmas which is less than two hours away. Next year, hopefully, I will be home. For now, though, I ponder in my cage.

Todd, my old cellie from Eagleview who was redesignated here at Martinsburg, is now in the cell with Red Dog and me. The first time I met Todd was in early March when he was in my unit at the pen. He had just shot up some heroin into his hand and his hand was as big as a basketball. "I missed," he said. Now Todd is back in the hole for Christmas and under investigation for drugs.

A lot has happened. At least it seems like a lot to me. When the days are filled with hours of nothing, small occurrences seem larger than they are. Diane has sent me a nice Christmas card. I've also received cards from my mother, Susie, Suzy, Tom, Aunt Peggy, Gram and Gramp, Mr. & Mrs. O'Sullivan and cousin Sarah and Jerry.

My unit team, though, did not share the same holiday spirit when they delivered my custody classification form. It appears I am in a bad way according to the official government form. I attempted to point out the custody classification was dated July 95 and was a little outdated. This was met with the usual head scratching and guttural, incomprehensible grunts. My only hope lies in the hands of Mr. Sneezin, my unit manager. He seems like a decent sort of guy.

Now is the time I should wax philosophical I suppose, but in truth, my heart's not in it. It appears that I will be spending my last eight months in at the U.S.P. in Lompoc, California.

Diane says Mike's buying her a diamond. Her card says, "I won't forget you" which I take to be good-bye.

It's 10:36 and I'm tired, depressed, discouraged and more and more feeling like the world is involved in some giant conspiracy to torment me. But I am the gum on the shoe of my tormentors. I am the flea on the dog that is oppression and I will continue to surf the waves of good and bad times.

Sometimes chicken.

Sometimes feathers.

December 25, 1995

Santa Claus did not make it to prison again this year. However, the B.O.P. presented us with a bag of junk food and cookies and egg nog last night. I've never seen anything like it.

I'm listening to Christmas music and this has lifted my spirits somewhat from last night. My cellie, Red Dog, utilized his orderly perks to get on the phone today and called both Todd's mother and my mother. My Christmas message? "Love you plenty, send me twenty." As in dollars.

The radio seemed to push the image of Christmas as being tough in a blue and difficult time. I guess things are tough all over. I cringe to think of the kids who do without this year.

Christmas to me is not about wanting or giving. Rather it is about family and togetherness. Christmas is not about money. It's about the only thing that money can't buy. Christmas is about love. Most children are conditioned to believe that the more Christmas presents they receive, the more their parents love them. Of course, it's not true. Love, or the lack of love, is the only thing in the world that will make a rich kid poor or a poor child rich.

December 29, 1995

The year has almost come to an end. My last full year in prison. Nineteen ninety-five was a fairly memorable calendar, albeit not one I would mention in mixed company.

My ride with the Federal Bureau of Prisons is about to come to a halt. The trip could not be compared to a jaunt aboard the Love Boat. More likely, the B.O.P. is comparable to the Exxon Valdez. I am certain that high up in the infrastructure, Gilligan himself is at the helm cheerfully whistling something about a three hour tour. I am also certain that the politicians who latched onto the "War on Drugs" battle cry must have overlooked a long term study on the effects and consequences of mass incarceration. From what I have seen throughout my imprisonment it boils down to treatment and amenities of the convict.

The politicians speak of harsher sentences and less amenities for the prisoners to make themselves look good. But no one speaks for the prisoner. Any opinion of or about a prisoner is tainted. It has been my experience that the crime does not matter. A "prisoner" seems to be defined as a rapist or murderer or bum who deserves whatever it is he gets.

In my case, I went through all the stages and have a couple more to go. Once you wade through the misery and struggle through the calendars, the remorse is long gone. I've paid my dues.

If prison is about checks and balances, then I'm even. I've reached a point where I've come full circle and although I've changed, I'm chomping at the bit to have my freedom back. Sure, I've got some self righteous anger, but there are positive outlets to direct it towards. My future and my daughter's future are all that concern me now. I pray to God I never come back to prison. I wouldn't wish it on my worst enemy.

I have some fear about getting out and screwing up. But fears are meant to be faced.

The worst part about prison isn't the violence or the loneliness or the separation from your people. The worst part of it for me was facing myself and being thrust into a totally alien environment where adjustment means survival. It drives some men to buggery, some men to madness and still others into the gaping black hole of heroin addiction. It's abrasive, but it's beatable. There are locks on the doors, but there are also keys.

When I mention survival, I mean it in a very broad sense. For the most part, you have to make a pretty serious screw up to get whacked. Common sense rules the playground most of the time.

I've got anywhere from two to eight months left, depending on my halfway house placement, which doesn't look good.

My agenda for right now and into the future indefinitely consists of but four words and two parts. It is the prisoner's mantra.

Get out.

Stay out.

December 31, 1995

Snow falls outside my window as I prepare to welcome 1996 with open arms. Already there is talk of spring and soon the rains will come to wash away the remains of winter.

The thoughts of spring remind me of my own rebirth with my release. I have spent three years preparing for 1996, unlocking the doors of my mind. I have made progress and learned much about myself and about life.

Nobody is ever alone. We all suffer the silent indignity of oppression to varying degrees. My peers are not only behind these walls. They are across the nation and around the world. Your manacles might be the physical limitations of a small town or a bad relationship. Maybe you've fallen into a daily pattern that is harder to break out of than any prison. The chains that prevent us from the pursuit of our dreams, the boundaries that inhibit our real desires in life, these are the walls of our real prisons.

Inside these stone walls I've come to realize freedom as a state of mind. The manacles can be slipped, the chains can be broken.

Through my search for inner peace I have faced all the wars that rage inside me. Some I conquered. Some I did not conquer. At times I have become quite discouraged and lost my focus. But most important, I never gave up. We only fail when we stop trying.

As I write this, I realize that this will be my last entry. Perhaps I have found that which I sought, a deeper understanding of myself, a small sliver of color in the pattern of the kaleidoscope. The words of T. S. Elliot come to mind:

> We shall not cease from exploration
> And the end of all our exploring
> Will be to arrive where we started
> And know the place for the first time.

The end becomes the beginning.